Microsoft® Office Excel® 2010

Level 3 (Second Edition)

Microsoft® Office Excel® 2010: Level 3 (Second Edition)

Part Number: 084678
Course Edition: 1.0

NOTICES

What is the Microsoft Office Specialist Certification Program?

The Microsoft Office Specialist (MOS) Certification Program enables candidates to show that they have something exceptional to offer - proven expertise in Microsoft® Office applications. The MOS Certification Program is the only Microsoft-approved certification program of its kind. The MOS Certification exams focus on validating specific skill sets within each of the Microsoft® Office system programs. The candidate can choose which exam(s) they want to take according to which skills they want to validate. The available MOS exams include:

- MOS: Microsoft® Office Word 2010
- MOS: Microsoft® Office Excel 2010
- MOS: Microsoft® Office PowerPoint 2010
- MOS: Microsoft® Office Outlook 2010
- MOS: Microsoft® Office Access 2010
- MOS: Microsoft® SharePoint 2010

For more information:

 HELP US IMPROVE OUR COURSEWARE

Your comments are important to us. Please contact us at Element K Press LLC, 1-800-478-7788, 500 Canal View Boulevard, Rochester, NY 14623, Attention: Product Planning, or through our Web site at **http://support.elementkcourseware.com**.

To learn more about MOS exams, visit **www.microsoft.com/learning/en/us/certification/mos.aspx**.

Athens Tech
Online Courses
Continuing Ed
Economic Development

Most Classes - 6 weeks $112
Not credit courses

Microsoft® Office Excel® 2010: Level 3 (Second Edition)

Lesson 1: Streamlining Workflow

Lesson 2: Collaborating with Other Users

Lesson 3: Auditing Worksheets

Lesson 4: Analyzing Data

About This Course

Your training in Microsoft® Office Excel® 2010 has provided you with a solid foundation in the basic and intermediate skills for using the software. You used Excel to perform tasks such as running calculations on data and sorting and filtering numeric data. In this course, you will extend your knowledge into some of the more specialized and advanced capabilities of Excel by automating some repeated tasks, troubleshooting errors, sharing workbooks with others in a secure manner, applying advanced analysis techniques to more complex data sets, and sharing Excel data with other applications.

In addition to basic data analysis features, Excel provides you with advanced data analysis and troubleshooting techniques that will help you extract accurate values from static data by summarizing and forecasting values that are not readily apparent. Excel also allows you to share your workbooks with other users in a secure manner, enabling a collaborative work environment.

This course can also benefit you if you are preparing to take the Microsoft Office Specialist (MOS) Certification exams for Microsoft® Excel® 2010. Please refer to the CD-ROM that came with this course for documents that map exam objectives to the content in the Microsoft Office Excel courseware series. To access the mapping documents, insert the CD-ROM into your CD-ROM drive and at the root of the CD, double-click ExamMappingCore.doc or ExamMappingExpert.doc to open a mapping document. In addition to the mapping documents, two assessment files per course can be found on the CD-ROM to check your knowledge. To access the assessments, at the root of the course part number folder, double-click 084678s3.doc to view the assessments without the answers marked, or double click 084678ie.doc to view the assessments with the answers marked.

If your course manual did not come with a CD-ROM, please go to **http://www.elementk.com/courseware-file-downloads** to download the files.

Course Description

Target Student

This course was designed for students desiring to gain the skills necessary to create macros, collaborate with others, audit and analyze worksheet data, incorporate multiple data sources, and import and export data.

Course Prerequisites

To ensure your success, we recommend that you first take the following Element K courses or have equivalent knowledge:

■ *Microsoft® Office Excel® 2010: Level 1 (Second Edition)*

■ *Microsoft® Office Excel® 2010: Level 2 (Second Edition)*

Course Objectives

In this course, you will automate some common Excel tasks, apply advanced analysis techniques to more complex data sets, troubleshoot errors, collaborate on worksheets, and share Excel data with other applications.

You will:

● Enhance productivity and efficiency by streamlining the workflow.

● Collaborate with other workbook users.

● Audit worksheets.

● Analyze data.

● Work with multiple workbooks.

● Import and export data.

● Integrate Excel data with the web.

Certification

This course is designed to help you prepare for the following certification.

Certification Path: MOS: Microsoft Office Excel 2010 Exam 77–882

Certification Path: MOS: Microsoft Office Excel 2010 Expert Exam 77–888

This course is one of a series of Element K courseware titles that addresses Microsoft Office Specialist (MOS) certification skill sets. The MOS and certification program is for individuals who use Microsoft's business desktop software and who seek recognition for their expertise with specific Microsoft products.

How to Use This Book

As a Learning Guide

This book is divided into lessons and topics, covering a subject or a set of related subjects. In most cases, lessons are arranged in order of increasing proficiency.

The results-oriented topics include relevant and supporting information you need to master the content. Each topic has various types of activities designed to enable you to practice the guidelines and procedures as well as to solidify your understanding of the informational material presented in the course.

At the back of the book, you will find a glossary of the definitions of the terms and concepts used throughout the course. You will also find an index to assist in locating information within the instructional components of the book.

In the Classroom

This book is intended to enhance and support the in-class experience. Procedures and guidelines are presented in a concise fashion along with activities and discussions. Information is provided for reference and reflection in such a way as to facilitate understanding and practice.

Each lesson may also include a Lesson Lab or various types of simulated activities. You will find the files for the simulated activities along with the other course files on the enclosed CD-ROM. If your course manual did not come with a CD-ROM, please go to **http:// elementkcourseware.com** to download the files. If included, these interactive activities enable you to practice your skills in an immersive business environment, or to use hardware and software resources not available in the classroom. The course files that are available on the CD-ROM or by download may also contain sample files, support files, and additional reference materials for use both during and after the course.

As a Teaching Guide

Effective presentation of the information and skills contained in this book requires adequate preparation. As such, as an instructor, you should familiarize yourself with the content of the entire course, including its organization and approaches. You should review each of the student activities and exercises so you can facilitate them in the classroom.

Throughout the book, you may see Instructor Notes that provide suggestions, answers to problems, and supplemental information for you, the instructor. You may also see references to "Additional Instructor Notes" that contain expanded instructional information; these notes appear in a separate section at the back of the book. PowerPoint slides may be provided on the included course files, which are available on the enclosed CD-ROM or by download from **http://elementkcourseware.com**. The slides are also referred to in the text. If you plan to use the slides, it is recommended to display them during the corresponding content as indicated in the instructor notes in the margin.

The course files may also include assessments for the course, which can be administered diagnostically before the class, or as a review after the course is completed. These exam-type questions can be used to gauge the students' understanding and assimilation of course content.

As a Review Tool

Any method of instruction is only as effective as the time and effort you are willing to invest in it. In addition, some of the information that you learn in class may not be important to you immediately, but it may become important later on. For this reason, we encourage you to spend some time reviewing the topics and activities after the course. For additional challenge when reviewing activities, try the "What You Do" column before looking at the "How You Do It" column.

As a Reference

The organization and layout of the book make it easy to use as a learning tool and as an after-class reference. You can use this book as a first source for definitions of terms, background information on given topics, and summaries of procedures.

Course Icons

Icon	Description
	A **Caution Note** makes students aware of potential negative consequences of an action, setting, or decision that are not easily known.
	Display Slide provides a prompt to the instructor to display a specific slide. Display Slides are included in the Instructor Guide only.
	An **Instructor Note** is a comment to the instructor regarding delivery, classroom strategy, classroom tools, exceptions, and other special considerations. Instructor Notes are included in the Instructor Guide only.
	Notes Page indicates a page that has been left intentionally blank for students to write on.
	A **Student Note** provides additional information, guidance, or hints about a topic or task.
	A **Version Note** indicates information necessary for a specific version of software.

Course Requirements

Hardware

For this course, you will need one computer for each student and the instructor. Each computer should have the following minimum hardware configuration:

- 1 GHz Pentium-class processor or faster.
- A minimum of 1 GB of RAM is recommended.
- 20 GB hard disk or larger. You should have at least 1 GB of free hard disk space available for Office 2010 installation.
- A DVD-ROM drive.
- A keyboard and mouse or other pointing device.
- A 1024 x 768 resolution SVGA monitor is recommended.
- Network cards and cabling for local network access.
- Internet access.
- A printer (optional) or an installed printer driver.
- A projection system to display the instructor's computer screen.

Software

- Microsoft® Office Professional Plus 2010 Edition
- Microsoft® Windows® XP Professional with Service Pack 3

    This course was developed using the Windows XP operating system. If you use Windows Vista or Windows 7, you might notice some slight differences when keying in the course.

- Windows Rights Management Services (RMS) Client with Service Pack 2.

Class Setup

Initial Class Setup

For initial class setup:

1. Install Windows XP Professional on an empty partition.

    ■   Leave the Administrator password blank.

    ■   For all other installation parameters, use values that are appropriate for your environment (see your local network administrator for details).

2. On Windows XP Professional, disable the **Welcome** screen. (This step ensures that students will be able to log on as the Administrator user regardless of what other user accounts exist on the computer.)

    a. Click **Start** and choose **Control Panel→User Accounts.**

    b. Click **Change The Way Users Log On And Off.**

    c. Uncheck **Use Welcome Screen.**

    d. Click **Apply Options.**

3. If necessary, on Windows XP Professional, install Service Pack 3. Use the Service Pack installation defaults.

4. On the computer, install a printer driver (a physical print device is optional). Click **Start** and choose **Printers and Faxes.** Under **Printer Tasks,** click **Add a Printer** and follow the prompts.

    If you do not have a physical printer installed, right-click the printer and choose **Pause Printing** to prevent any print error message.

5. Run the **Internet Connection Wizard** to set up the Internet connection as appropriate for your environment if you did not do so during installation.

6. Display known file type extensions.

    a. Open **Windows Explorer** (right-click **Start** and then choose **Explore.**)

    b. Choose **Tools→Folder Options.**

    c. On the **View** tab, in the **Advanced Settings** list box, uncheck **Hide Extensions For Known File Types.**

    d. Click **Apply,** and then click **OK.**

    e. Close **Windows Explorer.**

7. Log on to the computer as the Administrator user if you have not already done so.

8. Perform a complete installation of Microsoft Office Professional Plus 2010.

9. In the **User Name** dialog box, click **OK** to accept the default user name and initials.

10. In the **Microsoft Office 2010 Activation Wizard** dialog box, click **Next** to activate the Office 2010 application.

11. When the activation of Microsoft Office 2010 is complete, click **Close** to close the **Microsoft Office 2010 Activation Wizard** dialog box.

12. In the **User Name** dialog box, click **OK.**

13. In the **Welcome To Microsoft 2010** dialog box, click **Finish.** You must have an active Internet connection in order to complete this step. Here, you have to select the **Download And Install Updates From Microsoft Update When Available (Recommended)** option so that whenever there is a new update it gets automatically installed on your system.

14. After the Microsoft Update is run, in the **Microsoft Office** dialog box, click **OK.**

15. If necessary, minimize the **Language** bar.

16. On the course CD-ROM, open the 084678 folder. Then, open the Data folder. Run the 084678dd.exe self-extracting file located in it. This will install a folder named 084678Data on your C drive. This folder contains all the data files that you will use to complete this course. If your course did not come with a CD, please go to **http:// elementkcourseware.com** to download the data files.

Within each lesson folder, you may find a Solution folder. This folder contains solution files for the lesson's activities and lesson lab, which can be used by students to check their end results.

For activities that require complex class setup requirements, simulations are provided. Within each lesson folder, you may find a Simulations folder. If you wish, you may run the simulations provided to perform the activities in class or to review after class.

Install Windows Rights Management Services (RMS)

To install Windows Rights Management Services (RMS):

1. Launch the Microsoft Office Excel 2010 application.

2. Select the **File** tab, and in the Backstage view, in the **Permissions** section, from the **Protect Workbook** drop-down list, select **Restrict Permission by People→Manage Credentials.**

3. In the **Microsoft Office** message box, click **Yes.**

4. In the **File Download — Security Warning** message box, click **Run.**

5. In the **Internet Explorer — Security Warning** message box, click **Run** to execute the file.

6. In the **Windows Rights Management Client with Service Pack 2** dialog box, on the **Welcome to the Windows Rights Management Client with Service Pack 2 Setup Wizard** page, click **Next.**

7. On the **License Agreement** page, select the **I Agree** option and click **Next.**

8. On the **Confirm Installation** page, click **Next.**

9. On the **Installation Complete** page, click **Close.**

10. In the Backstage view, in the **Permissions** section, from the **Protect Workbook** drop-down list, select **Restrict Permission by People→Manage Credentials.**

11. In the **Service Sign-Up** dialog box, select **Yes, I want to sign up for this free service from Microsoft** and click **Next.**

12. In the **Security Alert** message box, click **OK.**

13. In the **Windows Rights Management** wizard, on the **Welcome to the Information Rights Management Configuration Wizard** page, select **Yes, I have a Windows Live ID** and click **Next.**

14. In the **Sign in to Windows Live** page, in the **Sign in to IRM** section, in the **Email address** text box, type in your Hotmail or Windows Live ID, and in the **Password** text box, type the password. Select **Always ask for my email address and password** and then click **Sign in.**

15. On the **Select computer type** page, verify that **This is a private computer** is selected and click **I accept.**

16. On the **Completing to the Information Rights Management Configuration Wizard** page, click **Finish.**

Customize the Windows Desktop

Customize the Windows desktop to display the **My Computer** and **My Network Places** icons.

1. On the desktop, right-click and choose **Properties.**

2. Select the **Desktop** tab.

3. Click **Customize Desktop.**

4. In the **Desktop Items** dialog box, check **My Computer** and **My Network Places.**

5. Click **OK** and click **Apply.**

6. Close the **Display Properties** dialog box.

Before Every Class

1. Log on to the computer as the Administrator user.

2. Delete any existing data file from the C:\084678Data folder.

3. Extract a fresh copy of the course data files from the CD-ROM provided with the course manual, or download the data files from **http://elementkcourseware.com**

List of Additional Files

Printed with each activity is a list of files students open to complete that activity. Many activities also require additional files that students do not open, but are needed to support the file(s) students are working with. These supporting files are included with the student data files on the course CD-ROM or data disk. Do not delete these files.

(General)
File - Options - Change Color & Font

File - Options - Save
 Auto Save Setting
  Time & Location

Right Click on
Program when
Open - Pin to
 Tasbar

Right Click on Task Bar
Select Options to Display
 in task Bar
  Sum
  Average
  Min
  ETC...

1 | Streamlining Workflow

Lesson Time: 1 hour(s), 20 minutes

Lesson Objectives:

In this lesson, you will enhance productivity and efficiency by streamlining the workflow.

You will:

- Update workbook properties.
- Create a macro.
- Edit a macro.
- Apply conditional formatting.
- Add data validation criteria.

Introduction

While managing workbooks in Microsoft® Office Excel® 2010, you may have found some common tasks that are repetitive. You can simplify the methods of performing these tasks in Excel. In this lesson, you will streamline your workflow.

As an experienced Excel user, there may be times when you need to automate frequently performed tasks, restrict the type of data entered in cells, or format data based on predefined criteria. Streamlining your workflow by tailoring the Excel environment to your job needs can increase your productivity and improve your efficiency.

TOPIC A

Update Workbook Properties

You are familiar with performing basic operations in Excel workbooks. But first, you should be able to locate your workbook by using specific properties or information, such as its title or summary. In this topic, you will modify a workbook's properties.

Searching for a workbook can become tedious if no specific information is available about its authors or contents. By updating workbook properties and attaching specific information, locating the workbook or identifying its contents becomes a lot easier.

Workbook Properties

The **[Workbook Name] Properties** dialog box contains five tabs for specifying the properties of a workbook.

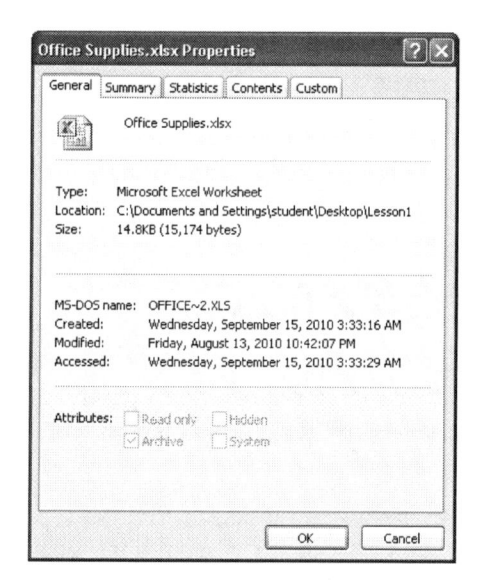

Figure 1-1: *The [Workbook Name] Properties dialog box allows you to observe or specify the properties of a workbook.*

Tab	Description
General	Identifies the file name, type, location, size, MS-DOS name; creation, modification, and access dates; and attributes such as whether the file is read-only. You cannot alter this information from within the **[Workbook Name] Properties** dialog box. The system supplies this information.
Summary	Allows you to specify the file title, subject, author, manager, company, category, keywords, and hyperlink base.
Statistics	Lists system information such as the creation date, last modified date, last accessed date, and last printed date. It also identifies the name of the person who last saved the file, the revision number (if applicable), and the total editing time (if applicable). The data on this tab cannot be edited.

Tab	Description
Contents	Identifies the total number of worksheets by name. The data on this tab cannot be edited.
Custom	Allows you to attach specific information to the file, such as the destination, editor, language, and so on. Apart from the suggested options available on the tab, it is possible to add a property name of your own.

Display Workbook Properties

Workbook properties are displayed in the **Backstage View** when the **Info** option is selected. They can also be displayed using the **[Workbook Name] Properties** dialog box, by selecting the **File** tab and then selecting **Advanced Properties** from the **Properties** drop-down list, in the right pane of the **Info** tab.

Keywords

Keywords that are entered for a workbook are used to index the file. This allows the file to be easily found when the keywords are used as search terms when searching for a file.

The Document Panel

The **Document Panel** displays the properties of an Excel workbook in a panel below the Ribbon and enables you to add or edit the workbook's properties. Specifying the workbook properties enables you to easily identify and organize workbooks.

Property	Used to Identify
Author	The name of the individual who has authored the workbook.
Title	The name of the workbook.
Subject	The topic of the contents of the workbook.
Keywords	A word or set of words that describe the workbook.
Category	A category in which the workbook can be classified.
Status	The status of the content.
Comments	The summary or abstract of the contents of the workbook.

How to Update Workbook Properties

Procedure Reference: Update Workbook Properties Using the [Workbook Name] Properties Dialog Box

To update workbook properties:

1. In the open workbook, select the **File** tab, and in the Backstage view, from the **Properties** drop-down list, select **Advanced Properties.**

2. In the **[Workbook Name] Properties** dialog box, modify the desired properties.

    *   On the **Summary** tab, specify the necessary details in the respective text boxes.

    *   On the **Custom** tab, specify the custom properties.

        a. Either select an existing name in the **Name** list box, or type a new name in the **Name** text box to specify a name for the custom property.

        b. If necessary, from the **Type** drop-down list, select **Text, Date, Number,** or **Yes or no**, to limit the type of value that can be entered.

        c. In the **Value** text box, type the value of the custom property. If you selected **Yes or no** from the **Type** drop-down list, select the **Yes** or **No** option.

        d. Click **Add.**

 The **Link to content** check box allows you to store the custom property in an existing bookmark within the document.

3. Click **OK** to close the **[Workbook Name] Properties** dialog box.

4. Save the document to store the new properties with the file.

Procedure Reference: Update Workbook Properties in the Backstage View

To update workbook properties in the Backstage view:

1. In the open workbook, select the **File** tab to display the Backstage view.

2. In the right pane, edit the information related to the workbook.

    *   If necessary, click **Add a title** and type a title of your choice.

    *   If necessary, click **Add a tag** and type keywords that you want to add to the workbook.

    *   If necessary, click **Add a category** and type a category for the workbook.

    *   If necessary, in the related people section, click **Add an author** and type the name of the author.

    *   If necessary, click **Show All Properties** to display additional properties.

        *   To add comments, click **Add comments** and enter comments.

        *   To define the status of the workbook, click **Add Text** corresponding to the **Status** field and type the required text.

        *   To specify a subject for the file, click the text **Specify a subject** corresponding to **Subject** field and type a subject for the workbook.

        *   To specify a **Hyperlink Base** for the file, click **Add Text** corresponding to **Hyperlink Base** field and type the required text.

        *   To specify a company name for the file, click **Specify the company** corresponding to **Company** field and type the company name.

Procedure Reference: Manipulate Workbook Properties Using the Document Panel

To manipulate workbook properties using the document panel:

1. In the open workbook, select the **File** tab to display the Backstage view.
2. In the Backstage view, from the **Properties** drop-down list, select **Show Document Panel.**
3. In the Document panel, enter the information related to the workbook.
   - In the **Author** text box, type the name of the author.
   - In the **Title** text box, type a title of your choice.
   - In the **Subject** text box, type a subject for the workbook.
   - In the **Keywords** text box, type the keywords that you want to add to the workbook.
   - In the **Category** text box, type a category for the workbook.
   - In the **Status** text box, type the required text to define the status of the workbook.
   - In the **Comments** text box, enter comments.
4. If necessary, from the **Document Properties** drop-down list, select **Advanced Properties** to display the **[Workbook Name] Properties** dialog box.
5. Close the **[Workbook Name] Properties** dialog box.
6. If necessary, close the Document panel.
7. In the Backstage view, see the information entered.

Procedure Reference: Modify the Default Settings in Excel

To modify the default settings:

1. Select the **File** tab, and in the **Backstage View**, select **Options.**
2. In the **Excel Options** dialog box, make the necessary changes.
   - In the right pane, select the **General** category and choose the required settings.
     - In the **When creating new workbooks** section, from the **Use this font** drop-down list, select the font you want to use as the default font for all new worksheets.
     - From the **Font size** drop-down list, select the font size you want to set as the default font for all new worksheets.
     - If desired, from the **Default view for new sheets** drop-down list, select the preferred default view.
     - In the **Include this many sheets** spin box, specify a value for the number of sheets to be displayed in a workbook and click **OK.** By default, 255 is the maximum number of worksheets a workbook can contain.
   - In the right pane, select the required options.
     - Select the **Formulas** category and choose the settings for formulas.
     - Select the **Proofing** category and choose the settings for autocorrection and spellcheck.
     - Select the **Save** category and choose the settings related to saving workbooks.
     - Select the **Language** category and set the language preferences.

- Select the **Advanced** category and set the options related to editing, cutting, copying, and pasting, image size and quality, print, chart, and display options for worksheets and workbooks.
- Select the **Customize Ribbon** category and choose the appropriate settings for the Ribbon.
- Select the **Quick Access Toolbar** category and choose the appropriate settings for the Quick Access Toolbar.
- Select the **Add-Ins** category and choose the Add-Ins that you want to install.
- Select the **Trust Center** category and choose the appropriate settings for **Trust Center.**

3. In the **Excel Options** dialog box, click **OK**, and in the **Microsoft Excel** warning box, click **OK** to quit and restart Excel.

4. Open Excel to test the updated default settings.

Compatibility Mode

Compatibility Mode is a feature that allows users to open workbooks that were created in Excel 97-2003 in Excel 2010. Files created in Excel 97-2003 are automatically opened in Compatibility Mode, and display "Compatibility Mode" in square brackets next to the file name in the Excel title bar. Most of the new features of Excel 2010 are not available in Compatibility Mode, and the files edited in this mode are saved in the Excel 97-2003 file format (.xls). Because Excel 2007 uses the same file format as Excel 2010, Excel 2007 workbooks do not open in Compatibility Mode.

Convert a Workbook to the Excel 2010 File Format

A workbook opened in Compatibility Mode can be converted to the Excel 2010 format by selecting the **File** tab and selecting the **Convert** button on the **Info** tab. When you convert a workbook, it is replaced with a copy of the workbook in the current file format (.xlsx or .xlsm).

Procedure Reference: Change the Default File Storage Location

To change the default file storage location:

1. If necessary, create a folder in the location where you want to store files by default.
2. Display the **Excel Options** dialog box.
3. In the **Excel Options** dialog box, select the **Save** category.
4. In the right pane, in the **Default File Location** text box, type the path where you want to save files.
5. In the **Excel Options** dialog box, click OK.

ACTIVITY 1-1

Updating Workbook Properties

Data Files:

C:\084678Data\Streamlining Workflow\Sales Data Canada.xlsx

Before You Begin:

Open the Microsoft Excel 2010 application.

Scenario:

As Josh Duvane, an employee, you are developing a workbook titled Sales Data Canada. Your manager, Roberta Williams, wants you to enter some details about the creation and editing of this file so that others will get to know about it. She wants to list her name as the manager of the file, your name as the author of the file, and Mary Coleman as the editor of the file. Additionally, she wants to easily locate the file using words such as "Canada," "Sales," and "Vendor Code."

---

1. Add a title to the workbook.

   a. Display the **Open** dialog box, navigate to the C:\084678Data\Streamlining Workflow folder, and open the Sales Data Canada.xlsx file.

   b. Select the **File** tab, and in the Backstage view, from the **Properties** drop-down list, select **Advanced Properties.**

   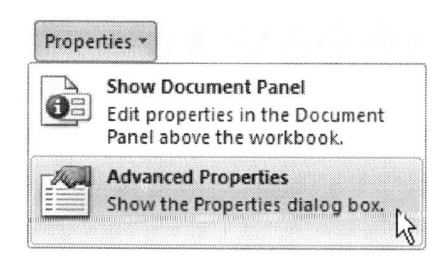

   c. In the **Sales Data Canada.xlsx Properties** dialog box, select the **Summary** tab.

   d. On the **Summary** tab, in the **Title** text box, type *Highest Sales Canada*

---

2. Add the author, manager, company name, and keywords to the workbook.

   a. In the **Author** text box, type *Josh Duvane*

   b. In the **Manager** text box, type *Roberta Williams*

   c. In the **Company** text box, type *Our Global Company*

   d. In the **Keywords** text box, type *Canada, Sales, Vendor Code*

---

3. Add a custom property listing Mary Coleman as the editor of the workbook.

   a. Select the **Custom** tab.

---

    b.   In the **Name** list box, scroll down and select **Editor.**

    c.   Verify that **Text** is selected by default in the **Type** drop-down list.

    d.   In the **Value** text box, type *Mary Coleman*

    e.   Click **Add** to display the modified editor details in the **Properties** area, and click **OK.**

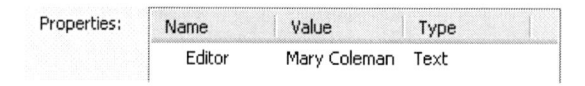

4.   View the properties of the workbook.

    a.   In the Backstage view, in the right pane, from the **Properties** drop-down list, select **Advanced Properties.**

    b.   On the **Custom** tab, verify that the updated custom details are displayed.

    c.   Select the **Summary** tab and verify that the details related to title, author, manager, company, and keywords are displayed as entered and click **OK.**

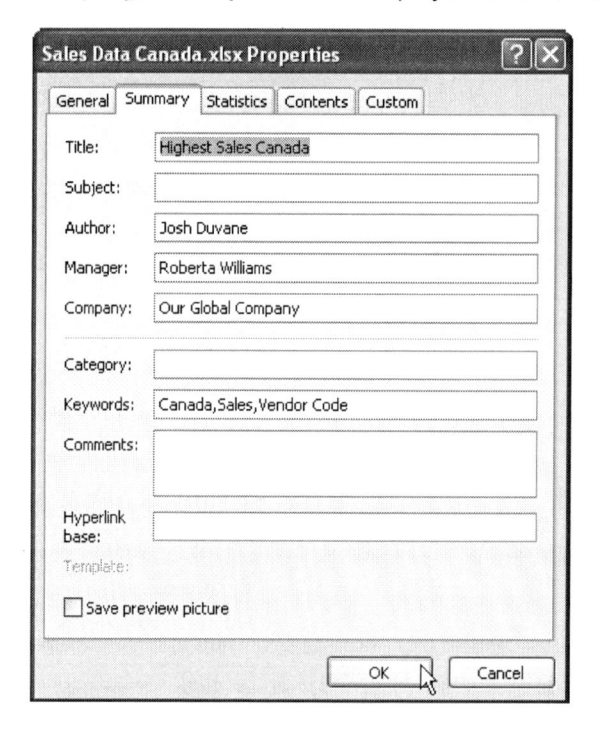

    d.   In the Backstage view, in the right pane, click the **Show All Properties** link to view properties in the Backstage view.

    e.   Save the document as *My Sales Data Canada* and close it.

TOPIC B

Create a Macro

You know that certain tasks in Excel become repetitive. Automating such tasks helps you to perform them with minimal interaction. In this topic, you will create a macro.

Workbooks containing many sheets usually carry some standard text on every sheet; for example, the contact information. It can be tedious to include such information on all sheets of a workbook. Creating macros to handle such tasks will be of great help. Macros automate complex tasks and ensure their precise replication.

Macros

Definition:

A *macro* is a task automation tool that executes a set of commands to automate a series of frequently used steps. Each macro is uniquely identified by a name. A macro-enabled Excel workbook has .xlsm as the file extension. You can use the macro recorder to record a sequence of actions, and then perform the tasks by using the macro name or a simple command assigned to the macro. The set of commands in the recorded macro is converted into a Visual Basic programming code that can be edited if required. Macros can be stored in the Personal Macro Workbook, a new workbook, or in the current workbook. Macros that are stored in the Personal Macro Workbook can be used in any workbook.

Example:

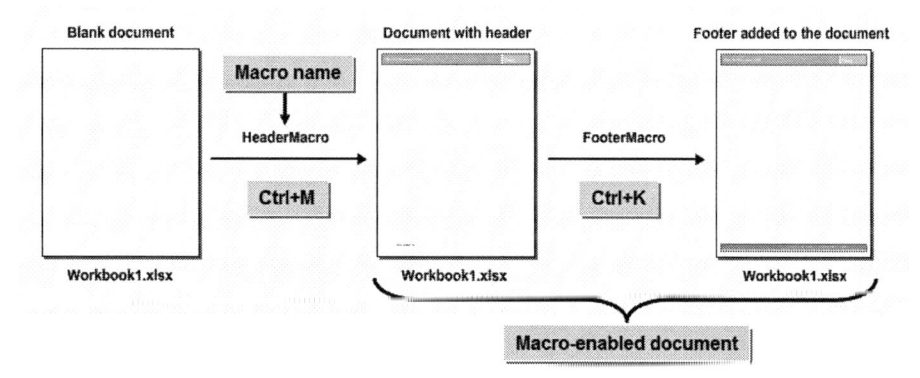

Figure 1-2: Adding a header and footer to a worksheet using macros.

The Record Macro Dialog Box

The **Record Macro** dialog box is used to specify details about a macro and to start recording the macro. You can specify details such as the macro name, shortcut key for running the macro, location in which the macro will be stored, and description of the macro in the **Record Macro** dialog box. The **Record Macro** dialog box can be displayed from the **Macros** drop-down list on the **View** tab.

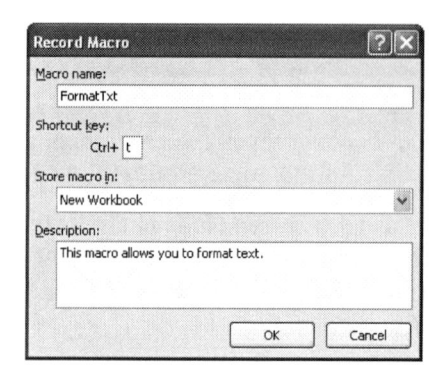

Figure 1-3: *A macro name, shortcut key, and description entered in the Record Macro dialog box.*

Macro Recording for Chart Elements

In Microsoft Office Excel 2007, recording a macro while formatting a chart will not produce any macro code. However, in Excel 2010, you can record the formatting changes to a chart as a macro and apply them to another chart.

Macro Naming Rules

There are certain rules to follow when you create macro names:

* The name must begin with a letter.

* The name must not contain spaces.

* The name can contain letters, numbers, and the underscore character.

* The name should not be in conflict with the name of another object in the worksheet or workbook, or any built-in name.

If any of these rules are not followed, you will receive an invalid procedure name error message.

Auto_Open Macros

Macros can be configured to run automatically by saving them with the name Auto_Open. Macros so named will run whenever you open a workbook containing them.

Macro Referencing

There are two types of referencing used in macros: absolute and relative. In *absolute referencing*, actions are recorded by taking the absolute position of cells. Therefore, the macro will perform the actions in the same cell positions, irrespective of the position of the cell pointer.

In *relative referencing*, actions are recorded relative to cell positions. For instance, if you record a macro that moves the cursor to cell A5, with cell A1 selected, and then if you enter some text, absolute reference will insert the text in cell A5, irrespective of the selected cell. Relative referencing, on the other hand, would place the text in the fourth cell to the right in the same row. By default, macros are recorded using absolute referencing. To use relative referencing, you need to choose the option **Use Relative References** from the **Macros** drop-down list before recording a macro.

How to Create a Macro

Procedure Reference: Record a Macro

To record a macro:

1. Select a worksheet where you want to begin recording a macro.

2. If necessary, to use relative referencing, on the **View** tab, in the **Macros** group, from the **Macros** drop-down list, select **Use Relative References.**

3. On the **View** tab, in the **Macros** group, from the **Macros** drop-down list, select **Record Macro.**

4. In the **Record Macro** dialog box, in the **Macro Name** text box, type a name for the macro.

5. If necessary, in the **Record Macro** dialog box, in the **Macro Name** text box, type *Auto_ Open* to run the macro automatically when the file is opened.

6. In the **Shortcut Key** text box, type a letter to add a shortcut key for the macro.

 Ctrl appears by default when you open the **Record Macro** dialog box to specify a short-cut key. This combination is a quick way to run a macro in a worksheet.

7. From the **Store Macro In** drop-down list, select a location where the macro will be saved.

   - Select **Personal Macro Workbook** to store the macro in the Personal workbook that is created by default when you open Excel and to use the macro in the other workbooks.

   - Select **New Workbook** to store and use the macro in a new workbook.

   - Select **This Workbook** to store and use the macro in the current workbook.

8. If necessary, in the **Description** text box, add a description of the macro.

9. Click **OK** to begin recording the macro.

10. Perform the tasks you want to record in the macro.

11. Stop the recording.

    - Click the **Stop Recording** button on the **Status Bar.**

    - Or, on the **View** tab, in the **Macros** group, from the **Macros** drop-down list, and select **Stop Recording.**

12. On the **File** tab, choose **Save As**, and from the **Save As** drop-down list, select the **.xlsm** file extension to save the macro along with the workbook.

Procedure Reference: Create a Custom Macro Button on the Quick Access Toolbar

To create a custom macro button on the Quick Access toolbar:

1. Display the **Excel Options** dialog box.

2. In the **Excel Options** dialog box, select the **Quick Access Toolbar** tab.

3. In the **Choose commands from** drop-down list, select **Macros.**

4. In the **Choose commands from** list box, select the macro that you created, and click **Add** to add it to the Quick Access toolbar.

5. In the **Excel Options** dialog box, click **OK** to close the dialog box.

[handwritten: Add Macro to Quick Access Toolbar]

Procedure Reference: Run Macros Using the Macros Dialog Box

To run macros using the **Macros** dialog box:

1. Choose a worksheet to which you want to apply the macro.
2. On the **View** tab, in the **Macros** group, from the **Macros** drop-down list, select **View Macros.**
3. In the **Macro** dialog box, in the macro list box, select the macro you want to apply.
4. Click **Run.**

Procedure Reference: Run a Macro When a Workbook is Opened

To run a macro when a workbook is opened:

1. On the **Developer** tab, in the **Code** group, click **Visual Basic.**
2. If necessary, in the **Microsoft Visual Basic for Applications** window, in the **Project – VBAProject** pane, expand the **Microsoft Excel Objects** folder.
3. Double-click **ThisWorkbook.**
4. In the right pane, from the **General** drop-down list, select **Workbook.**
5. From the **Open** drop-down list, verify that **Open** is selected.
6. Write the necessary macro code and save it.
7. Close the **Microsoft Visual Basic for Applications** window.
8. Save the document and exit the Excel 2010 application.
9. Open the same document to run the macro.

Procedure Reference: Run a Macro When a Button is Clicked

To run a macro when a button is clicked:

1. On the **View** tab, in the **Macros** group, click **Macros.**
2. In the **Macros** dialog box, in the **Macro name** text box, enter a name for the macro, and click **Create.**
3. In the **Microsoft Visual Basic for Applications** window, write the macro code and save it.
4. Close the **Microsoft Visual Basic for Applications** window.
5. Display the **Excel Options** dialog box, and in the dialog box, select **Customize Ribbon.**
6. Create a new group.
7. From the **Choose Commands from** drop-down list, select **Macros.**
8. Add the command with the macro name that you created to the custom group, and click **OK.**
9. On the Ribbon, click the button to run the macro.

Procedure Reference: Assign a Macro to a Command Button

To assign a macro to a command button:

1. On the **Developer** tab, in the **Controls** group, from the **Insert** drop-down list, in the **ActiveX Controls** section, select **Command Button.**
2. Click anywhere on the worksheet to insert it.
3. In the worksheet, double-click the command button that is inserted to open the **Microsoft Visual Basic for Applications** window.
4. Type the macro code and save it.

5. Close the **Microsoft Visual Basic for Applications** window.
6. Run the macro.
   - On the **Developer** tab, in the **Controls** group, click **Design Mode** to exit the design mode.
   - Click the command button to run the macro.

ACTIVITY 1-2
Creating a Macro

Data Files:

C:\084678Data\Streamlining Workflow\Office Supplies.xlsx

Before You Begin

The Excel application is open.

Scenario:

You are assisting the accounts manager in creating a report that tracks the expenditure on office supplies for different departments in various locations. The workbook consists of four worksheets, and your manager wants you to apply the same formatting to all of them.

You want to make the following changes to the Australian, European, North American, and Summary sheets:

- Change the font color and font size of the cell that contains each worksheet's title to Blue and 24 pts respectively.

- Bold, italicize, and underline the column headings.

- Format the numerical data to currency.

Rather than making manual changes to all four sheets, you decide to format one of the sheets, record and automate actions on the remaining sheets by using a shortcut.

---

1. Begin recording a new macro in the Office Supplies workbook.

   a. Display the **Open** dialog box, navigate to the C:\084678Data\Streamlining Workflow folder, and open the Office Supplies.xlsx file.

   b. Select the European, North American, and Summary worksheets to observe that they have data formatted similar to the Australian worksheet.

   c. Select the Australian worksheet, and on the **View** tab, in the **Macros** group, from the **Macros** drop-down list, select **Record Macro.**

   d. In the **Record Macro** dialog box, in the **Macro name** text box, type *SheetFormat*

   e. Observe that **Ctrl +** is indicated by default before the text box in the **Shortcut key** section and, in the text box, type *F*

    Macro shortcut keys are case sensitive. These steps have been written to use an uppercase F as the shortcut key. If you use a lowercase f the Shift key will not be used when running the macro.

f. In the **Store macro in** drop-down list, verify that **This Workbook** is selected to store the macro in the current workbook.

g. In the **Description** text box, type *Format Worksheets* and click **OK** to begin recording the macro.

h. At the left end of the status bar, observe that a stop button is displayed, indicating the macro recording has started.

2. In the Australian worksheet, change the font size and color of the title.

a. Select cell **A1.**

b. On the **Home** tab, in the **Font** group, from the **Font Size** drop-down list, select **24.**

c. Click the **Font Color** drop-down arrow, and in the displayed gallery, in the **Standard Colors** section, select **Blue.**

3. Add bold, italic, and underline formatting to the column headings.

a. Select the range **A3:E3.**

b. In the **Font** group, click the **Bold** button.

c. Click the **Italic** button.

d. Click the **Underline** button

4. Apply currency formatting to the numerical data.

a. Select the range **B4:E9.**

b. In the **Number** group, from the **Number Format** drop-down list, select **Currency.**

5. Stop recording the macro.

a. Select the **View** tab.

b. In the **Macros** group, from the **Macros** drop-down list, select **Stop Recording.**

c. At the left end of the status bar, observe that the stop button is replaced with the begin recording button indicating that no macros are currently recording.

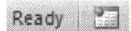

6. Run the macro on the European worksheet.

   a. Display the **European** worksheet.

   b. On the **View** tab, from the **Macros** drop-down list, select **View Macros.**

   c. In the **Macro** dialog box, observe that the **SheetFormat** macro is selected. Click **Run.**

   d. Observe that the macro performs all the recorded actions.

European Division

Item	QTR 1	QTR 2	QTR 3	QTR 4
Hardware	$3,500.00	$4,800.00	$3,400.00	$2,500.00
Software Upgradation	$300.00	$200.00	$250.00	$300.00
Furniture	$250.00	$400.00	$500.00	$700.00
Accessories	$180.00	$250.00	$200.00	$300.00
Totals:	$4,230.00	$5,650.00	$4,350.00	$3,800.00

7. Apply the macro to the North American and Summary worksheets using the keyboard shortcut.

   a. Display the **North American** worksheet and press **Ctrl+Shift+F** to apply the macro using the keyboard shortcut.

   b. Display the **Summary** worksheet and press **Ctrl+Shift+F.**

   c. Observe that the shortcut key applies the recorded actions to the **Summary** worksheet.

Summary

Item	QTR 1	QTR 2	QTR 3	QTR 4
Hardware	$12,400.00	$13,400.00	$9,100.00	$8,400.00
Software	$1,000.00	$1,150.00	$1,000.00	$1,000.00
Furniture	$950.00	$1,200.00	$1,400.00	$1,100.00
Accessories	$580.00	$700.00	$500.00	$650.00
Totals:	$14,930.00	$16,450.00	$12,000.00	$11,150.00

8. Save the workbook as a macro-enabled workbook.

   a. Display the **Save As** dialog box, type the file name as *My Office Supplies* and click **Save.**

   b. In the **Microsoft Excel** message box, observe the message indicating that these features can only be saved in a macro-enabled workbook and click **No.**

c.   From the **Save as type** drop-down list, select **Excel Macro-Enabled Workbook (*.xlsm)** and click **Save.**

TOPIC C
Edit a Macro

Now that you have created a macro in Excel, you can go further and make changes to the macro. Modifying a macro helps to meet specific requirements. In this topic, you will edit a macro.

When using a macro for common tasks such as applying multiple formats to the contents of a cell, you may find that one of the settings in the macro needs updating, though the other settings work fine. In such cases, it is best to edit the macro rather than rerecord it. Editing macros eliminates the need to rerecord complex actions.

Visual Basic for Applications

Visual Basic for Applications (VBA) is the programming language used for creating macros in Microsoft Office 2010 applications. When you record a macro, Excel automatically translates the keystrokes and commands into VBA code.

 If you are familiar with the VBA programming language and syntax, you can create macros directly in VBA.

VBA Modules

Each macro consists of a block of VBA code. Macro code is grouped in larger VBA code blocks known as *modules*. Documents and templates can contain one or more modules, and modules can contain one or more macros.

The Visual Basic Editor

The *Visual Basic Editor* is an add-in application you can use to load, view, and edit the VBA code of a macro. The application window has its own interface, menu bar, and Help system.

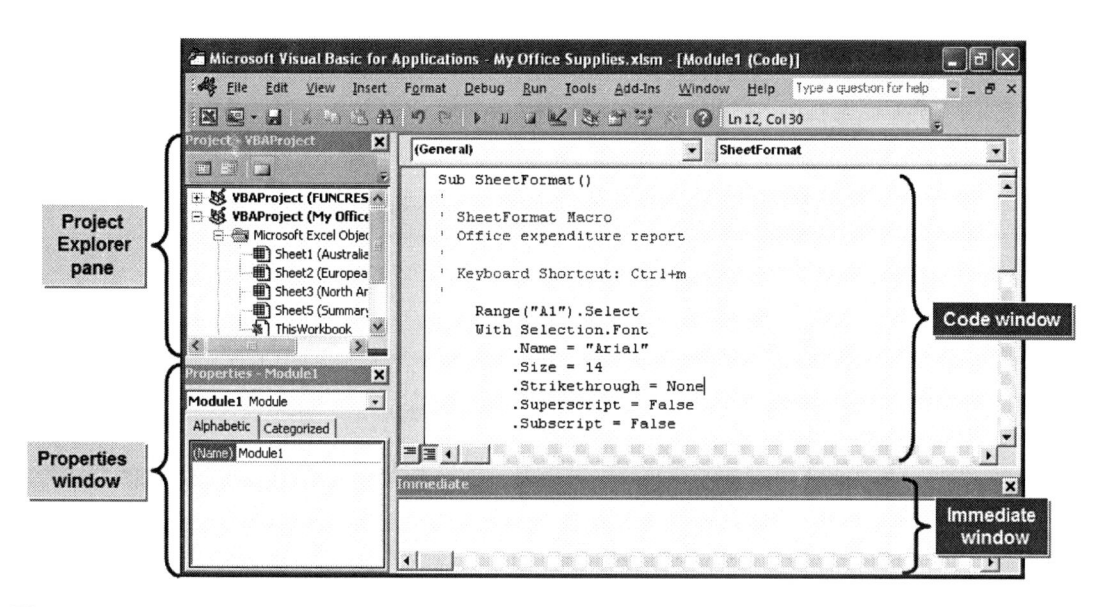

Figure 1-4: *A macro code block in the Visual Basic Editor window.*

The Visual Basic Editor window is made up of various components. The components can be displayed or hidden by using the **View** tab of the Visual Basic Editor application window.

Component	Description
Project Explorer	A hierarchical interface listing VBA modules in all open documents and templates. The normal template is listed as Normal. Open documents appear as Project objects. Open templates appear as TemplateProject objects.
Properties Window	Lists the properties of the object selected in the Project Explorer. A property is a characteristic of the object. For example, one property of a VBA module is the module's name.
Code	Displays the VBA code of the selected project for editing.
Immediate Window	Displays information resulting from debugging statements in the code or from commands typed directly into the window.

Macro Settings

You can set a security level to protect a macro by choosing the options in the **Macro Settings** category of the **Trust Center** dialog box.

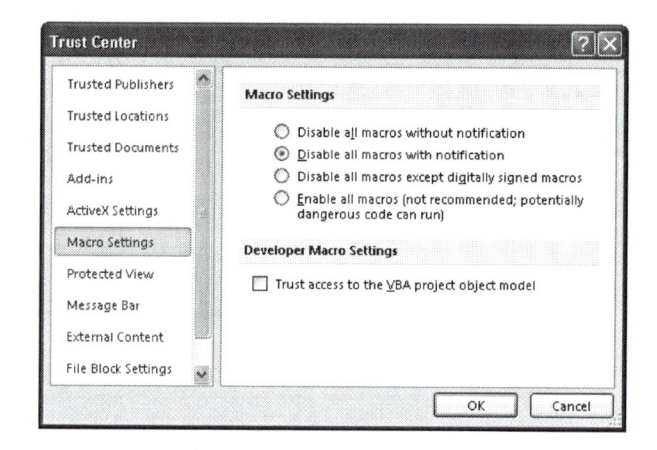

Figure 1-5: The different macro settings in the Trust Center dialog box.

Option	Description
Disable all macros without notification	Disables all macros in the workbook and their security alerts. Only the macros stored in documents in a trusted location are allowed to run.
Disable all macros with notification	Disables all macros but not their security alerts. This is the default setting. This setting allows you to choose which macro to run.
Disable all macros except digitally signed macros	Disables all macros except those that are digitally signed by a trusted publisher.
Enable all macros	Enables all macros in the workbook. This lowers the security of the computer, making it vulnerable to malicious code. This option is not recommended as it may allow potentially dangerous code in the macro to run.
Trust access to the VBA project object model	Enables macros to access the core Microsoft Visual Basic objects, methods, and properties. This option is for developers only, as it poses a security hazard.

How to Edit a Macro

Procedure Reference: Adjust Macro Security Settings

To adjust macro settings:

1. On the **File** tab, select **Options.**

2. In the **Excel Options** dialog box, in the left pane, click **Trust Center** and then click **Trust Center Settings.**

3. In the **Trust Center** dialog box, select the level of macro security you desire and click **OK** to save the macro security settings.

4. Close the **Excel Options** dialog box.

Procedure Reference: Edit a Macro

To edit a macro:

1. Open the worksheet with the macro you want to edit.

2. If necessary, enable macros in a document.

   a. In the **Security Warning** panel, click **Options.**

   b. In the **Microsoft Office Security Options** dialog box, select the **Enable This Content** option and click **OK.**

3. On the **View** tab, in the **Macros** group, from the **Macros** drop-down list, select **View Macros.**

4. In the **Macro** dialog box, in the **Macro Name** list box, select the macro you want to edit and click **Edit.**

5. Make changes to the macro in the corresponding code window of the macro.

6. Return to Excel.

7. Run the newly edited macro to test its functionality.

8. Save the file.

ACTIVITY 1-3
Editing a Macro

Before You Begin:

The My Office Supplies.xlsm file is open.

Scenario:

You have created a macro, but there are a few things you would like to change:

- The font size 24 for the worksheet titles is too large and you want to reduce it to 14.

- Remove the underline formatting for the range A3:E3.

You do not want to waste time in rerecording the entire macro. You just want to make these changes.

1. Open the SheetFormat macro in the Visual Basic Editor.

   a. On the **View** tab, in the **Macros** group, from the **Macros** drop-down list, select **View Macros.**

   b. In the **Macro** dialog box, verify that **SheetFormat** is selected by default, and click **Edit** to open the macro code in the Visual Basic Editor.

2. Edit the macro to decrease the font size of the worksheet title in cell A1 to 14 pts.

   a. Maximize the My Office Supplies.xlsm - Module1 (Code) window.

   b. Below the `Range("A1").Select` statement, in the `.Size` line of the `With` statement, double-click **24** and type *14*

   ```
   Range("A1").Select
   With Selection.Font
       .Name = "Arial"
       .Size = 14
   ```

3. Remove the underline formatting for range A3:E3.

   a. Below the `Range("A3:E3").Select` statement, in the `Selection.Font.Underline` line, double-click `xlUnderlineStyleSingle` and type **False**

   ```
   Range("A3:E3").Select
   Selection.Font.Bold = True
   Selection.Font.Italic = True
   Selection.Font.Underline = xlUnderlineStyleSingle
   ```

   b. On the toolbar, click the **Save** button to update the file with the edited macro.

   c. Close the Visual Basic Editor.

4. Update the workbook using the edited macro.

    a.   Select the **Australian** worksheet.

    b.   Press **Ctrl+Shift+F** to apply the updated macro to the sheet.

    c.   Observe that the edited format has been applied to the worksheet.

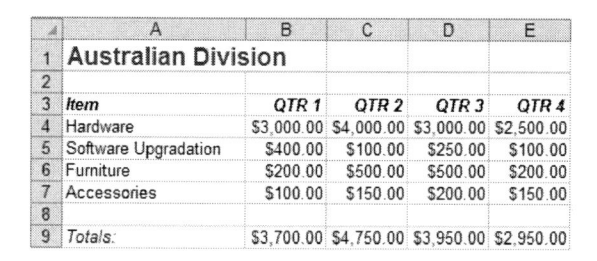

	A	B	C	D	E
1	Australian Division				
2					
3	Item	QTR 1	QTR 2	QTR 3	QTR 4
4	Hardware	$3,000.00	$4,000.00	$3,000.00	$2,500.00
5	Software Upgradation	$400.00	$100.00	$250.00	$100.00
6	Furniture	$200.00	$500.00	$500.00	$200.00
7	Accessories	$100.00	$150.00	$200.00	$150.00
8					
9	Totals:	$3,700.00	$4,750.00	$3,950.00	$2,950.00

    d.   Apply the updated macro to other worksheets in the workbook.

    e.   Save the file as ***My New Office Supplies*** in the XLSM format.

TOPIC D
Apply Conditional Formatting

In the previous topic, you automated frequently performing tasks on a worksheet. Now you can go a step further and change data appearance based upon the criteria set. In this topic, you will apply conditional formatting.

Applying conditional formatting to a worksheet allows you to quickly identify specific information that meets a given criterion. A worksheet with conditional formatting applied will make it easier to identify and differentiate between the data within it.

Conditional Formatting

Definition:

Conditional formatting is a formatting technique that applies a specified format to a cell or range of cells based upon a set of predefined criteria. In Excel, the cells to be formatted can contain numeric or textual data. The condition for formatting can be set using default or user-defined rules.

Example:

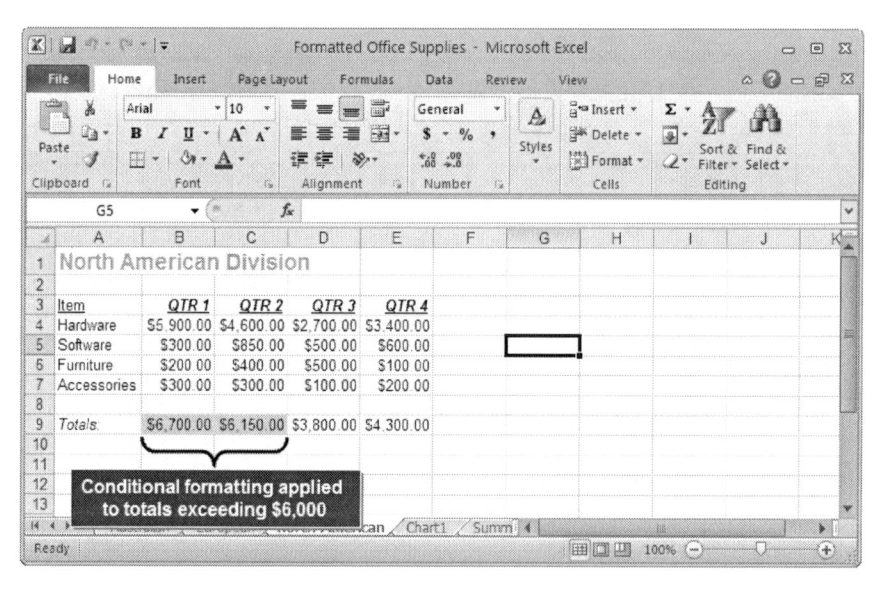

Figure 1-6: *Applying conditional format allows users to distinguish between groups of data on a worksheet.*

Conditional Formats

Excel provides different types of conditional formats that can be applied using the **Conditional Formatting** option in the **Styles** group on the **Home** tab.

Format	Used To
Highlight Cell Rules	Quickly find specific cells within a range of cells. You can format those cells based on a comparison operator. This format is applied by selecting the desired option displayed in the **Highlight Cell Rules** submenu.
Top/Bottom Rules	Find the highest and lowest values in a range of cells based on a cut-off value you specify. This format is applied by selecting the desired option in the **Top/Bottom Rules** submenu.
Data Bars	View the value of a cell relative to other cells. The length of the data bar represents the value in the cell. This format is applied by selecting a data bar format from the **Data Bars** gallery. A data bar can be customized if required.
Color Scales	Visually represent data distribution and variation. The shade of the color in this format represents higher, middle, or lower values. This format is applied by selecting a color scale format from the **Color Scales** gallery. A color scale can be customized if required.
Icon Sets	Annotate and classify data into three or five categories. Each category is represented by an icon. This format is applied by selecting an icon set type from the **Icon Sets** gallery. An icon set can be customized if required.

The Conditional Formatting Rules Manager Dialog Box

The **Conditional Formatting Rules Manager** dialog box is used to define one or more conditional format rules for data sets. This dialog box can be used to create, edit, and delete a rule. It also lists all the rules in a worksheet. This dialog box can be accessed from the **Conditional Formatting** drop-down list on the Ribbon.

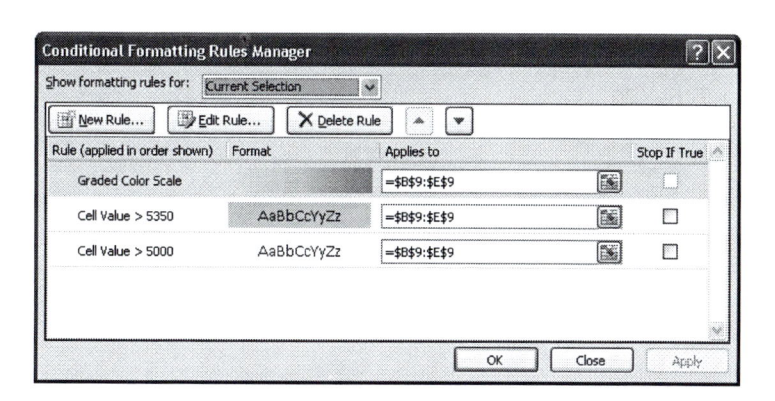

Figure 1-7: *Conditional formatting rules can be set using the Conditional Formatting Rules Manager dialog box.*

The New Formatting Rule Dialog Box

The **New Formatting Rule** dialog box lists six types of conditional formatting rules that you can apply.

Rule Type	Description
Format all cells based on their values	Cells are formatted based on their values. You need to specify the minimum and maximum values for which the formatting needs to be applied. It cannot be used for text data.
Format only cells that contain	Cells are formatted based on their numeric, text, or date type content.
Format only top or bottom ranked values	Used for selecting the top or bottom percentage of cells from the range that will be formatted.
Format only values that are above or below average	Only cells that are above or below the average value are formatted.
Format only unique or duplicate values	Used for applying conditional formatting to cells containing unique or duplicate values.
Use a formula to determine which cells to format	Used for conditionally formatting the cells based on a formula.

The Edit Formatting Rule Dialog Box

The formatting rules can be edited by using the **Edit Formatting Rule** dialog box. To change the formatting criteria, you have to select the rule type and edit the description.

Clear Rules

The **Clear Rules** submenu, located in the **Conditional Formatting** drop-down list, can be used for removing the conditional formatting rules. This submenu contains options for deleting conditional formatting from a worksheet, selected cells, tables, or PivotTables.

How to Apply Conditional Formatting

Procedure Reference: Apply Conditional Formatting

To apply conditional formatting:

1. Select a cell or cells to which you want to apply the formatting.

2. On the **Home** tab, in the **Styles** group, click **Conditional Formatting.**

3. From the **Conditional Formatting** drop-down list, select a conditional format type.

   - Select **Highlight Cells Rules** and from the **Highlight Cells Rules** submenu, select a rule. In the displayed dialog box, enter a value for comparison and specify a formatting color to highlight cells.

   - Select **Top/Bottom Rules** and from the **Top/Bottom Rules** submenu, select a rule . In the displayed dialog box, enter a value for the number of values to be formatted and specify a formatting color to be applied to the highest or lowest values in a range of cells.

   - Select **Data Bars** and from the **Data Bars** submenu, select a data bar type to display the values as bars of proportional length.

   - Select **Color Scales** and from the **Color Scales** submenu, select a color scale to differentiate data values visually.

   - Select **Icon Sets** and from the **Icon Sets** submenu, select an icon set to classify data into three to five categories and apply an icon to each data classification.

Procedure Reference: Create a New Conditional Formatting Rule

To create a new conditional formatting rule:

1. On the **Home** tab, in the **Styles** group, click **Conditional Formatting.**

2. Display the **New Formatting Rules** dialog box.

   - Display the **New Formatting Rules** dialog box using the **Conditional Formatting Rules Manager** dialog box.

     a. Select **Manage Rules.**

     b. In the **Conditional Formatting Rules Manager** dialog box, if necessary, select an option from the **Show formatting rules for** drop-down list to display all rules in a particular location.

     c. Click **New Rule.**

   - Or, from the **Conditional Formatting** drop-down list, select **New Rule.**

3. In the **Select a rule type** section, select the desired option.

   - Select **2–Color Scale** to compare a range of cells by using a gradient of 2 colors.

   - Select **3–Color Scale** to compare a range of cells by using a gradient of 3 colors.

   - Select **Data Bar** to compare values in a range of cells by representing them as bars of proportional length.

   - Select **Icon Sets** to classify data into three to five categories and assign an icon to each category.

4. In the **Edit The Rule Description** section, format cells based on their values.

    ●   From the **Format Style** drop-down list, select a format style.

    ●   From the **Minimum and Maximum Type** drop-down lists, select **Lowest Value, Number, Percent, Formula,** or **Percentile.**

    ●   In the **Minimum and Maximum Value** text boxes, select or enter a value.

    ●   From the **Color** drop-down lists, select a color for the minimum and maximum values.

    ●   In the **Bar Appearance** section, specify a fill type, fill color, border type, border color, and bar direction.

    ●   From the **Icon Style** gallery, select a category to classify data.

    ●   In the **Display each icon according to these rules** section, select a comparison operator, enter a value, and specify the type of data for each icon.

5. Preview the format and click **OK** to apply the new conditional format.

Procedure Reference: Edit an Existing Conditional Formatting Rule

To edit an existing conditional formatting rule:

1. On the **Home** tab, in the **Styles** group, from the **Conditional Formatting** drop-down list, select **Manage Rules.**

2. In the **Conditional Formatting Rules Manager** dialog box, if necessary, select an option from the **Show Formatting Rules For** drop-down list to display all rules in a particular location.

3. In the **Rule** pane, select the rule you want to edit.

4. Click **Edit Rule.**

5. In the **Edit Formatting Rule** dialog box, edit the properties and settings of the rules.

6. Click **OK** to close the **Edit Formatting Rule** dialog box.

7. In the **Conditional Formatting Rules Manager** dialog box, click **OK** to update the rule for the data.

Procedure Reference: Clear a Conditional Formatting Rule

To clear a conditional formatting rule:

1. Select a cell, worksheet, table, or PivotTable with a conditional formatting rule applied.

2. On the **Home** tab, in the **Styles** group, from the **Conditional Formatting** drop-down list, select **Clear Rules,** and from the submenu, select an option.

    ●   Select **Clear Rules from Selected Cells** to clear rules from the selected cell.

    ●   Select **Clear Rules from Entire Sheet** to clear rules from the entire worksheet.

    ●   Select **Clear Rules from This Table** to clear rules from the selected table.

    ●   Select **Clear Rules from This PivotTable** to clear rules from the selected PivotTable.

Procedure Reference: Apply Conditional Formatting Using Conditional Logic Formulas

To apply conditional formatting using a formula:

1. On the **Home** tab, in the **Styles** group, from the **Conditional Formatting** drop-down list, select **Manage Rules.**

2. In the **New Formatting Rule** dialog box, in the **Select a rule to format** section, select **Use a formula to determine which cells to format.**

3. In the **Edit the Rule Description** section, in the **Format values where this formula is true** list box, enter a conditional logic formula containing the `IF()` or `IFERROR ()` function.

4. If necessary, in the **Edit the Rule Description** section, click **Format** and using the tabs and options provided in the **Format Cells** dialog box, choose the required settings and click **OK.**

5. In the **New Formatting Rule** dialog box, click **OK** to apply the conditional format.

Conditional Logic Functions

Conditional logic functions result in either a True or False value for a given condition. Conditional Logic functions are created using the `IF()` or `IFERROR()` function. For instance, if you want to conditionally format cells in the range **A1:A5** that have a value greater than **1000**, you would enter the formula as `=IF(OR(A1>1000, A2>1000, A3>1000, A4>1000,A5>1000))`.

Procedure Reference: Delete a Conditional Formatting Rule

To delete a conditional formatting rule:

1. On the **Home** tab, in the **Styles** group, from the **Conditional Formatting** drop-down list, select **Manage Rules.**

2. If necessary, in the **Conditional Formatting Rules Manager** dialog box, select an option from the **Show formatting rules for** drop-down list to display all rules in a particular location.

3. In the **Conditional Formatting Rules Manager** dialog box, in the **Rule** pane, select the rule you want to delete.

4. Click **Delete Rule** to delete the conditional formatting rule.

Procedure Reference: Sort Data Using Conditional Formatting

To sort data using conditional formatting:

1. On the **Home** tab, in the **Editing** group, click **Sort & Filter.**

2. From the **Sort & Filter** drop-down list, select **Custom Sort.**

3. In the **Sort** dialog box, from the **Sort By** drop-down list, select the column you want to sort.

4. From the **Sort** drop-down list, select the type of sort.
   - Select **Values** to sort by cell value.
   - Select **Cell Color** to sort by cell color.
   - Select **Font Color** to sort by font color.
   - Select **Cell Icon** to sort by an icon set.

5. From the **Order** drop-down list, select the order option in which you would like to sort.

6. If necessary, click **Add Level**, and specify the value, cell color, font color, or cell icon for the next sort level.

7. Click **OK** to sort the data.

Procedure Reference: Filter Data Using Conditional Formatting

To filter data using conditional formatting:

1. Select the column to which conditional formatting has been applied.

2. On the **Home** tab, in the **Editing** group, click **Sort & Filter.**

3. From the **Sort & Filter** drop-down list, click **Filter** to display the arrow in the column header.

4. Click the column header filter drop-down arrow, and from the **Filter By Color** submenu, choose the color by which you want to filter a column.

ACTIVITY 1-4
Creating a Conditional Format

Before You Begin
The My New Office Supplies.xlsm file is open.

Scenario:
You created a workbook containing details of the amount spent on office supplies in three regions. Due to budget constraints, the management has decided that for the North American region, total spending above $5,000 in any quarter should be highlighted.

1. Select the range displaying totals of each quarter in the North American worksheet tab.

   a. Select the **North American** worksheet.

   b. Select the range **B9:E9**.

2. Apply a condition to the North American quarterly totals so that any amount exceeding $5,000 will be formatted in red.

   a. On the **Home** tab, in the **Styles** group, from the **Conditional Formatting** drop-down list, select **Highlight Cells Rules→Greater Than.**

   b. In the **Greater Than** dialog box, in the **Format cells that are GREATER THAN** text box, type *5000*

   c. From the **with** drop-down list, select **Light Red Fill**, and click **OK** and then click cell **G9** to deselect the range **B9:E9.**

   d. Observe that the values in cells **B9** and **C9** are displayed in light red color as the values are greater than 5000.

   > $7,000.00 $6,050.00 $3,700.00 $4,400.00

   e. Save the file and close it.

ACTIVITY 1-5
Editing Conditional Formats

Data Files:

C:\084678Data\Streamlining Workflow\Product Sales.xlsx

Before You Begin

The Excel application is open.

Scenario:

On the Summary worksheet of the Product Sales workbook, you applied conditional formatting to the Totals row to highlight values greater than $5,000. Later, you decide to modify the conditional formatting to apply a 2-color scale that shows lower values in orange and higher values in yellow, a format that you have applied for quarterly sales and annual sales in the OGC-Sales worksheet. Also, in the OGC-Sales worksheet, you decide to remove the conditional formatting for the Annual Totals column.

---

1. Apply the data bar conditional formatting to the Totals row in the Summary worksheet.

   a. Display the **Open** dialog box, navigate to the C:\084678Data\Streamlining Workflow folder, and open the Product Sales.xlsx file.

   b. Verify that the **Summary** worksheet is selected and select the range **B9:E9.**

   c. On the **Home** tab, in the **Styles** group, from the **Conditional Formatting** drop-down list, select **Manage Rules**, and in the **Conditional Formatting Rules Manager** dialog box, click **Delete Rule** and then click **New Rule.**

   d. In the **New Formatting Rule** dialog box, in the **Edit the Rule Description** section, in the **Format Style** drop-down list, verify that **2-Color Scale** is selected.

   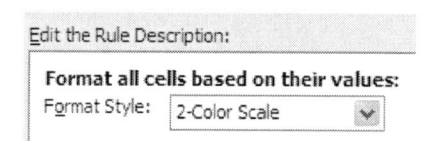

   e. Observe that the color for the lowest value is orange and for the highest value is yellow, and click **OK.**

   f. In the **Conditional Formatting Rules Manager** dialog box, click **OK** to apply formatting to the data set.

   g. Click any cell outside the range to deselect the range **B9:E9.**

   h. On the worksheet, observe that the data is formatted according to the new conditional format rule by displaying the Quarter 3 total in yellow because it is the highest value and the Quarter 4 total in orange because it is the lowest value.

---

2. Apply a conditional formatting rule to the Annual Totals column in the OGC-Sales worksheet to highlight the highest value.

    a. Display the **OGC-Sales** worksheet.

    b. Select the range **R5:R12.**

    c. On the **Home** tab, in the **Styles** group, from the **Conditional Formatting** drop-down list, select **Manage Rules.**

    d. Observe that the existing rule is displayed in the **Conditional Formatting Rules Manager** dialog box.

    e. In the **Conditional Formatting Rules Manager** dialog box, in the **Rule** pane, select the **Graded Color Scale** rule.

    f. Click **Edit Rule** to edit the rule.

    g. In the **Edit Formatting Rule** dialog box, in the **Select a Rule Type** section, select **Format only top or bottom ranked values.**

    h. In the **Edit the Rule Description** section, in the **Format Values that rank in the** drop-down list, verify that **Top** is selected, and in the text box, double-click the number **10** and type *1*

    i. In the **Preview** section, click **Format.**

    j. In the **Format Cells** dialog box, select the **Fill** tab, and in the **Background Color** section, select light blue and click **OK.**

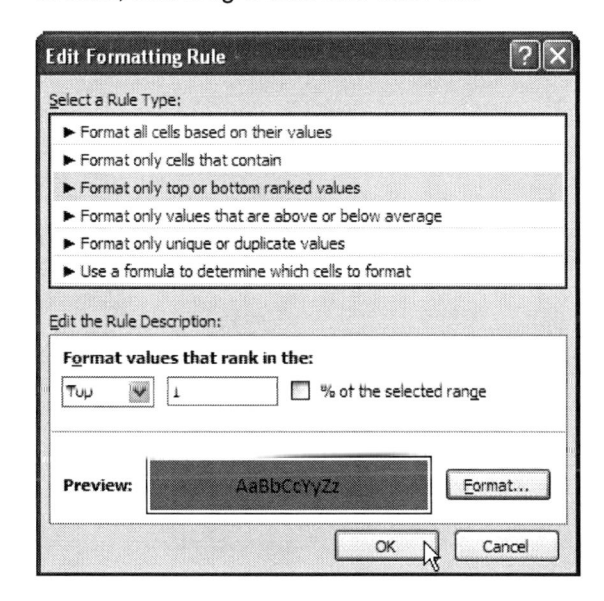

    k. In the **Edit Formatting Rule** dialog box, click **OK** to apply the formatting rule, and in the **Conditional Formatting Rules Manager** dialog box, click **OK.**

3. Apply a conditional formatting rule to the Annual Totals column in the OGC-Sales worksheet to highlight the lowest value.

    a. Verify that the range R5:R12 is selected.

    b. On the **Home** tab, in the **Styles** group, from the **Conditional Formatting** drop-down list, select **Top/Bottom Rules,** and in the displayed submenu, select **Bottom 10 Items.**

c. In the **Bottom 10 Items** dialog box, in the **Format cells that rank in the BOTTOM** text box, double-click the number **10** and type *1*

d. From the **Format cells that rank in the BOTTOM** drop-down list, select **Light Red Fill** and click **OK.**

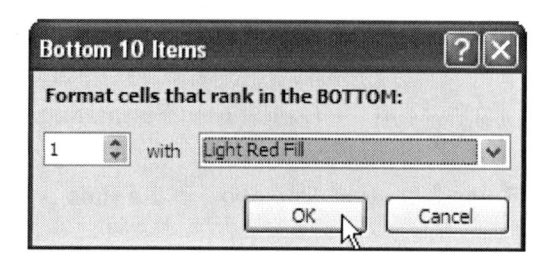

e. Click any cell outside the range to deselect the selected range.

f. Observe that the highest value is in blue and the lowest value in light red.

g. Save the file as *My Product Sales*

ACTIVITY 1-6
Sorting and Filtering Conditionally Formatted Data

Before You Begin:
The My Product Sales.xlsx file is open.

Scenario:
You want to group the total monthly sales data in the OGC–Total Sales by Month worksheet based on the color format applied. After grouping data, you want the workbook to display only the data grouped by a certain color.

1. Group data by cell color.

   a. Display the **OGC-Total Sales by Month** worksheet.

   b. Observe that a pink colored format has been applied to sales data over $970.

   c. On the **Home** tab, in the **Editing** group, from the **Sort & Filter** drop-down list, select **Custom Sort.**

   d. In the **Sort** dialog box, in the **Column** section, from the **Sort by** drop-down list, select **(Column B).**

   e. From the **Sort On** drop-down list, select **Cell Color.**

   f. Verify that pink is displayed in the **Order** drop-down list, which indicates that the cells having that color will appear on top upon sorting. Click **OK** to sort data.

   Total Sales

January	$975
February	$1,100
March	$1,000
April	$990
June	$1,100
July	$1,653
December	$1,230
May	$930
August	$874
September	$789
October	$878
November	$960

   [handwritten: Select Range cell first]

2. Filter the data listed in pink color and retain only the data listed in green color.

   a. On the **Home** tab, in the **Editing** group, from the **Sort & Filter** drop-down list, select **Filter.**

   b. Observe that a filter drop-down arrow is added to cells **A1** and **B1.**

   c. Click the filter drop-down arrow in the cell **B1**, and from the menu, choose **Filter by Color.**

d. From the **Filter by Color** submenu, in the **Filter by Cell Color** section, select the green color filter to display only the data listed in green on the worksheet.

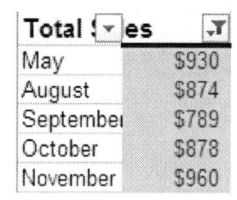

Total Sales	
May	$930
August	$874
September	$789
October	$878
November	$960

e. Save the file as *My Sorted Product Sales* and close it.

TOPIC E

Add Data Validation Criteria

You worked with worksheets that store various types of data. Forcing certain cells in the worksheet to accept only a specific type of data helps you to have greater control over the input. In this topic, you will add a data validation criterion.

Applying data validation rules in worksheets ensures that all input values fall within a specified range. The validation criteria will help improve the integrity of your data by forcing specified cells to accept only a specific type of data.

Data Validation

Definition:

Data validation is a technique used for restricting the input value or type of data based on a specific set of criteria. Cells with data validation criteria applied to them can accept data that meets the validation criteria. Any attempt to store data of a type other than that defined in the criteria will result in an error message. Data validation can include a user-defined input message, to indicate the type of data that a cell or range can contain.

Example:

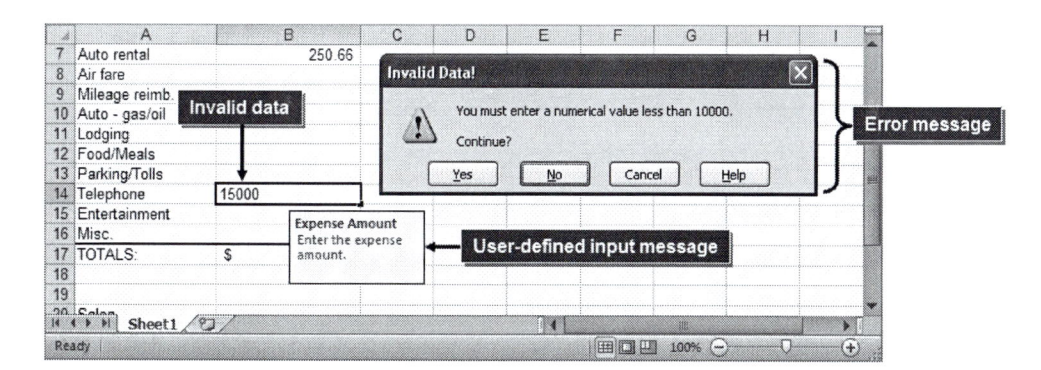

Figure 1-8: Data validation restricts the type of data that can be entered.

The Data Validation Dialog Box

The **Data Validation** dialog box has three tabs to specify the settings, input message, and error alert for data that can be entered in a cell.

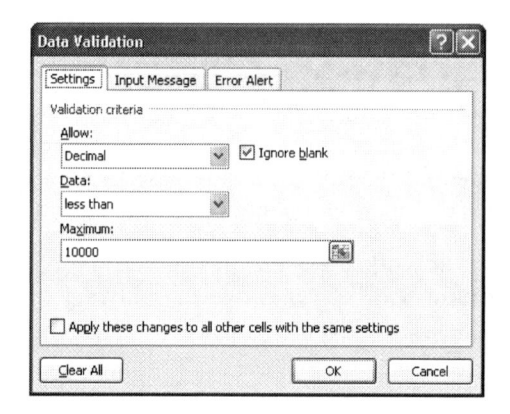

Figure 1-9: *The Data Validation dialog box specifies the criteria for data validation.*

Tab	Function
Settings	Allows you to set the permitted value type such as the decimal, date, and time. The range of data that can be entered in a cell is also set here. It is also possible to create a drop-down list by using the options on this tab.
Input Message	Allows you to set a specific title and description of data to be entered in a cell.
Error Alert	Allows you to specify a style, title, and description of an error alert that pops up if the input data does not meet the specified criteria.

Types of Error Alerts

Excel allows you to set any of three error alert styles.

Icon	Type	Description
	Stop	Restricts users from entering invalid data in a cell.
	Warning	Warns the users that they have entered invalid data, but does not restrict them from entering it.
	Information	Informs the users that they have entered invalid data, but accepts the entered values.

How to Add Data Validation Criteria

Procedure Reference: Add a Data Validation Rule

To add a data validation rule:

1. In an Excel worksheet, select the range to which you want to apply data validation.
2. On the **Data** tab, in the **Data Tools** group, click **Data Validation.**
3. In the **Data Validation** dialog box, on the **Settings** tab, set the criteria for a valid entry.
   - From the **Allow** drop-down list, select the type of validation you want.
     - Select **Any value** to accept any value either a number or text.
     - Select **Whole number** to restrict the data entry only to whole numbers within a specified range.
     - Select **Decimal** to restrict the data entry only to decimal numbers within a specified range.
     - Select **List** to restrict the data entry only to values in a specified list of values.
     - Select **Date** to restrict the data entry only to dates within a specified time frame.
     - Select **Time** to restrict the data entry only to time within a specified time frame.
     - Select **Text Length** to restrict the data entry only to text of a specified length.
     - Select **Custom** to calculate values in a cell using a specified formula.
   - From the **Data** drop-down list, select a comparison operator.
   - In the **Minimum and/or Maximum** text boxes, set the desired values for valid data entries.
4. On the **Input Message** tab, create an optional message.
   - In the **Title** text box, type a title for the message.
   - In the **Input Message** text area, type the required message.
5. If necessary, on the **Error Alert** tab, make changes to the default error message.
   - From the **Style** drop-down list, select an error icon.
   - In the **Title** text box, enter a title for the error message.
   - In the **Error Message** text area, type the desired error message.
6. Click **OK** to add data validation.
7. Test the data validation rule.

Procedure Reference: Create a Drop-Down List from a Range of Cells

To create a drop-down list from a range of cells:

1. In an Excel workbook, create a list of valid entries for the drop-down list.
2. Select the range of valid entries.
3. At the left end of the **Formula Bar**, in the **Name** text box, type a name for the selected list.
4. Select a cell where the drop-down list should appear.
5. In the **Data Validation** dialog box, select the **Settings** tab.
6. From the **Allow** drop-down list, select **List.**
7. In the **Source** text box, type the equals sign and enter the reference name in the list you created. All items in the reference list will become part of the drop-down list.

8. Verify that the **In-cell Drop-down** check box is checked to ensure that the drop-down arrow will appear within the cell.

9. If necessary, on the **Input Message** tab, create a message.

10. If necessary, on the **Error Alert** tab, create a message for invalid data entries.

11. Click **OK.**

ACTIVITY 1-7
Adding Data Validation Rules

Data Files:

C:\084678Data\Streamlining Workflow\Monthly Expenses.xlsx

Before You Begin
The Excel application is open.

Scenario:
You are creating a workbook that tracks monthly travel expenses for employees. You decide to implement the following restrictions on data in the range of cells showing expense values.

- Force the expense amounts entered to accept only numerical values less than 10,000.
- Display a short note describing the correct data the cells can store.
- Return an error message if a user tries to enter an invalid value as an expense amount.
- Allow the user to select a valid entry for department name from a drop-down list.
- Restrict the destination name entered to eight characters.

---

1. For the range B7:B16, set the validation criteria to accept decimal values less than 10,000.

    a. Display the **Open** dialog box, navigate to the C:\084678Data\Streamlining Workflow folder, and open the Monthly Expenses.xlsx file.

    b. Select the range **B7:B16.**

    c. On the **Data** tab, in the **Data Tools** group, click **Data Validation.**

    d. In the **Data Validation** dialog box, on the **Settings** tab, from the **Allow** drop-down list, select **Decimal.**

    e. From the **Data** drop-down list, select **less than.**

    f. In the **Maximum** text box, type *10000*

---

2. Create a message to be displayed on any cell of the selected range.

    a. In the **Data Validation** dialog box, select the **Input Message** tab.

    b. In the **Title** text box, type *Expense Amount*

    c. In the **Input message** text area, type *Enter the expense amount*

---

3. Set the error alert for invalid data.

    a. In the **Data Validation** dialog box, select the **Error Alert** tab.

---

b. Observe that **Show error alert after invalid data is entered** check box is checked by default, and verify that **Stop** is selected in the **Style** drop-down list.

c. In the **Title** text box, type *Invalid Data*

d. In the **Error message** text area, type *You must enter a numerical value less than 10000.* and click **OK.**

e. Observe that the message and title are displayed when a cell in the range B7:B16 is selected.

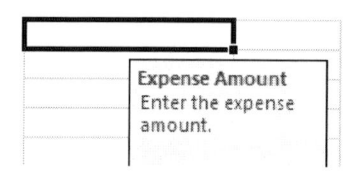

4. Create a drop-down list for entering a valid department name.

a. Select cell **B5.**

b. Display the **Data Validation** dialog box.

c. In the **Data Validation** dialog box, on the **Settings** tab, from the **Allow** drop-down list, select **List.**

d. In the **Source** text box, specify the range *=A20:A24* and click **OK** to create a drop-down list for cell **B5.**

e. Click the drop-down arrow to display the department names in the drop-down list, and click the drop-down arrow again.

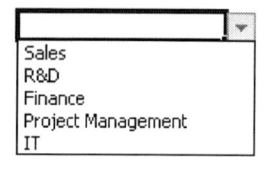

5. Create a data validation rule that restricts the length of characters allowed in a cell to six.

a. Select cell **B3.**

b. Display the **Data Validation** dialog box.

c. On the **Settings** tab, from the **Allow** drop-down list, select **Text length.**

d. From the **Data** drop-down list, select **less than or equal to.**

e. In the **Maximum** text box, type *6* to limit the number of characters to six.

f. On the **Input Message** tab, in the **Input message** text area, type *Enter an employee code with six or fewer characters.*

g. Click **OK** to apply the data validation rule.

h. Observe that the message is displayed because the cell is selected.

6. Test the data validation rules.

a. In cell **B3,** enter an employee code with seven characters.

b. In the **Microsoft Excel** message box, click **Retry.**

c. Type *MKT123* and press **Enter** to enter valid data into the cell.

d. Select cell **B5,** and from the drop-down list, select **Sales.**

e. Select cell **B7,** and enter a value greater than 10,000 to view the error alert.

f. In the **Invalid Data** warning box, click **Retry.**

g. In cell **B7,** enter *9990.50* to enter valid data into the cell.

h. Save the file as *My Monthly Expenses* and close it.

Lesson 1 Follow-up

In this lesson, you streamlined your workflow and increased your productivity by customizing the properties of a workbook. You also created macros and applied data validation to cells. These features will help you to save time and protect the integrity of data.

1. **For what types of applications would you use macros?**

2. **What are the various properties of a workbook that you might need to customize?**

2 | Collaborating with Other Users

Lesson Time: 1 hour(s), 40 minutes

Lesson Objectives:

In this lesson, you will collaborate with other workbook users.

You will:

- Protect files.
- Share a workbook.
- Set revision tracking.
- Review tracked revisions.
- Merge workbooks.
- Administer digital signatures.
- Restrict document access.

Introduction

You worked on developing a workbook. You would now like to include other people in the development process. In this lesson, you will collaborate with others.

In a work environment, there may be instances where you may need to collaborate with other users and work on a common file. Protecting your workbook will help you to share your data with other users in a secure manner.

TOPIC A
Protect Files

You streamlined your workflow to help you work more efficiently. Now, you have some Excel files to share with others, while ensuring that the data in the files is safe. In this topic, you will protect your files.

You might have come across instances where you thought of sharing a workbook with others. However, you may not want everyone who views the worksheet to edit the data or layout of the workbook in any way. Protecting a workbook before sharing it will ensure that the data is secure and can be modified by only trusted sources.

The Collaboration Process

In Excel, the collaboration process involves four stages: protecting, saving, sharing, and reviewing.

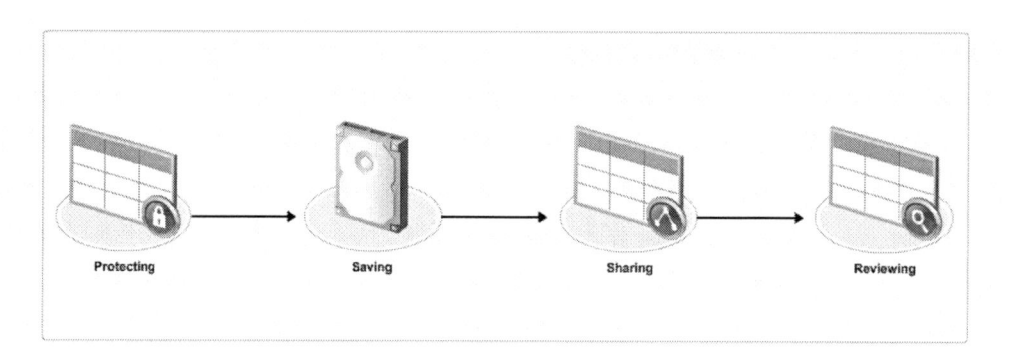

Figure 2-1: *Various stages in the collaboration process.*

Stage	Description
Protecting	Users protect the worksheet to ensure that other users do not alter the elements in the sheet.
Saving	Users save the workbook as a shared workbook, which can be placed at a common location so that it can be accessed by all persons working on the workbook.
Sharing	Users share the workbook to allow other users to make changes.
Reviewing	Users review the workbook to view and incorporate the changes made by others.

Worksheet Protection

In Excel, you can protect worksheets by locking and hiding cells. You can neither edit the content in locked cells nor display the content from hidden cells on the Formula bar. You can protect cells by checking the **Locked** and **Hidden** check boxes, on the **Protection** tab, in the **Format Cells** dialog box. The lock and hide options come into effect only when the worksheet is protected by using the **Protect Sheet** option, in the **Changes** group, on the **Review** tab. By default, all cells in a new workbook are locked.

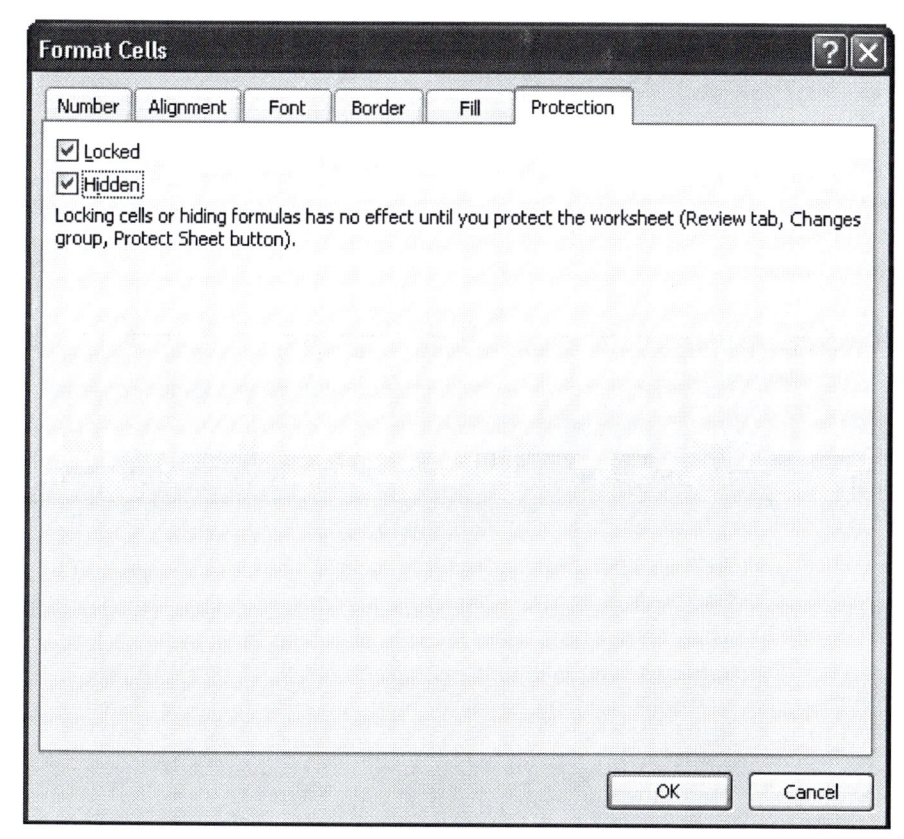

Figure 2-2: The Format Cells dialog box displaying the options to lock and hide cells.

File Protection Options

Excel has two security options for protecting a workbook against unauthorized opening and modification. Additionally, you can set a password to protect the worksheet structure and window layout of workbooks. Users without the password are not allowed to either move a worksheet or alter the display of windows in a workbook.

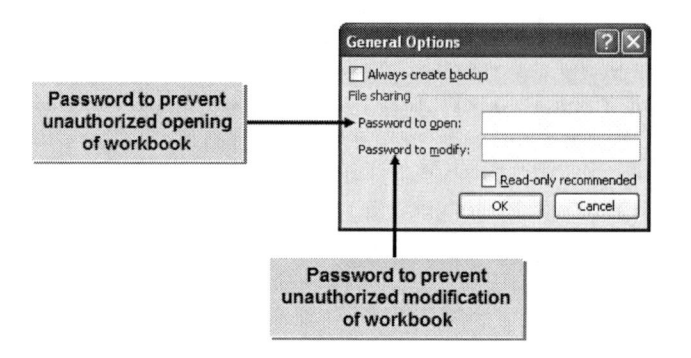

Figure 2-3: *User can protect files by setting up passwords for opening and modifying them.*

The Changes Group

The **Changes** group on the **Review** tab has options to protect, share, edit, and track changes in either a worksheet or a workbook.

Option	Description
Protect Sheet	Allows you to specify the options that help to protect a worksheet.
Protect Workbook	Prevents new sheets from being created and limits the access of a workbook to specific users.
Share Workbook	Allows different users to access a workbook from different locations and contribute to the completion of the workbook. The workbook needs to be saved in a folder, which can be shared over a network. However, a workbook with tables cannot be shared. Either worksheets with tables need to be converted to ranges, or XML mapping needs to be removed.
Protect and Share Workbook	Allows you to protect a workbook, and at the same time share it among multiple users on the network. The workbook can be protected by specifying a password, which prevents users from turning off track changing.
Allow Users to Edit Ranges	Allows users to edit ranges of protected cells. This option can be used only if the computer is connected to a Microsoft Windows domain.
Track Changes	Allows you to track all the changes made to the workbook.

The Protect Workbook Option

The **Protect Workbook** option in the **Changes** group of the **Review** tab allows you to restrict permission to edit or access a workbook. This option displays the **Protect Structure and Windows** dialog box, which you can use to protect the structure of the workbook, and ensures that the workbook window always opens in the same size and position. Restrictions are placed by specifying a password that must be entered before making any modification.

How to Protect Files

Procedure Reference: Protect Worksheets

To protect worksheets:

1. In the **Format Cells** dialog box, set the desired protection level.

    a. Select the range of cells you want to lock.

    b. On the **Home** tab, in the **Cells** group, from the **Format** drop-down list, select **Format Cells.**

    c. In the **Format Cells** dialog box, select the **Protection** tab.

    d. On the **Protection** tab, lock or hide the selected range of cells.

    - Check **Locked** to lock the cells.

     By default, the cells in a worksheet are locked. You can only lock the cells that were previously unlocked.

    - Check **Hidden** to hide the formulas in cells.

    e. Click **OK** to close the dialog box and save the settings.

2. Set the desired permission levels.

    a. On the **Review** tab, in the **Changes** group, click **Protect Sheet.**

    b. If necessary, in the **Protect Sheet** dialog box, in the **Password to unprotect sheet** text box, type a password.

    c. In the **Protect Sheet** dialog box, in the **Allow all users of this worksheet to** list box, check the tasks you want users to perform and click **OK.**

    d. If necessary, retype your password for confirmation and click **OK.**

    e. Click **OK** to close the **Protect Sheet** dialog box and save the settings.

Procedure Reference: Allow Users to Edit Specific Cell Ranges in a Password-Protected Worksheet

To allow users to edit specific cell ranges in a password-protected worksheet:

1. On the **Review** tab, in the **Changes** group, click **Allow users to Edit Ranges.**

2. In the **Allow Users to Edit Ranges** dialog box, click **New.**

3. In the **New Range** dialog box, in the **Title** text box, type a title for the range.

4. Specify the range of cells that users can edit.

    - In the **Refers to cells** text box, type the cell range or;

    - Click the **Range Selection** button and select the desired range.

5. In the **Range Password** text box, type a password and click **OK.**

6. In the **Confirm Password** dialog box, retype the password for confirmation and click **OK.**

7. In the **Allow Users To Edit Ranges** dialog box, click **Apply** and then click **OK.**

Procedure Reference: Remove Specific Content from a Workbook

To remove specific content from a workbook by inspecting it:

1. Select the **File** tab.

2. In the Backstage view, in the **Prepare for Sharing** section, from the **Check for Issues** drop-down list, select **Inspect Document.**

3. If necessary, in the **Microsoft Excel** message box, click **Yes** to save the latest changes made to the workbook.

4. In the **Document Inspector** dialog box, check the check boxes corresponding to the content you want to inspect in the workbook and click **Inspect.**

5. Review the results displayed by the **Document Inspector** dialog box corresponding to the content you want to remove and select the **Remove All** option corresponding to each type of content that you want to remove.

6. If necessary, click **Reinspect** to inspect the workbook again.

7. Click **Close.**

Procedure Reference: Protect the Structure and Window Layout of Workbooks

To protect the structure and window layout of workbooks from being altered:

1. On the **Review** tab, in the **Changes** group, click **Protect Workbook.**

2. In the **Protect Structure and Windows** dialog box, in the **Protect Workbook For** section, specify the type of protection.
   - Check the **Structure** check box to restrict users from adding, editing, or deleting worksheets.
   - Check the **Windows** check box to ensure that the window always opens in the same size and position.

3. In the **Password (Optional)** text box, type a password to restrict access and then click **OK.**

4. Retype the password and click **OK** to confirm it.

Procedure Reference: Protect Workbooks from Being Opened or Modified

To protect workbooks from being opened or modified:

1. Open the workbook you want to protect.

2. On the **File** tab, select **Save As.**

3. In the **Save As** dialog box, navigate to the folder in which you want to save the file.

4. From the **Tools** drop-down list, select **General Options.**

5. In the **General Options** dialog box, in the **File Sharing** section, specify a password to open or modify a workbook.
   - In the **Password to open** text box, type a password to open the file.
   - In the **Password to modify** text box, type a password to modify the file.

6. Click **OK,** and in the **Confirm Password** text box, retype the passwords for confirmation and then click **OK.**

7. Click **Save.**

ACTIVITY 2-1
Protecting a Worksheet

Data Files:

C:\084678Data\Collaborating with Others\Display.xlsx

Before You Begin:
The Excel application is open.

Scenario:
You are the regional head for the western region of Our Global Company (OGC) LLC. You created a report on the sales achieved by each sales person and wanted to send it to the human resources department. You also need to send a copy of it to all sales personnel for their information. You decide to modify the settings in such a way that anyone can open the file, select a cell or range of cells, and make formatting changes to the worksheet, but only the person with whom you share the password can make changes to the numerical data stored in the worksheet.

---

1. Lock the contents in the worksheet and hide the formulas.

   a. Display the **Open** dialog box, navigate to the C:\084678Data\Collaborating with Others folder and open the Display.xlsx file.

   b. Select range **A1:S11.**

   c. On the **Home** tab, in the **Cells** group, from the **Format** drop-down list, select **Format Cells.**

   d. In the **Format Cells** dialog box, select the **Protection** tab.

   e. Observe that the **Locked** check box is checked because this is the default setting in Excel and also observe the message stating that the setting comes into effect only when the worksheet is protected.

   f. Check the **Hidden** check box, and then click **OK** to secure data and to hide formulas.

   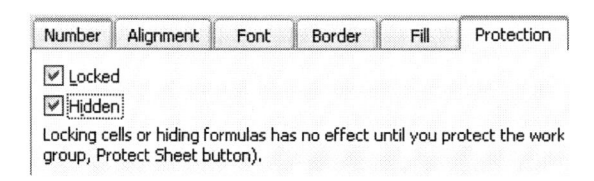

2. Protect the worksheet with a password, permitting only the selection and formatting of cells.

   a. On the **Review** tab, in the **Changes** group, click **Protect Sheet.**

   b. In the **Protect Sheet** dialog box, in the **Password to unprotect sheet** text box, type *password*

You can also set your own password, but be sure to use the password you set, when you are prompted to enter the password later in the activity.

    c.   In the **Allow all users of this worksheet to** list box, verify that the **Select locked cells** and **Select unlocked cells** check boxes are checked.

    d.   Check the **Format cells** check box and click **OK**.

    e.   In the **Confirm Password** dialog box, in the **Reenter password to proceed** text box, type *password* and click **OK**.

3.   Test your settings.

    a.   Select cell **B6**.

    b.   Observe that the **Formula Bar** remains blank because the cells were hidden by using the option on the **Protection** tab of the **Format Cells** dialog box.

    c.   Enter any number in cell **E5**.

    d.   Observe that the **Microsoft Excel** warning box opens, indicating that you are trying to change the content of a protected cell. Click **OK**.

    e.   Select the range **A5:A9**.

    f.   On the **Home** tab, in the **Font** group, click the **Italic** button to italicize the salespersons' names.

    g.   Observe that although you are not allowed to change the content of cells, you are able to format the font.

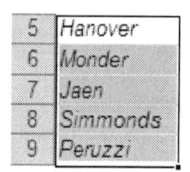

4.   Verify if users with the password can edit the worksheet.

    a.   On the **Review** tab, in the **Changes** group, click **Unprotect Sheet**.

    b.   In the **Unprotect Sheet** dialog box, in the **Password** text box, type *password* and click **OK**.

    c.   Change the value in cell **S3** to *230*

    d.   Observe that Excel allows you to modify the value if you use the password.

    e.   Save the workbook as *My Display*

ACTIVITY 2-2
Allowing Users to Edit a Specific Range

Before You Begin:
The My Display.xlsx file is open.

Scenario:
You need to give a copy of the My Display file to the sales and finance managers to update the worksheet data. The sales manager has to update the sales amount for each salesperson and the finance manager has to update the Bonus table which defines the bonus eligibility for salespersons. You want to provide rights to the sales manager to make changes in the worksheet. While the finance manager needs to unlock the Bonus table with a password that you had shared such that other cells are not editable.

---

1. Allow only the sales amounts to be edited.

   a. On the **Review** tab, in the **Changes** group, click **Allow Users to Edit Ranges.**

   b. In the **Allow Users to Edit Ranges** dialog box, click **New,** and in the **New Range** dialog box, in the **Title** text box, type *Sales* and press **Tab.**

   c. In the **Refers to cells** text box, type *=B5:M9* and click **OK.**

---

2. Define the entire range of cells in the Bonus table as editable with a password.

   a. In the **Allow Users to Edit Ranges** dialog box, click **New,** and in the **New Range** dialog box, in the **Title** text box, type *Bonus Table* and press **Tab.**

   b. In the **Refers to cells** text box, type *=R7:S11* and press **Tab.**

   c. In the **Range password** text box, type *p@ss!bonus* and click **OK.**

   d. In the **Confirm Password** dialog box, in the **Reenter password to proceed** text box, type *p@ss!bonus* and click **OK.**

---

3. Protect the worksheet.

   a. In the **Allow Users to Edit Ranges** dialog box, click **Protect Sheet.**

   b. In the **Protect Sheet** dialog box, in the **Password to unprotect sheet** text box, type *password* and click **OK.**

   c. In the **Confirm Password** dialog box, in the **Reenter password to proceed** text box, type *password* and click **OK.**

---

4. Test the applied settings.

   a. Enter *17* into cell F5 to observe that any cell within the range B5:M9 is editable without a password.

   b. Enter *235* into cell R8.

---

c.   Observe that the **Unlock Range** dialog box is displayed, prompting you to type a password for editing the cell. In the **Unlock Range** dialog box, in the **Enter the password to change this cell** text box, type *p@ss!bonus* and click **OK.**

d.   Enter *235* into cell R8.

e.   Observe that you are able to edit the worksheet after entering the correct password.

f.   Save the workbook as *My Display Range*

ACTIVITY 2-3
Protecting a Workbook

Before You Begin
The My Display Range.xlsx file is open.

Scenario:
As the regional sales head at OGC LLC, you are working on the western regional sales data of the company. You want to let your coworkers contribute to the workbook, but you do not want anyone to modify the structure of the workbook. You also want to ensure that only users with the password can open the workbook.

1. Protect the workbook's structure and windows using a password.

   a. On the **Review** tab, in the **Changes** group, click **Protect Workbook.**

   b. In the **Protect Structure and Windows** dialog box, observe that the **Structure** check box is checked by default, and check the **Windows** check box to ensure that the layout of the window always remains the same.

   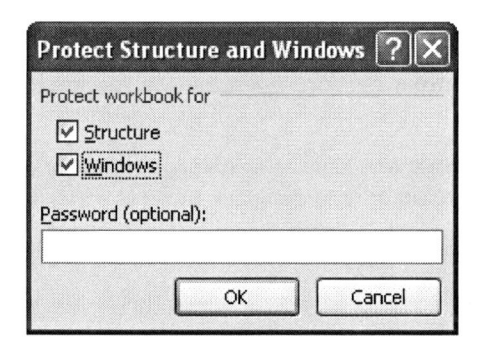

   c. In the **Password (optional)** text box, type *p@ssstruct!* and click **OK.**

   d. In the **Confirm Password** dialog box, type *p@ssstruct!* and click **OK.**

2. Try to modify the structure and window layout of the workbook.

   a. Right-click the **West** worksheet.

   b. Observe that the options to modify the worksheet are disabled.

   c. Select the **View** tab.

   d. In the **Window** group, observe that the options to modify the layout of the window are disabled.

3. Save the workbook with a password for opening it.

   a. Display the **Save As** dialog box.

   b. In the **File name** text box, type *My Regional Sales*

c.   In the **Save As** dialog box, from the **Tools** drop-down list, select **General Options.**

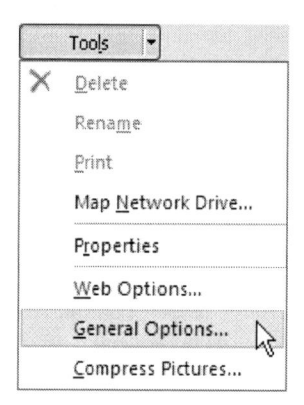

d.   In the **General Options** dialog box, in the **Password to open** text box, type *p@ssopen!* and click **OK.**

e.   In the **Confirm Password** dialog box, type *p@ssopen!* and click **OK** to confirm the password.

f.   Click **Save.**

g.   Close the file.

4.   Test the password-protected workbook.

a.   On the **File** tab, in the **Recent Workbooks** section, open the My Regional Sales.xlsx file.

b.   In the **Password** dialog box, observe that a message is displayed indicating that the My Regional Sales.xlsx workbook is protected.

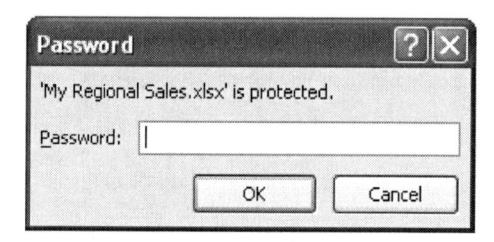

c.   In the **Password** dialog box, in the **Password** text box, type *p@ssopen!* and click **OK.**

d.   Observe that the workbook is now open.

e.   Close the file.

TOPIC B
Share a Workbook

You applied protection features to your workbook. Now, you are ready to let others access it and work on it. In this topic, you will share a workbook through the SharePoint server.

You have created a workbook that many people in your organization will need to use. Sharing the workbook through email may result in multiple copies from different users, which may be difficult to consolidate. Working on a single copy stored at a common location will help all users to make their changes on the same file.

The SharePoint® Server

Microsoft® Office SharePoint® Server 2010 is a collaboration and content management server that is integrated with the Office 2010 suite. It acts as a repository of documents where files can be saved and accessed from different locations. The SharePoint server tracks the work done on a file by maintaining information on users and file versions. This server also acts as a common platform for hosting content from the Internet and an intranet. The SharePoint server can also be used to control access and content modification permissions for files stored on the server.

Microsoft Office SharePoint Server 2010 vs. Microsoft SharePoint Foundation 2010

Microsoft SharePoint Foundation 2010 is a collaboration software product from Microsoft. This software enables individuals working on a project team or in a functional group to share information and communicate with one another from a central location. It allows users to work in a web-based collaborative environment. It provides specialized websites that contain elements, including a central calendar; task lists; discussion boards; wikis, blogs; and libraries of documents, photos, and forms. Microsoft SharePoint Foundation 2010 is suitable for small teams and projects whereas Microsoft Office SharePoint Server 2010 is an enterprise-level server with additional functionalities such as advanced search capabilities and personalized sites for users to share information.

Shared Workbooks

Definition:

A *shared workbook* is a workbook that is set up and saved to allow multiple users to share it over a network. Each person who opens a shared workbook can see the changes that were made by other users. The data in the workbook can be changed by multiple users, and all the changes can be highlighted during review if the workbook is shared. When a workbook is shared, the text "Shared" appears on the title bar of the workbook.

 A shared workbook may not support certain Excel features such as deleting worksheets, merging cells, or splitting cells.

Example:

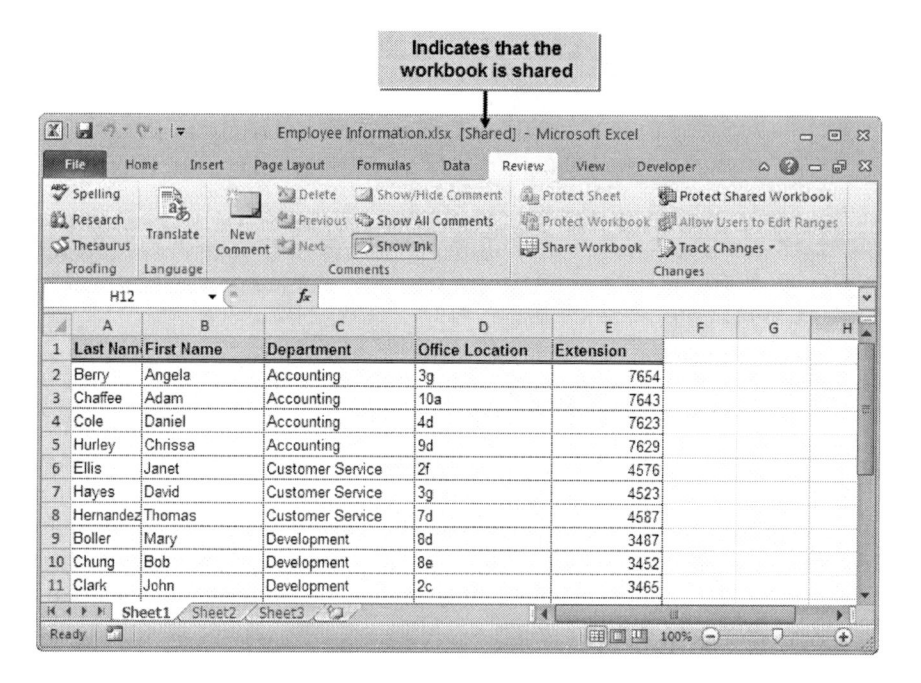

Figure 2-4: Sharing of worksheets allows multiple users to collaborate on a workbook.

Save and Send Options

You can choose the storage location for shared workbooks using the **Save & Send** option on the **File** tab.

Option	Allows Users To
Send Using E-mail	Send a copy of a worksheet through email. The changes made by each user need to be copied manually. It is also possible to send a PDF or XPS copy of the workbook through email. However, other users cannot easily make modification to PDF or XPS copies.
Save to Web	Save a file on Windows Live SkyDrive, a shared folder on the web that can be accessed by using a Windows Live ID or a Hotmail ID. Users have to share the link to the file path through email.
Save to SharePoint	Collaborate by storing a file at a location in the SharePoint server. Similar to SkyDrive, users need to share the link to the file path through email.

The Save to Windows Live Feature

Excel 2010 allows you to save your workbooks directly to the web using your Windows Live SkyDrive account. Windows Live SkyDrive provides 25 GB of online space to store your documents, and enables you to access documents from any computer at any location. Using the Save to Windows Live SkyDrive feature, you can view, edit, or download documents, create and share multiple folders, set permissions on folders, add comments to documents, and track versions of documents.

Windows Live SkyDrive

Windows Live SkyDrive is a service provided by Microsoft that allows users with a Windows Live ID to store and share files on the web.

How to Share a Workbook

Procedure Reference: Create a Shared Workbook

To create a shared workbook:

1. Open the file you want to share.
2. On the **Review** tab, in the **Changes** group, click **Share Workbook.**
3. In the **Share Workbook** dialog box, on the **Editing** tab, check **Allow changes by more than one user at the same time. This also allows workbook merging** to permit multiple users to contribute to the workbook.
4. Set options on the **Advanced** tab.
   - In the **Track Changes** section, select the required options to display the track change history.
   - In the **Update Changes** section, select the required options to update changes regularly.
   - In the **Conflicting changes between users** section, select the required options to specify the changes to be retained.
   - In the **Include in personal view** section, select the required options to specify print and filter settings.
5. Click **OK.**
6. In the **Microsoft Excel** warning box, click **OK** to save the workbook.

Procedure Reference: Publish a Shared Workbook to the SharePoint Server Through the Excel Interface

To publish a shared workbook on the SharePoint server using the Excel interface:

1. Open the file that you want to place on the SharePoint server.
2. Select the **File** tab and select **Save & Send.**
3. In the **Save & Send** section, select **Save to SharePoint,** and in the **Save to SharePoint** section, uncheck **Open with excel in the browser** and click **Save As.**

 If the **Open with excel in the browser** check box is checked, then the file will automatically open in a browser after the upload to server is complete.

4. In the **Save As** dialog box, mention the file name and click **Save** to place the file on the server.

Procedure Reference: Upload a Workbook to the SharePoint Server Using the SharePoint Interface

To upload a workbook to the SharePoint server using the SharePoint interface:

1. In the Address bar of the browser window, type the address of your SharePoint website.
2. On the **Home** page, below the **Shared Documents** section, click **Add document.**
3. In the **Upload Document** dialog box, in the **Name** section, click **Browse,** navigate to the file that needs to be uploaded, and click **OK** to upload the file to SharePoint server from your computer.
4. In the **Version Comments** text area, click and type a comment and click **OK.**

Procedure Reference: Share a File Located on the SharePoint Server with Other Users

To share a file located on the SharePoint server with other users:

1. In the Address bar, type the address of your SharePoint website.
2. On the **Home** page, in the **Shared Documents** section, check the required file.
3. On the **Library Tools Documents** contextual tab, in the **Share & Track** section, click **E-mail a link** to open the default email client application.
4. The link to the file will be added to the email. Enter the email IDs of all users with whom you want to collaborate on the workbook and send an email. Other users can access the shared file by clicking the link received through email.

Procedure Reference: Upload a Workbook to Windows Live SkyDrive

To upload a workbook to Windows Live SkyDrive:

1. Open the workbook that you want to upload.
2. On the **File** tab, select **Save & Send.**
3. In the **Save & Send** section, click **Save to Web.**
4. In the **Save to Windows Live** section, click **Sign In** and enter your Windows Live credentials.
5. In the **My Folders** section, choose the folder in which you want to save the file and click **Save As.**
6. In the **Save As** dialog box, enter a name for the workbook and click **Save.**

Procedure Reference: Share a Workbook Located on the Windows Live SkyDrive with Other Users

To share a workbook located on the Windows Live SkyDrive with other users:

1. In the Address bar, type *http://skydrive.live.com*
2. Enter your Windows Live login credentials.
3. Navigate to the folder containing the document you want to share and check the check box corresponding to the document.
4. From the **Share** drop-down list, select **Edit permissions** to change the permissions of the workbook.
5. In the **Add specific people** section, in the **Enter a name or an e-mail address** text box, enter the email IDs of users with whom you want to share the file and click **Save** to set permissions.
6. In the **Send a notification** section, click **Send.** Users can open the shared document for editing by clicking the link received through email.

Procedure Reference: Change the File Type Using the Save & Send Option

To change the file type using the **Save & Send** option:

1. Open the workbook for which you want to change the file type.
2. On the **File** tab, select **Save & Send.**
3. In the **File Types** section, change the file type by selecting one of the options.
   - Click **Change File Type,** and in the right pane, select the required file type, and in the **Save As** dialog box, enter the file name and click **Save.**
   - Click **Create PDF/XPS document,** and in the right pane, click **Create/Publish PDF,** and in the **Publish as PDF or XPS** dialog box, mention the file name, select either **PDF** or **XPS Document** and click **Publish** to convert the file into the PDF or XPS format.

ACTIVITY 2-4
Sharing a Workbook

Data Files:

C:\084678Data\Collaborating with Others\Simulations\Sharing a Workbook_guided.exe

Simulation:

This is a simulated activity. In this simulation, SharePoint Server 2010 has been configured with the URL **http://dc**

Scenario:

You need to share the Phonelist.xlsx file that contains the name, department, office, and phone extension information of employees. This is an informal list that each department manager in the company will need to update periodically. Because each manager needs to access the file, you decide to share the workbook and save it in a designated location on the network. You also decide to keep the history of track changes for 15 days.

After saving the file on the server, you ask the manager of the Accounts department to add details of Jaco Prestia, a new employee in the Accounts department, to the Phonelist.xlsx file. Jaco is in office 9f and his phone extension is 2699. After making changes, the manager informs you so that you can verify the changes.

---

1. To launch the simulation, browse to the C:\084678Data\Collaborating with Others\ Simulations folder.

---

2. Double-click the **Sharing a Workbook_guided.exe** file.

---

3. Maximize the simulation window.

---

4. Follow the on-screen steps for the simulation.

---

5. When you have finished this activity, close the simulation window.

TOPIC C
Set Revision Tracking

You shared data in workbooks. You want to set tracking options in order to track any changes made to a given worksheet or workbook. In this topic, you will set revision tracking.

You have a worksheet that other people in your organization will be manipulating. However, your business process dictates that you need to know who has made changes to the worksheet, when they made those changes, and what the changes were. By setting revision tracking, you can keep close track of who has made alterations to a given worksheet or workbook and what those alterations were.

Revision Tracking

Definition:

Revision tracking is a formatting technique used to track any changes made to a workbook. Once a workbook is set to revision tracking mode, it becomes a shared workbook. Revision tracking is not a default option; it needs to be enabled for the changes to be highlighted. It tracks details such as the person who made the change, the date and time when the change was made, and where in the workbook the change was made.

Example:

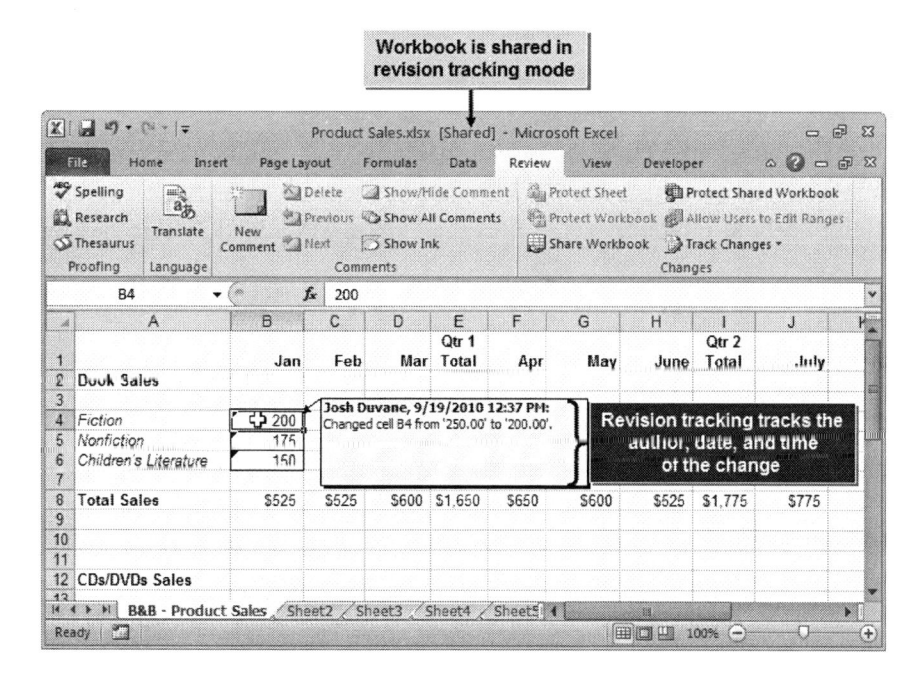

Figure 2-5: *The revision tracking feature allows users to track revisions made to a worksheet.*

The Highlight Changes Dialog Box

The **Highlight Changes** dialog box is used to set highlighting options for revision tracking. This dialog box allows users to enable track changing in the workbook. You can also set options to track changes based on who made the changes, when they were made, and where in the worksheet they were made.

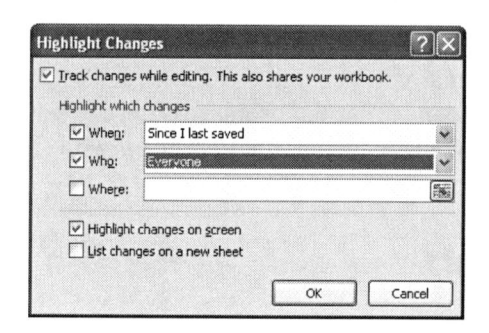

Figure 2-6: *Users can highlight changes made by other users using the Highlight Changes dialog box.*

How to Set Revision Tracking

Procedure Reference: Set Revision Tracking Using the Track Changes Option

To set revision tracking using the **Track Changes** option:

1. On the **Review** tab, in the **Changes** group, from the **Track Changes** drop-down list, select **Highlight Changes** to display the **Highlight Changes** dialog box.

2. Check **Track changes while editing.** This also shares your workbook to enable the track changes options.

3. In the **Highlight which changes** section, set the **When, Who,** and **Where** parameters as needed.

    ●   Check **When** and select an option from the **When** drop-down list, to specify the period for which the changes need to be highlighted.

    ●   Check **Who** and select an option from the **Who** drop-down list, to specify whose changes need to be highlighted.

    ●   Check **Where** and enter the range of cells in the **Where** text box, for which the changes need to be highlighted.

4. Check **Highlight changes on screen** to view changes on the same worksheet, or check **List changes on a new sheet** to view changes on a new sheet.

5. Click **OK**, and in the message box that prompts you to save changes in the workbook, click **OK**.

Procedure Reference: Set Revision Tracking Using the Protect and Share Workbook Command

To set revision tracking using the **Protect and Share Workbook** command:

1. On the **Review** tab, in the **Changes** group, click **Protect and Share Workbook.**

2. In the **Protect Shared Workbook** dialog box, check the **Sharing with track changes** check box and click **OK.**

Procedure Reference: Display All Changes Made to a Workbook

To display all changes made to a workbook:

1. Open a file with the changes made to it.
2. From the **Track Changes** drop-down list, select **Highlight Changes.**
3. In the **Highlight Changes** dialog box, uncheck the **When, Who,** and **Where** check boxes to view all changes.
4. If necessary, on the cells that have a small triangle at the top-left corner, hover the mouse pointer to view the revision note displaying information on the changes made by the user.

ACTIVITY 2-5
Setting Revision Tracking

Data Files:

C:\084678Data\Collaborating with Others\Product Sales.xlsx

Before You Begin:

The Excel application is open.

Scenario:

You are asked to create a report that shows the annual sales of all products. You have entered data relating to the sales of books and DVDs. Though you have data for the sales of electronic items, you are busy with some other task. Therefore, you ask the manager of the electronics department to fill in the necessary details in a format similar to the sales of books and DVDs. You have shared the document with the manager of the electronics department and now decide to enable the track changes option so that you can validate the entries before accepting them.

1. Set revision tracking in the Product Sales workbook using the **Highlight Changes** option.

    a. Display the **Open** dialog box, navigate to the C:\084678Data\Collaborating with Others folder and open the Product Sales.xlsx file.

    b. On the **Review** tab, in the **Changes** group, from the **Track Changes** drop-down list, select **Highlight Changes.**

    c. In the **Highlight Changes** dialog box, in the **Highlight which changes** section, check the **Who** check box.

    d. Observe that the **Everyone** option is selected by default in the **Who** drop-down list and click **OK.**

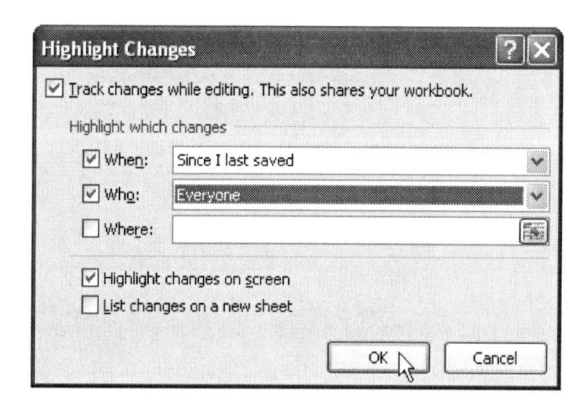

    e. In the **Microsoft Excel** message box, click **OK.**

2. Test the applied revision tracking feature.

    a. In cell **A24,** enter *Electronics*

    b. Place the mouse pointer over cell **A24.**

c. Observe that a comment box is displayed showing details of the modification made by you.

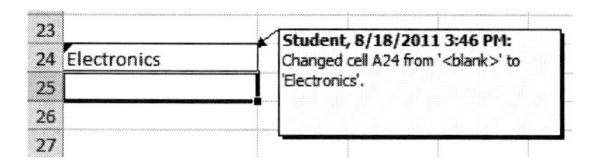

d. Save the file as ***My Product Sales*** and close it.

TOPIC D
Review Tracked Revisions

You set revision tracking for your files. The next step is to see what changes were made to the file, and to accept or reject them as required. In this topic, you will review tracked revisions.

You created a workbook, set revision tracking, and sent the workbook for review. You have now received the workbook back from one of your colleagues, and are in the process of checking whether or not any of the changes made are viable. By reviewing tracked revisions, you can be sure that any revisions made to a file are correct before the core content of the file is changed.

The Accept/Reject Changes Option

The **Accept/Reject Changes** option allows you to decide which changes you want to retain and which to discard after a tracked review. Selecting this option displays the **Select Changes to Accept or Reject** dialog box. Options regarding which changes to be selected, such as when the changes were made, who made the changes, and where the changes were made in the workbook, can be set using the dialog box. When you click **OK,** the **Accept or Reject Changes** dialog box is displayed with the details of the changes made to the workbook. It also has options to accept or reject the changes.

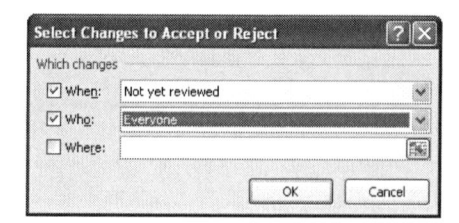

Figure 2-7: *The Accept/Reject changes option allows you to accept or reject the changes made by other users.*

How to Review Tracked Revisions

Procedure Reference: Accept or Reject Tracked Changes

To accept or reject tracked changes:

1. On the **Review** tab, in the **Changes** group, from the **Track Changes** drop-down, select **Accept/Reject Changes.**

2. In the **Microsoft Excel** message box, click **OK** to save the workbook.

3. In the **Select Changes to Accept or Reject** dialog box, in the **Which Changes** section, specify changes you want to make.

   - Select **When** to display changes by specifying when the changes were made.
   - Select **Who** to display changes by specifying who made the changes.
   - Select **Where** to display changes by specifying the range of cells in which the changes were made.

4. Click **OK.**

5. In the **Accept or Reject Changes** dialog box, accept or reject changes as needed.

   - Click **Accept** to accept a change.
   - Click **Accept All** to accept all changes.
   - Click **Reject** to reject a change.
   - Click **Reject All** to reject all changes.
   - Click **Close** to close the dialog box.

 The **Accept or Reject Changes** dialog box will close automatically after the last change is accepted.

ACTIVITY 2-6
Accepting or Rejecting Tracked Changes

Data Files:

Reviewed Product Sales.xlsx

Before You Begin:

The Excel application is open.

Scenario:

You are ready to review any changes made to the Reviewed Product Sales workbook from Robin Smith, the manager of the electronics department. You will highlight the changes made, list the changes on a worksheet, and then accept them.

---

1. Highlight any changes made by Robin Smith.

    a. Display the **Open** dialog box, navigate to the C:\084678Data\Collaborating with Others folder and open the Reviewed Product Sales.xlsx file.

    b. On the **Review** tab, in the **Changes** group, from the **Track Changes** drop-down list, select **Highlight Changes**.

    c. In the **Highlight Changes** dialog box, from the **When** drop-down list, select **All.**

    d. Check the **Who** check box, and from the **Who** drop-down list, select **Robin Smith.**

    e. Verify that **Highlight changes on screen** is checked and click **OK.**

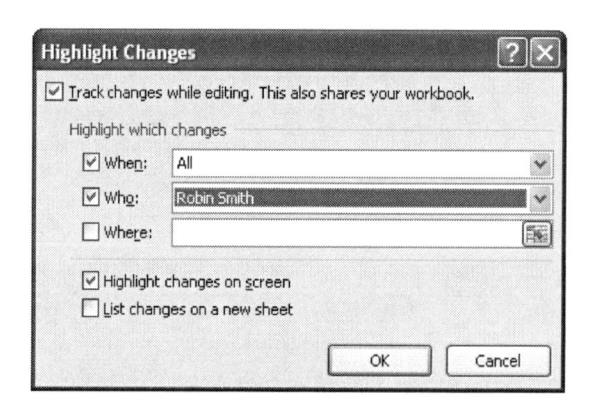

    f. Scroll down the worksheet.

g. Observe that the changes made by Robin Smith are highlighted in the worksheet.

24 Electronics				
25				
26 Toys	2000	2050	1900	$5,950
27 USB Drives	1500	1700	1950	$5,150
28 Musical Intruments	3000	2700	3000	$8,700
29 Head Phones	700	800	600	$2,100
30				
31 Total Sales	7200	7250	7450	21900
32				

2. Accept the changes.

a. On the **Review** tab, in the **Changes** group, from the **Track Changes** drop-down list, select **Accept/Reject Changes** to open the **Select Changes to Accept or Reject** dialog box.

b. In the **Who** drop-down list, observe that **Robin Smith** is selected and click **OK.**

c. Observe that on the worksheet, cell **A24** is selected as the first change, and in the **Accept or Reject Changes** dialog box, observe the change made to cell **A24** by Robin Smith.

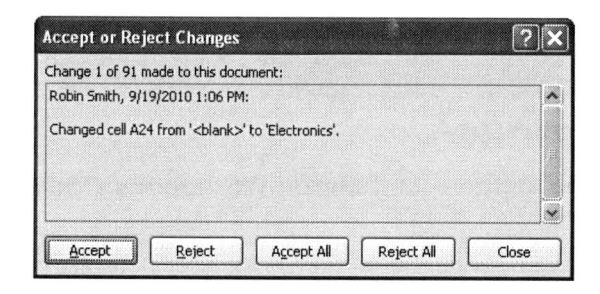

d. Click **Accept** to accept the first change and to move on to the next change.

e. Click **Accept All** to accept all changes.

f. In the **Changes** group, from the **Track Changes** drop-down list, select **Highlight Changes**, and in the **Highlight Changes** dialog box, uncheck the **Highlight changes on screen** check box, and click **OK.**

g. Save the file as *My Reviewed Product Sales* and close it.

TOPIC E
Merge Workbooks

You reviewed tracked changes in your workbook. Now, you have multiple related workbooks, and you would like to consolidate them into a single workbook. In this topic, you will merge workbooks.

There may be instances where you need to combine the contents of a set of similar workbooks into a single workbook, a process that can be tedious if done manually. Excel allows you to merge multiple copies of a workbook with different names into a single copy, thereby organizing related data.

The Compare and Merge Workbooks Feature

The **Compare and Merge Workbooks** feature allows users to merge multiple copies of a shared workbook. This option does not appear on the Ribbon by default, and it needs to be added to the **Quick Access** toolbar by using the **Excel Options** dialog box. The **Compare and Merge Workbooks** feature is activated only if the workbook is shared. The shared workbook that will contain the merge — and all of the other workbooks you want to merge into it — must be copies of the same shared workbook.

How to Merge Workbooks

Procedure Reference: Display the Compare and Merge Workbooks Option on the Quick Access Toolbar

To display the Compare and Merge Workbooks option on the Quick Access Toolbar:

1. Open any one of the copies of a shared workbook.
2. On the **File** tab, select **Options.**
3. In the **Excel Options** dialog box, click the **Customize Ribbon** category, and from the **Choose commands from** drop-down list, select **All Commands.**
4. In the **All Commands** list box, select **Compare and Merge Workbooks** and click **Add.**
5. Click **OK** to close the dialog box and to add the **Compare and Merge Workbooks** button to the Quick Access Toolbar.

Procedure Reference: Merge Workbooks

To merge workbooks:

1. Save different copies of the shared workbook in a folder along with the main copy.
2. Open the workbook with which you would like to merge other workbooks.
3. On the Quick Access Toolbar, click the **Compare and Merge Workbooks** button.
4. In the **Select Files to Merge into Current Workbook** dialog box, navigate to your folder and select the files you would like to merge with the open workbook and click **OK** to merge the workbooks.

ACTIVITY 2-7
Merging Workbooks

Data Files:

C:\084678Data\Collaborating with Others\Personnel Human Resources.xlsx, C:\084678Data\ Collaborating with Others\Personnel Accounting.xlsx, C:\084678Data\Collaborating with Others\Personnel Customer Service.xlsx, C:\084678Data\Collaborating with Others\Personnel Development.xlsx, C:\084678Data\Collaborating with Others\Personnel Engineering.xlsx, C:\084678Data\Collaborating with Others\Personnel Tech Support.xlsx

Before You Begin:

If you have already performed this activity, and want to perform it again, you will have to replace the six files used in the activity with a fresh set of the same files from the original data files provided for the course. If the files are not replaced, you will see a message stating that the compare and merge operation cannot be done with the existing files.

Scenario:

You created and shared an Excel workbook named Personnel Human Resources that acts as a contact list for employees. You have asked the managers of the accounting, customer service, development, engineering, and technical support department to update extension numbers for the employees in their respective departments. All managers have updated the file with the extension details of the employees in their departments and then renamed their versions of the file with their department names. You decide to make one file out of all the separate department files.

---

1. Add the Compare and Merge Workbooks button to the Quick Access Toolbar.

   a. Display the **Open** dialog box, navigate to the C:\084678Data\Collaborating with Others folder and open the Personnel Human Resources.xlsx file.

   b. Observe that **Sheet1** contains the extension details of only two employees in the human resources department. The extension details of employees in other departments are not listed.

   c. Save the workbook as *My Personnel Human Resources*

   d. On the **File** tab, select **Options**.

   e. In the **Excel Options** dialog box, in the left pane, select **Quick Access Toolbar**.

   f. In the **Customize the Quick Access Toolbar** pane, from the **Choose commands from** drop-down list, select **All Commands**.

   g. In the **All Commands** list box, scroll down, and select **Compare and Merge Workbooks,** and then click **Add.**

   h. Click **OK** to close the dialog box and to add the button to the Quick Access toolbar.

---

2. Merge the contents of files from each department with the Personnel Human Resources workbook.

---

a. On the Quick Access toolbar, click the **Compare and Merge Workbooks** button.

b. In the **Select Files to Merge Into Current Workbook** dialog box, select the **Personnel Accounting, Personnel Customer Service, Personnel Development, Personnel Engineering,** and **Personnel Tech Support** files.

c. Click **OK** to close the dialog box and to merge the files.

d. Observe that the workbook now displays the extension of all employees in the list. Close the file.

TOPIC F
Administer Digital Signatures

You adjusted security settings for a workbook in Excel. Workbooks with macros are sensitive files. When you send such files, recipients would prefer to verify the authenticity of the files. In this topic, you will administer digital signatures.

You have been receiving a large number of expense reports from a particular salesperson. When you call her, she denies ever sending the reports in question. You ask her to attach a digital signature to all of her future reports so that you can verify that they are coming from her. Digital signatures add an extra level of security to shared files by confirming the identity of the person who sends the files.

Digital Certificates

Definition:

A *digital certificate* is an electronic file that contains unique information about a specific person. It contains a serial number, the digital signature of the certificate-issuing authority, expiration dates, a name, and a copy of the certificate holder's public key so that a recipient can verify that the certificate is authentic. It is issued by a certification authority, *CA,* which is a trusted third party, or from your company's computer service professional. A digital certificate is also known as a digital ID because it is used to digitally sign a document.

Example:

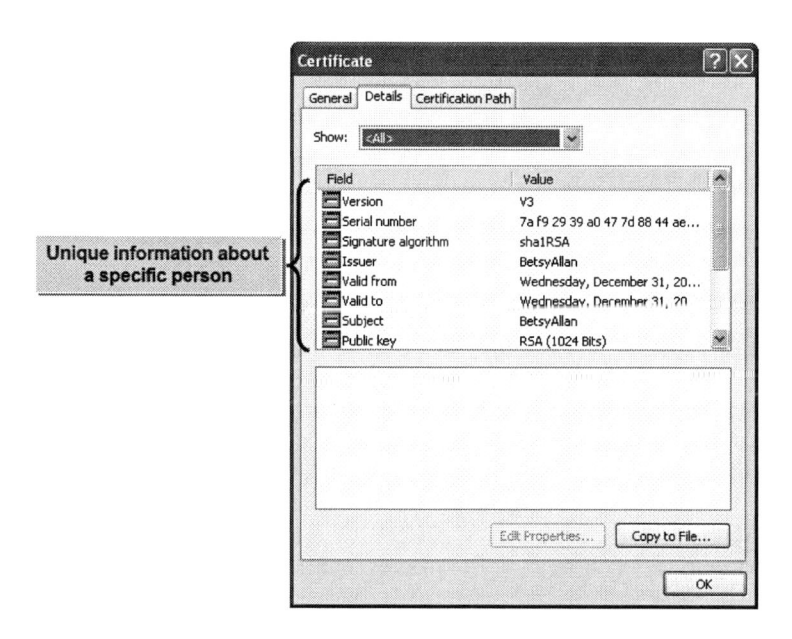

Figure 2-8: *Digital certificates are used by organizations and individuals to authenticate their files.*

Certificate Store

A certificate store is a folder in your system in which digital certificates are saved. Excel provides you options to either select the default certificate store depending on the type of certificate or manually select a location to open or save a certificate.

Digital Signatures

Definition:

A *digital signature* is a content authentication tool that authenticates the originator of a file, and ensures the integrity of digital documents. It validates the authenticity, integrity, and origin of the document. The digital signature is not visible within the contents of the workbook. The **Signature** icon on the **Microsoft Office Status Bar** at the bottom of the application window is indicative of the fact that the workbook has been digitally signed. When you open a document with a digital signature, the details will be visible in the **Signatures** pane of your workbook. Users cannot make modifications to a digitally signed document until the signature is removed.

Example:

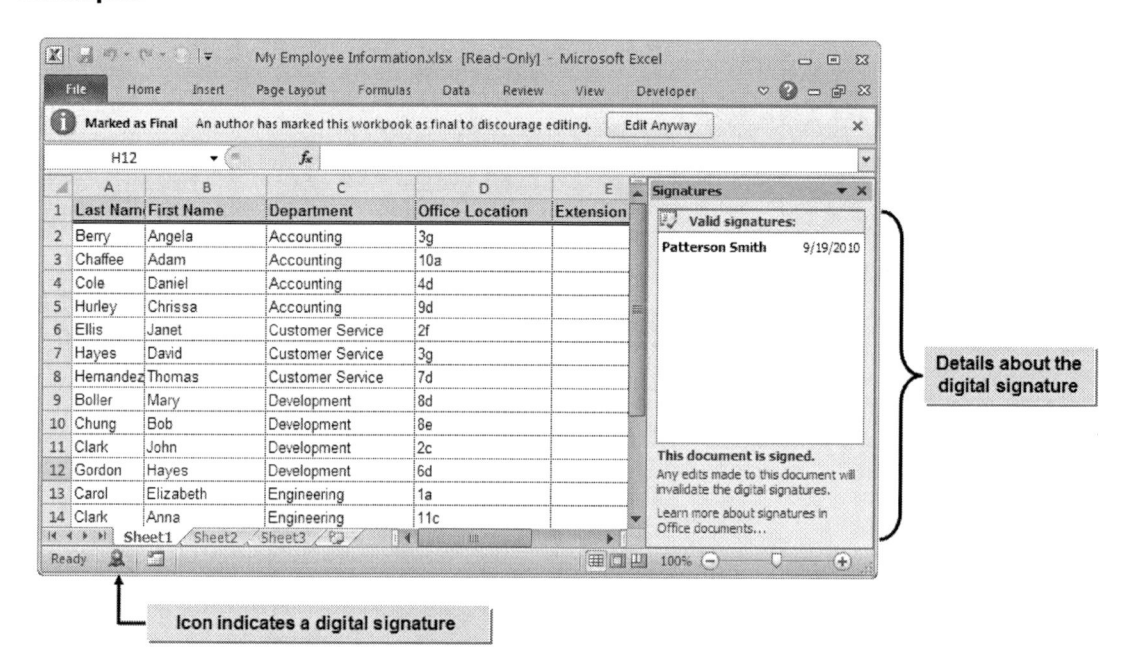

Figure 2-9: Digital signatures allow users to protect the integrity of their data.

Digitally Signed Macros

It is important that you run macros only if they are digitally signed because macros can contain malicious code that can be harmful to your computer thereby posing a threat to your system's security. You can choose your macro settings

Macro Settings	Description
Disable all macros without notification	The macros and its security alerts are disabled.
Disable all macros with notification	The macros are disabled, but its security alerts are displayed if the files contain macros.
Disable all macros except digitally signed macros	If a macro is digitally signed by a trusted publisher, it will run, else all other macros will be disabled displaying only the security alerts if the file contains macros.

Macro Settings	*Description*
Enable all macros (not recommended, potentially dangerous code can run)	All macros will run. This is harmful to your computer as few macros can contain malicious code.

How to Administer Digital Signatures

Procedure Reference: Add a Digital Signature to a File

To add a digital signature to a file:

1. On the **File** tab, in the Backstage view, click **Protect Workbook** and select **Add a Digital Signature.**

2. In the **Microsoft Excel** dialog box, click **OK.**

3. If necessary, create a digital ID.

    a. In the **Get a Digital ID** dialog box, select **Create your own digital ID.**

     The **Get a Digital ID** dialog box appears if you attempt to digitally sign a document without a digital certificate. This dialog box will appear only when you are signing it for the first time.

    b. In the **Create a Digital ID** dialog box, type the necessary information.

        A. In the **Name** text box, type a name.

        B. In the **E-mail Address** text box, type an email address.

        C. In the **Organization** text box, type the name of an organization or company.

        D. In the **Location** text box, type the geographic location.

4. In the **Sign** dialog box, in the **Purpose for signing this document** text box, enter the purpose for adding the digital signature.

5. If necessary, change the digital certificate.

    a. In the **Signing as** section, click **Change.**

    b. In the **Select Certificate** dialog box, select the desired certificate and click **OK.**

6. Click **Sign.**

7. In the **Signature Confirmation** message box, click **OK.**

Procedure Reference: Create a Digital Certificate Using the Digital Certificate for VBA Projects Tool

To create a self-issued certificate on the computer:

1. Choose **Start→All Programs→Microsoft Office→Microsoft Office Tools→Digital Certificate for VBA Projects.**

2. In the **Create Digital Certificate** dialog box, in the **Your Certificate's Name** text box, type a name for the certificate, and click **OK.**

3. In the **SelfCert Success** dialog box, click **OK.**

The certificates created using this method will be treated as untrusted as they have not been issued by a certified authority.

Procedure Reference: Install Another Person's Certificate on Your Computer

To install another person's certificate on your computer:

1. Upon opening a digitally signed file, in the **Security Warning** panel below the Ribbon, click **Options.**
2. If necessary, under **File sharing settings for this workbook,** click **Digital Signatures.**
3. In the **Microsoft Security Options** dialog box, in the **Signature** section, click **Show Signature Details.**
4. In the **Digital Signature Details** dialog box, on the **General** tab, click **View Certificate.**
5. In the **Certificate** dialog box, click **Install Certificate.**
6. On the **Certificate Import Wizard** screen, click **Next.**
7. On the **Certificate Store** page, select the desired storage location.
   - Select **Automatically select the certificate store based on the type of certificate.**
   - Select **Place all certificates in the following store to select the desired location.**
     a. Click **Browse** and choose the desired location.
     b. In the **Select Certificate Store** dialog box, select the certificate store you want to use and click **OK.**
8. Click **Next.**
9. Click **Finish.** In the dialog box that confirms a successful import, click **OK.**
10. In the **Certificate** dialog box, click **OK.**
11. In the **Digital Signature Details** dialog box, click **OK.**
12. In the **Microsoft Security Options** dialog box, select **Trust all documents from this publisher** and click **OK** to add the source as a trusted publisher.

Procedure Reference: Remove a Digital Signature from a File

To remove a digital signature from a file:

1. Open a file that has been digitally signed.
2. On the message bar below the Ribbon, click **View Signatures.**
3. Remove the signature.
   - In the **Signatures** pane, place the mouse pointer over the signature, click the drop-down arrow, and select **Remove Signature** or;
   - Right-click the signature and choose **Remove Signature.**
4. In the **Remove Signature** dialog box, click **Yes.**
5. In the **Signature Removed** message box, click **OK.**

ACTIVITY 2-8
Administering Digital Signatures

Data Files:

Employee Information.xlsx, Allan.xlsm

Before You Begin

1. Display the **Excel Options** dialog box.

2. In the left pane, select **Trust Center,** and in the right pane, click **Trust Center Settings.**

3. In the **Trust Center Settings** dialog box, in the **Macro Settings** section, select the **Disable all macros with notification** option and click **OK.**

Scenario:

You are Patterson Smith, and you need to digitally sign the Employee Information workbook so that when anyone receives the workbook they can be sure that it came from you. Since you do not have a signature, you decide to create your own digital signature that can be used for official communication within your organization. The second thing you need to do is to open the Allan workbook and install Betsy Allan's certificate on your computer, because you will be regularly corresponding with her.

---

1. Digitally sign the file.

   a. Display the **Open** dialog box, navigate to the C:\084678Data\Collaborating with Others folder and open the Employee Information.xlsx file.

   b. Save the file as *My Employee Information*

   c. Select the **File** tab, and in the Backstage view, in the **Permissions** section, choose **Protect Workbook→Add a Digital Signature.**

   d. In the **Microsoft Excel** message box, click **OK.**

   e. In the **Get a Digital ID** dialog box, select **Create your own digital ID** and click **OK.**

   f. In the **Create a Digital ID** dialog box, in the **Name** text box, select the existing text and type *Patterson Smith*

   g. In the **E-mail address** text box, type *PattersonSmith@ourglobalcompany.com*

   h. In the **Organization** text box, type *Our Global Company* and then click **Create.**

   i. In the **Sign** dialog box, in the **Signing as** section, observe that the name is displayed as **Patterson Smith,** and in the **Purpose for signing this document** text box, type *Confidential* and click **Sign.**

   j. In the **Signature Confirmation** message box, click **OK.**

k. Observe that a section named **Signed Workbook** appears in the Backstage view.

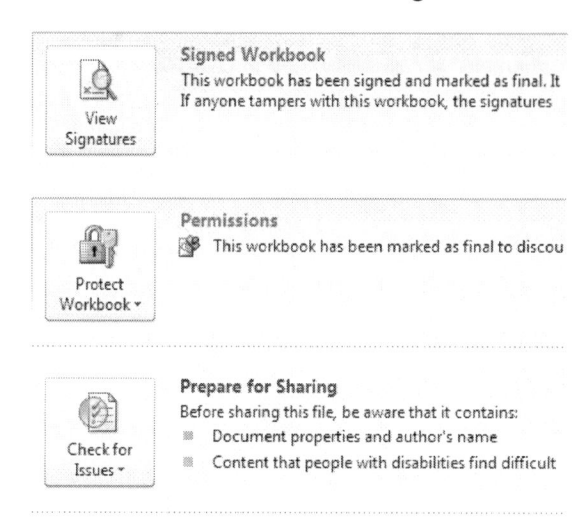

l. In the Backstage view, in the **Signed Workbook** section, click **View Signatures** to view the **Valid signatures** pane on the worksheet.

m. Observe that your signature is displayed in the **Valid signatures** pane. Also, observe that the file is opened in the read-only mode as a signature has been inserted into the worksheet.

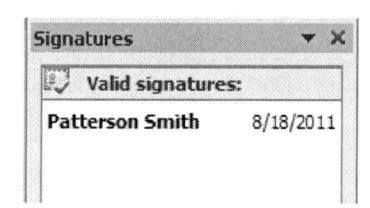

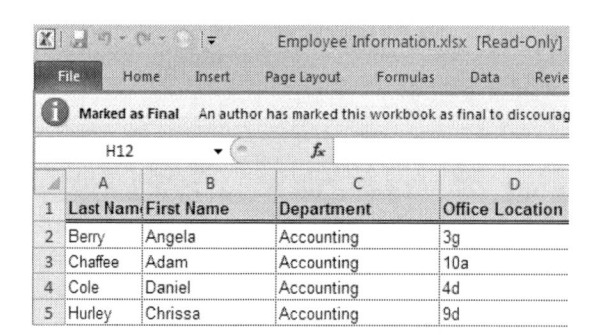

n. Close the **Signatures** pane.

o. Close the file.

2. Install the digital certificate present in the Allan workbook to your Trusted Root Certification Authorities store.

a. Navigate to the C:\084678Data\Collaborating with Others folder and open the Allan.xlsm file.

b. On the message bar below the Ribbon, observe the message stating that the macros in the file have been disabled as the file did not come from a trusted source.

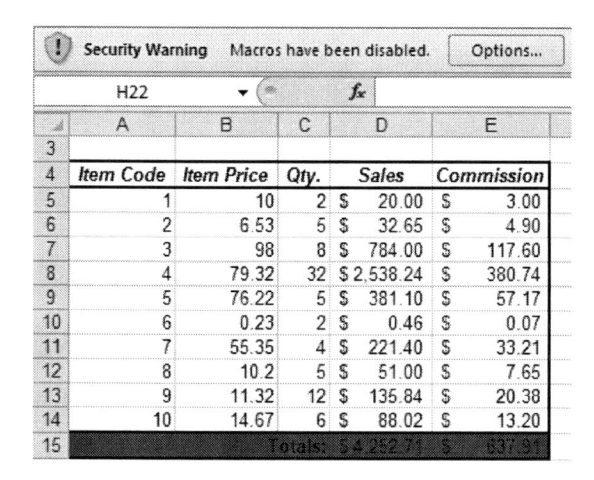

c. In the Backstage view, from the **Enable Content** drop-down list, select **Advanced Options.**

d. In the **Microsoft Office Security Options** dialog box, in the **Signature** section, observe that the file has been digitally signed by **BetsyAllan.**

e. In the **Signature** section, click the **Show Signature Details** link.

f. In the **Digital Signature Details** dialog box, on the **General** tab, click **View Certificate.**

g. In the **Certificate** dialog box, in the **Certificate Information** section, observe that the certificate icon is displayed with a "X" symbol as the certificate has not been installed on the computer and, therefore, cannot be trusted.

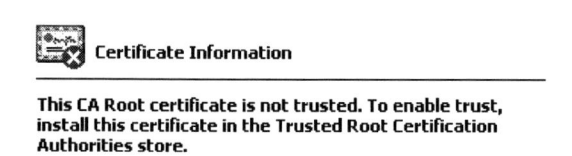

h. In the **Certificate** dialog box, click **Install Certificate.**

i. In the **Certificate Import Wizard,** click **Next.**

j. In the **Certificate Store** page, select **Place all certificates in the following store** and click **Browse.**

k. In the **Select Certificate Store** dialog box, select the **Trusted Root Certification Authorities** store, click **OK,** and on the **Certificate Store** page, click **Next.**

l. On the **Completing the Certificate Import Wizard** page, click **Finish.**

m. Observe that a **Security Warning** message box provides you with details of a digital thumbprint and asks you to contact the issuer and confirm with him or her that it is indeed their signature. Click **Yes,** and in the message box that confirms a successful import, click **OK.**

n. In the **Certificate** dialog box, click **OK.**

o. In the **Digital Signature Details** dialog box, click **OK.**

p. In the **Microsoft Office Security Options** dialog box, select the **Trust all documents from this publisher** option and click **OK.**

q. Observe that there is no message bar indicating that the macros are disabled. This is because Betsy Allan's signature is installed on your computer.

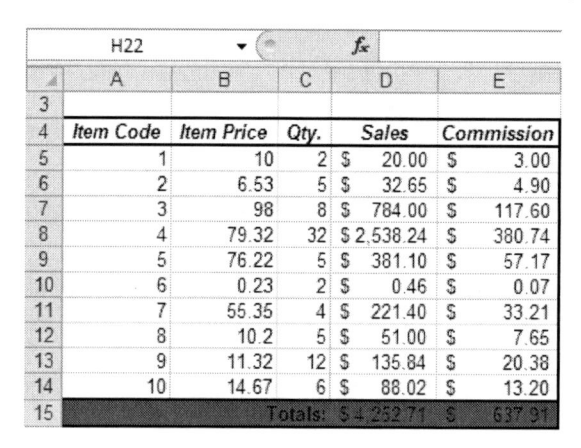

	A	B	C	D	E
3					
4	*Item Code*	*Item Price*	*Qty.*	*Sales*	*Commission*
5	1	10	2	$ 20.00	$ 3.00
6	2	6.53	5	$ 32.65	$ 4.90
7	3	98	8	$ 784.00	$ 117.60
8	4	79.32	32	$ 2,538.24	$ 380.74
9	5	76.22	5	$ 381.10	$ 57.17
10	6	0.23	2	$ 0.46	$ 0.07
11	7	55.35	4	$ 221.40	$ 33.21
12	8	10.2	5	$ 51.00	$ 7.65
13	9	11.32	12	$ 135.84	$ 20.38
14	10	14.67	6	$ 88.02	$ 13.20
15				Totals: $ 4,252.71	$ 637.91

3. View Betsy Allan's digital certificate installed on your computer.

a. Display the **Excel Options** dialog box.

b. Select **Trust Center,** and in the right pane, click **Trust Center Settings.**

c. In the **Trust Center** dialog box, select **Trusted Publishers,** and in the right pane, select **BetsyAllan.**

d. Click **View** to view the certificate information in the **Certificate** dialog box.

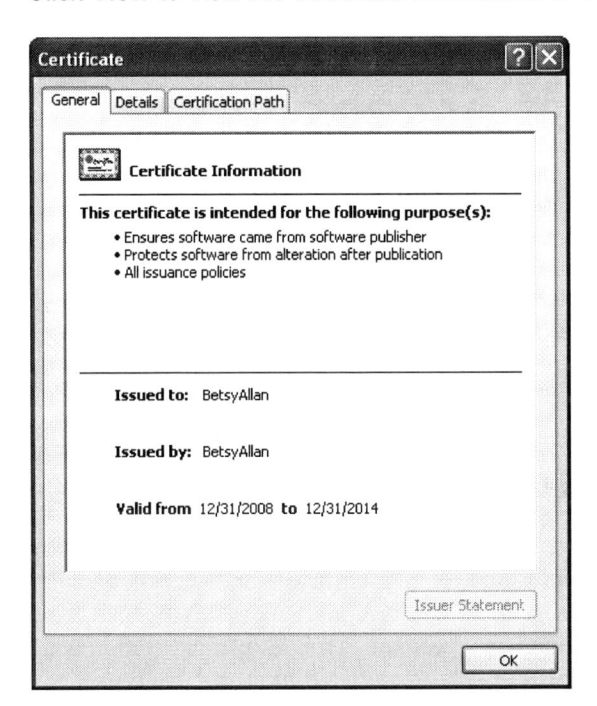

e. In the **Certificate Information** section, observe that the certificate icon is displayed without the "X" symbol as the certificate is listed in the **Trusted Publishers** category.

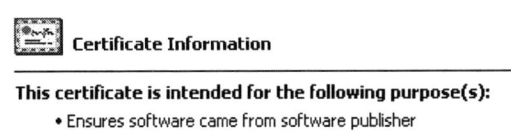

f. Click **OK** to close the **Certificate** dialog box.

g. Click **OK** to close the **Trust Center** dialog box.

h. Click **OK** to close the **Excel Options** dialog box.

i. Close the file without saving.

TOPIC G
Restrict Document Access

Digital signatures guarantee that files are from verifiable sources. But you will also want to ensure that the file has not been modified, either accidentally or on purpose. In this topic, you will restrict access to documents.

When you are creating a workbook by yourself, there is no need to worry about the security of its contents. But when you circulate it within a team, you will have to prevent unnecessary modification of the content. By restricting document permissions, you can ensure that the workbook is modified only by people to whom you assign permissions.

Information Rights Management

Information Rights Management (IRM) is a service that permits users and administrators to define permissions for others to access presentations, documents, and workbooks, as well as other Office suite application documents such as Outlook and Microsoft Access. The permissions assigned to a file are stored with the file's content. All data present within a document is bound by these permissions. The IRM also enables you to prohibit the printing, forwarding, or copying of sensitive data. The content also cannot be copied using the Print Screen mode of Windows. In addition, you can set an expiration date to restrict file access after a specific time frame. IRM is otherwise known as Digital Rights Management (DRM).

Windows Rights Management Services Client with Service Pack 2

If you are using Windows XP as the operating system for your computer, the Windows Rights Management Services Client with Service Pack 2, which is the IRM administrator, needs to be installed. The Rights Management account certificate becomes available on your system upon installation of the Windows Rights Management Services Client with Service Pack 2. Organization-specific policies on copying, forwarding, and editing can be configured using the server. If you are using Windows Vista or Windows 7, the Windows Rights Management Services Client is configured by default during the installation of the operating system.

The Rights Management Account Certificate

For those who are not using the IRM administrator, there is an option for using your email address and password configured on .NET Passport, MSN, or Hotmail. Your email address is used to create the Rights Management account certificate that is downloaded to your computer. You can choose to download a standard certificate or a temporary certificate, depending on use. Once the Rights Management account certificate is downloaded, you can create user accounts, which is the addition of the email address of the persons to whom you will send your workbook. You can give the users full control over your workbook or restrict the users to read, print, or copy.

Standard and Temporary Certificates

You can choose to download a standard certificate or a temporary certificate when you are using your email address and password to download the Rights Management account certificate. If you are going to use the content in the workbook for a limited time, or if you are using a public computer to send your workbook, then the temporary certificate will suffice. Downloading the standard certificate enables you to create, use, and view restricted content on your PC. The certificate can also be renewed on its expiration.

The Mark As Final Option

The **Mark as Final** option enables you to certify a document as final, and protect it from further modifications. After marking a workbook final, all editing commands are disabled, and the workbook goes into a read-only mode. The status is displayed as **Marked as Final** in a message bar below the Ribbon, and the **Marked as Final** icon is displayed on the Microsoft Office Status Bar. A document that is marked final can still be edited. If edited, it is not marked as final anymore.

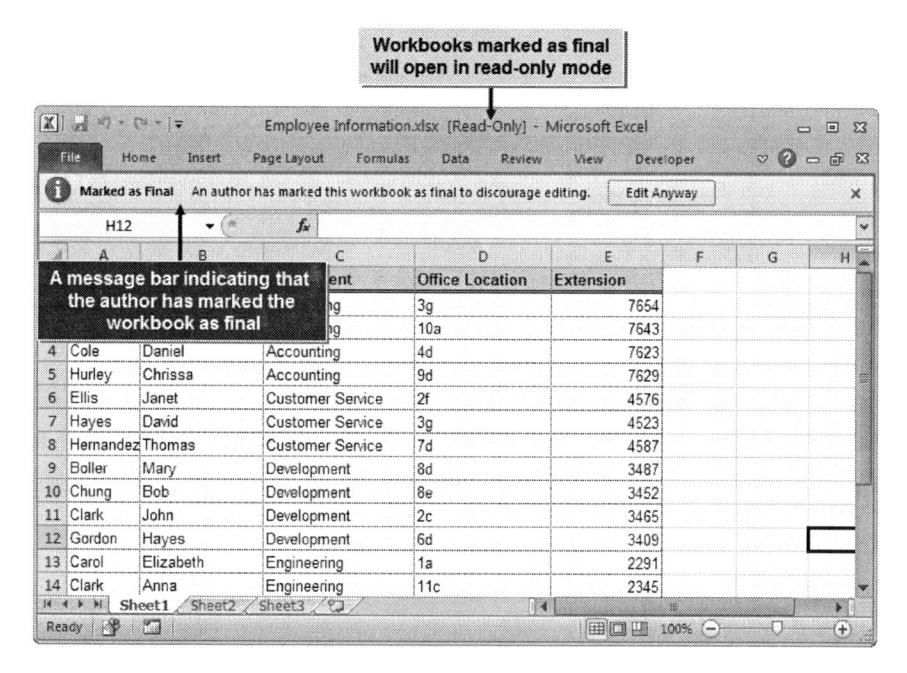

Figure 2-10: *You can discourage other users from editing a file by marking it as final.*

How to Restrict Document Access

Procedure Reference: Restrict Permission to the Contents in a File

To restrict permission to contents in a file:

1. Display the **Select User** dialog box.

   - On the **File** tab, choose **Protect Workbook→Restrict Permission by People→ Manage Credentials** or;

   - On the **Review** tab, in the **Changes** group, from the **Protect Workbook** drop-down list, select **Manage Credentials.**

2. In the **Select User** dialog box, select your user name and click **OK.**

3. In the **Permission** dialog box, check **Restrict permission to this workbook.**

4. Restrict permissions to users.

   - Grant read permission to users.

     - In the **Read** text box, type the email address of the user to whom you want to grant read-only rights or;

     - Click **Read,** and in the **Select Users or Groups** dialog box, enter the email address of the user to whom you want to grant read-only rights.

   - Grant change permission to users.

- In the **Change** text box, type the email address of the user to whom you want to grant editing rights or;
- Click **Change,** and in the **Select Users or Groups** dialog box, enter the email address of the user to whom you want to grant editing rights.

5. In the **Permission** dialog box, click **OK.**

6. If desired, click **More Options** and set additional options such as the expiry date of the permission and permission for printing and copying content.

7. If necessary, save the workbook.

Permission Levels

The three levels of permission allowed are read, change, and full control. However, you can change the permission levels given to a user depending on the requirements.

Level of Permission	Allows Users To
Read	Only read the document. They cannot edit, copy, or print it.
Change	Read, edit, and save changes to the document; however, they cannot print it.
Full control	Own full control of the document.

Procedure Reference: Set an Expiration Date for a File

To set an expiration date for a file:

1. If necessary, open the file.

2. On the **File** tab, choose **Protect Workbook→Restrict Permission by People→Manage Credentials.**

3. In the **Select User** dialog box, select your user name and click **OK.**

4. In the **Permission** dialog box, check the **Restrict permission to this workbook** check box and click **More Options.**

5. Under **Additional permissions for users,** check the **This workbook expires on** check box.

6. Select a date from the drop-down list or type a new date to specify the expiration date for the file and click **OK.**

Procedure Reference: View the Permissions Set for a User

To view the permissions set for a user:

1. Log into the computer with a user name for which you want to view permissions.

2. Open a workbook that is permission restricted.

3. In the **Microsoft Excel** message box, which states that permission is restricted to the worksheet, click **OK.**

4. On the message bar, click **View Permission.**

5. In the **My Permission** dialog box, note the permissions you have and click **OK.**

6. If you have rights to edit the workbook, make the desired changes to the workbook and save it.

Procedure Reference: Mark a Workbook as Final

To mark a workbook as final:

1. Open an existing workbook.

2. On the **File** tab, choose **Protect Workbook→Mark as Final.**

3. In the **Microsoft Excel** warning box, click **OK** to mark the workbook as final and save the file.

4. In the **Microsoft Excel** information box, click **OK.**

5. If necessary, select the **Home** tab and observe that the **Marked as Final** message bar is displayed below the Ribbon indicating that the file cannot be edited.

ACTIVITY 2-9
Restricting Document Access

Data Files:

Quarterly Sales.xlsx

Scenario:

The Quarterly Sales.xlsx workbook contains the quarterly sales data of the current financial year. You want to send it to Betsy Allan, the finance manager of your company, for review, and you also want to grant her permission to edit the workbook. Because this is confidential information, sharing the file could lead to some unnecessary tampering by external sources; therefore, you want to set permission in a way that only the financial manager can edit the document. You also want to set an expiry date for the document so that the document cannot be accessed or opened after a certain period of time.

1. Grant the change permission to Betsy Allan.

   a. Display the **Open** dialog box, navigate to the C:\084678Data\Collaborating with Others folder and open the Quarterly Sales.xlsx file.

   b. Select the **File** tab, and in the Backstage view, from the **Protect Workbook** drop-down list, choose **Restrict Permission by People→Manage Credentials.**

   c. In the **Select User** dialog box, verify that your user account is displayed and click **OK.**

   d. In the **Permission** dialog box, check **Restrict permission to this workbook.**

   e. In the **Change** text box, type *betsyallan@hotmail.com* to grant change permission to Betsy Allan.

    Students can enter the Hotmail or Windows Live ID of their partners in the classroom instead of the above mentioned address.

2. Set an expiration date for the workbook.

   a. In the **Permission** dialog box, click **More Options** to display the advanced permission options.

   b. In the **Additional permissions for users** section, check **This workbook expires on.**

   c. In the **This workbook expires on** text box, triple-click and type a date two months from the current date and click **OK** to set the expiration date.

   d. In the Backstage view, in the **Permissions** section, observe that the **Access to this workbook has been restricted to certain people** message is displayed.

   e. Save the file as *My Quarterly Sales* and close it.

ACTIVITY 2-10
Viewing the Permissions Set for a Workbook

Data Files:

C:\084678Data\Collaborating with Others\Simulations\Viewing the Permissions Set for a Workbook_guided.exe

Simulation:

This is a simulated activity. In this simulation, your email ID is betsy000allan@hotmail.com.

Scenario:

You are Betsy Allan and you have received the quarterly sales data from one of your team members. You verify that you have the permission to make changes to the workbook. You review it and notice that the Jazz music sales data for March is incorrect. Therefore, you make the necessary change and save the document.

1. To launch the simulation, browse to the C:\084678Data\Collaborating with Others\ Simulations folder.

2. Double-click the **Viewing the Permissions Set for a Workbook_guided.exe** file.

3. Maximize the simulation window.

4. Follow the on-screen steps for the simulation.

5. When you have finished the activity, close the simulation window.

ACTIVITY 2-11
Marking a Workbook as Final

Data Files:

Final.xlsx

Scenario:

You have created a workbook, incorporated the necessary changes, and got it approved by your manager. Before sending it to your client, you want to share it with your colleague, but you do not want her to make any changes to it.

---

1. Mark the workbook as final.

   a. Display the **Open** dialog box, navigate to the C:\084678Data\Collaborating with Others folder and open the Final.xlsx file.

   b. Save the file as *My Final*

   c. In the Backstage view, from the **Protect Workbook** drop-down list, select **Mark as Final.**

   d. In the **Microsoft Excel** warning box, click **OK** to mark the workbook as final and save the file.

   e. In the **Microsoft Excel** message box indicating that the document is the final version, click **OK.**

---

2. Check whether the workbook has been marked as final.

   a. In the Backstage view, in the **Permissions** section, observe that a message is displayed indicating that the workbook has been marked as final to discourage the editing of content.

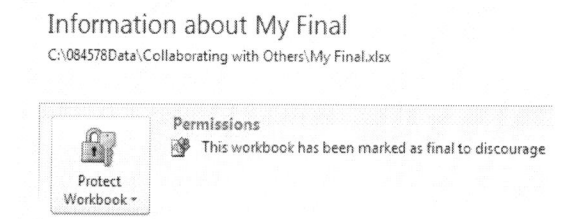

   b. Select the **Home** tab.

c. Observe that the file opens in read-only mode with a message displayed below the ribbon indicating that the file has been marked as final.

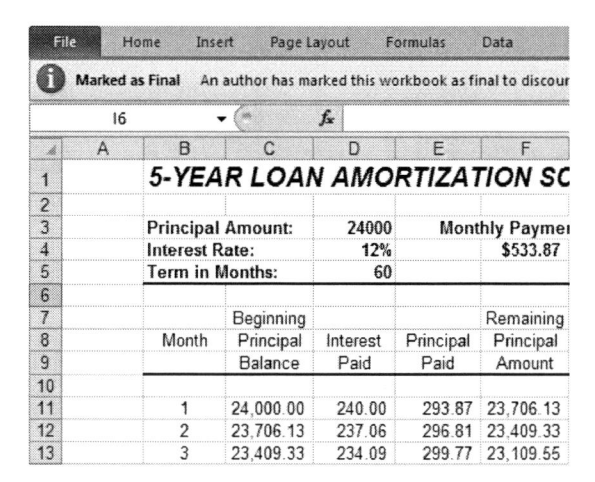

d. Close the workbook.

Lesson 2 Follow-up

In this lesson, you protected workbook data. You also shared a workbook with other users and merged multiple workbooks into a single workbook. The workbook sharing features are useful when multiple users are required to work on a workbook in a collaborative mode.

1. **What are the various types of applications for which you might need to share a workbook with multiple users?**

2. **What are the various security features available for securing a workbook?**

3 | Auditing Worksheets

Lesson Time: 1 hour(s)

Lesson Objectives:

In this lesson, you will audit worksheets.

You will:

- Trace cell precedents and dependents.
- Troubleshoot invalid data and formula errors.
- Watch and evaluate formulas.
- Create a data list outline.

Introduction

You interpreted data using Microsoft Excel 2010. Verifying the accuracy of data and formulas in a worksheet is a prerequisite for data interpretation. In this lesson, you will audit worksheets.

As an experienced Excel user, you know about the types of problems that errors in formulas or data can create. When it comes to working with multiple worksheets having complex formulas, the risk of error seepage is quite high. Using the advanced features in Excel, you can audit worksheets and ensure that all formulas, functions, and data work as intended.

TOPIC A
Trace Cells

You have worked with complex formulas. There are times when you know that your data is incorrect, and you cannot determine the nature of the problem. You will need to troubleshoot such problems with data. In this topic, you will trace cell precedents and dependents.

When you observe errors while working with a worksheet containing complex formulas, you have the option to trace cells rather than manually review each formula. Tracing the precedents and dependents of a cell helps you to validate a given formula and makes locating formulas and their dependent cells a lot easier.

Tracer Arrows

Definition:

Tracer arrows are graphics depicting the data flow between cells that contain values and those that contain formulas. These arrows point to the direction of the data flow. There are three types of tracer arrows: formula tracer arrows in solid blue, error tracer arrows in solid red, and external reference tracer arrows in dashed black lines pointing to a worksheet icon.

Example:

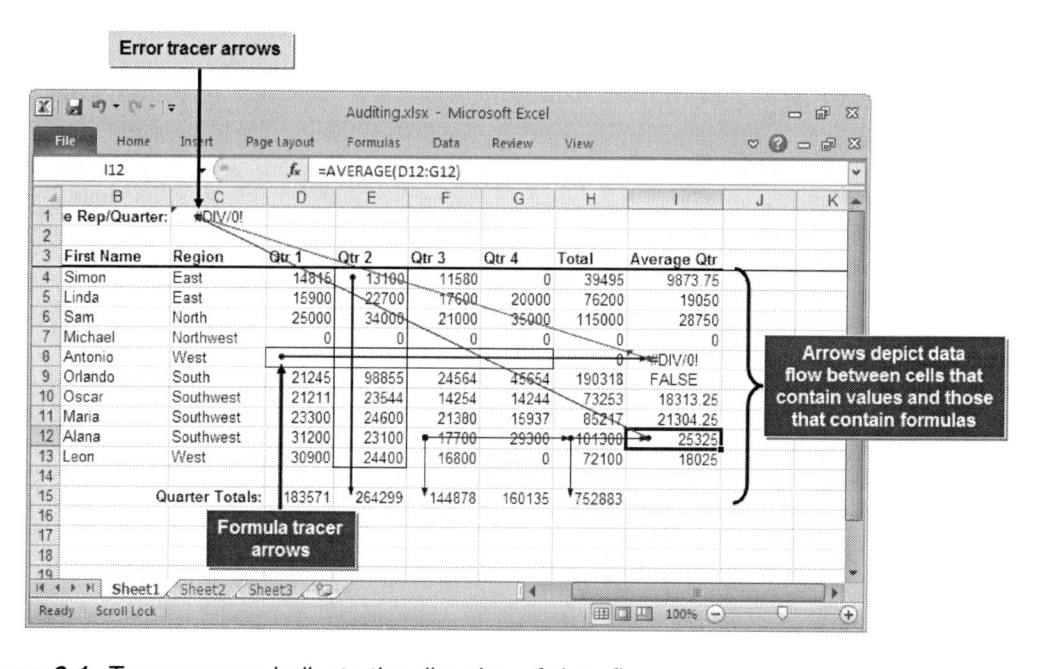

Figure 3-1: Tracer arrows indicate the direction of data flow.

Cell Precedents

Definition:

A *cell precedent* is a cell reference that supplies data to a formula. Arrows point to cells from where data is captured for the formula. The **Trace Precedents** button is used to check formulas and to graphically display or trace the relationship between cells and formulas using arrows.

Example:

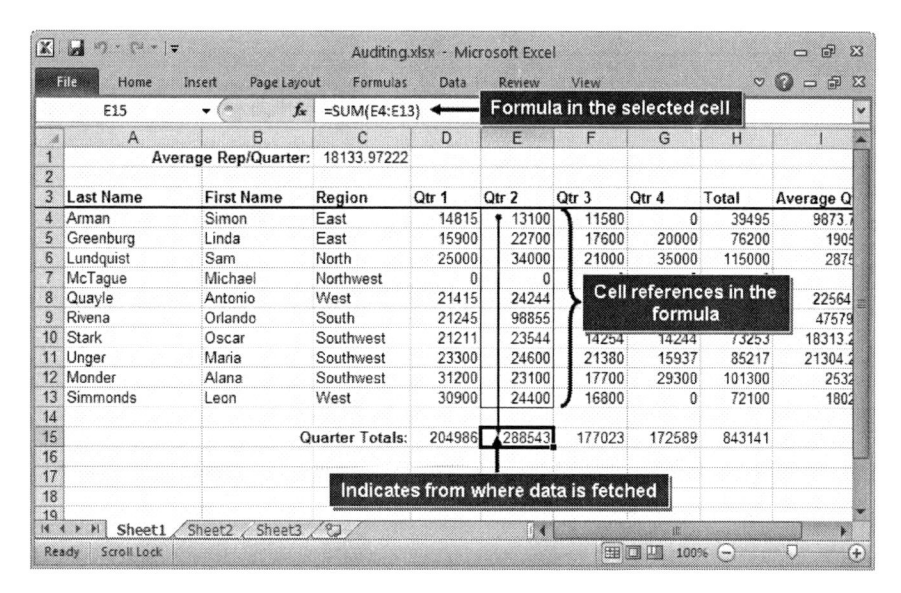

Figure 3-2: A cell precedent references data to a formula.

Cell Dependents

Definition:

A *cell dependent* is a cell that contains a formula referring to other cells. Arrows indicate the cells that are affected by the value of the currently selected cell. The cell containing the formula should not be included in the formula, and it should have a direct connection to the dependent cell. The dependent cell is highlighted by a red or blue arrow, depending on the error generated.

Example:

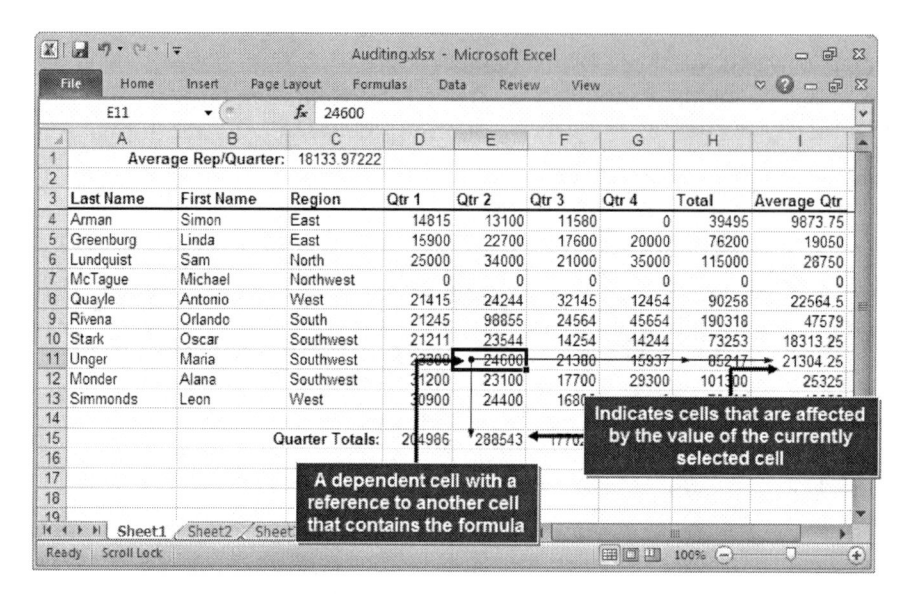

Figure 3-3: A cell dependent refers to other cells.

How to Trace Cell Precedents and Dependents

Procedure Reference: Trace Cell Precedents and Dependents

To trace cell precedents and dependents:

1. In a worksheet, select a cell that contains the formula or data for which you want to trace the precedent of dependent cells.

2. On the **Formulas** tab, in the **Formula Auditing** group, click **Trace Precedents** or **Trace Dependents** to trace the desired cells.

3. If necessary, double-click the tip of the tracer arrow to select the related cell or cell range.

4. If necessary, click **Trace Precedents** or **Trace Dependents** again to identify the next level of cells that provide data to the active cell.

5. In the **Formula Auditing** group, from the **Remove Arrows** drop-down list, select the necessary options in order to remove the arrows.

ACTIVITY 3-1
Tracing Cell Precedents and Dependents

Data Files:

C:\084678Data\Auditing Worksheets\Auditing.xlsx

Before You Begin:
The Excel application is open.

Scenario:
You have entered details of the first quarter sales. As this file will be distributed to a number of people, you want to make sure that the cell references used in the formula for calculating the first quarter sales as well as the grand total sales of all quarters are correct. You need to use arrows to indicate cells that are affected by the value of the cell corresponding to Alana Monder's quarter 1 sales. Finally, you need to view all relationships for the cell in the worksheet and identify the next level of cells that supply data to the active cell.

---

1. In the Auditing Workbook, trace the precedents for the first quarter sales.

    a. Display the **Open** dialog box, navigate to the C:\084678Data\Auditing Worksheets folder, and open the Auditing.xlsx file.

    b. Verify that cell D15 is selected, and on the **Formulas** tab, in the **Formula Auditing** group, click **Trace Precedents.**

    c. Observe that Excel draws a blue box around the range of cells referred by the formula. There is also a tracer arrow from the first cell in the precedent range that goes through the entire precedent range to the active cell.

3	Last Name	First Name	Region	Qtr 1	Qtr 2
4	Arman	Simon	East	$14,815.00	$13,100.00
5	Greenburg	Linda	East	$15,900.00	$22,700.00
6	Lundquist	Sam	North	$25,000.00	$34,000.00
7	McTague	Michael	Northwest	$25,476.00	$12,454.00
8	Quayle	Antonio	West	$31,454.00	$45,244.00
9	Rivena	Orlando	South	$13,455.00	$12,455.00
10	Stark	Oscar	Southwest	$21,141.00	$12,544.00
11	Unger	Maria	Southwest	$23,300.00	$24,600.00
12	Monder	Alana	Southwest	$31,200.00	$23,100.00
13	Simmonds	Leon	West	$30,900.00	$24,400.00
14					
15			Quarter Totals:	242641	224597

    d. Double-click the tip of the tracer arrow to select the entire precedent range.

e. Observe the range selected to calculate the first quarter total sales.

3	Last Name	First Name	Region	Qtr 1	Qtr 2
4	Arman	Simon	East	$14,815.00	$13,100.00
5	Greenburg	Linda	East	$15,900.00	$22,700.00
6	Lundquist	Sam	North	$25,000.00	$34,000.00
7	McTague	Michael	Northwest	$25,476.00	$12,454.00
8	Quayle	Antonio	West	$31,454.00	$45,244.00
9	Rivena	Orlando	South	$23,455.00	$12,455.00
10	Stark	Oscar	Southwest	$21,141.00	$12,544.00
11	Unger	Maria	Southwest	$23,300.00	$24,600.00
12	Monder	Alana	Southwest	$31,200.00	$23,100.00
13	Simmonds	Leon	West	$30,900.00	$24,400.00
14					
15			Quarter Totals:	242641	224597

2. Remove the precedent arrow.

   a. Select cell **D15.**

   b. In the **Formula Auditing** group, from the **Remove Arrows** drop-down list, select **Remove Precedent Arrows** to remove the precedent arrow.

3. Display two precedents for cell H15 and then remove all arrows.

   a. Select cell **H15.**

   b. In the **Formula Auditing** group, click **Trace Precedents** to view the precedent arrows.

   c. Click **Trace Precedents** again to view two levels of precedent arrows.

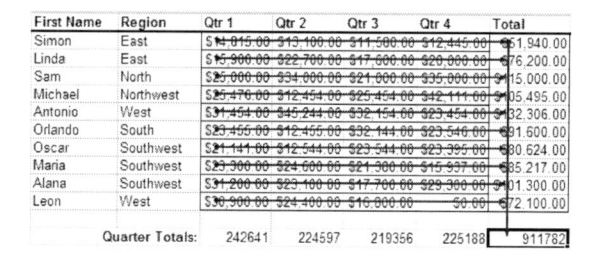

First Name	Region	Qtr 1	Qtr 2	Qtr 3	Qtr 4	Total
Simon	East	$14,815.00	$13,100.00	$11,580.00	$12,445.00	$51,940.00
Linda	East	$15,900.00	$22,700.00	$17,600.00	$20,000.00	$76,200.00
Sam	North	$25,000.00	$34,000.00	$21,000.00	$35,000.00	$115,000.00
Michael	Northwest	$25,476.00	$12,454.00	$25,454.00	$42,111.00	$105,495.00
Antonio	West	$31,454.00	$45,244.00	$32,154.00	$23,454.00	$132,306.00
Orlando	South	$23,455.00	$12,455.00	$32,144.00	$23,546.00	$91,600.00
Oscar	Southwest	$21,141.00	$12,544.00	$23,544.00	$23,395.00	$80,624.00
Maria	Southwest	$23,300.00	$24,600.00	$21,380.00	$15,937.00	$85,217.00
Alana	Southwest	$31,200.00	$23,100.00	$17,700.00	$29,300.00	$101,300.00
Leon	West	$30,900.00	$24,400.00	$16,800.00	$0.00	$72,100.00
	Quarter Totals:	242641	224597	219356	225188	911782

   d. Click **Remove Arrows** to remove the tracer arrows.

4. Trace all dependents for Alana Monder's quarter 1 sales.

   a. Select cell **D12** to select Alana Monder's first quarter sales.

   b. In the **Formula Auditing** group, click **Trace Dependents** to display the dependent tracer arrows.

   c. Observe that cell D12 has dependents referring to the total and average sales of all quarters pertaining to Alana Monder and to the quarter 1 totals.

First Name	Region	Qtr 1	Qtr 2	Qtr 3	Qtr 4	Total	Average Qtr
Simon	East	$14,815.00	$13,100.00	$11,580.00	$12,445.00	$51,940.00	$12,985.00
Linda	East	$15,900.00	$22,700.00	$17,600.00	$20,000.00	$76,200.00	$19,050.00
Sam	North	$25,000.00	$34,000.00	$21,000.00	$35,000.00	$115,000.00	$28,750.00
Michael	Northwest	$25,476.00	$12,454.00	$25,454.00	$42,111.00	$105,495.00	$26,373.75
Antonio	West	$31,454.00	$45,244.00	$32,154.00	$23,454.00	$132,306.00	$33,076.50
Orlando	South	$23,455.00	$12,455.00	$32,144.00	$23,546.00	$91,600.00	$22,900.00
Oscar	Southwest	$21,141.00	$12,544.00	$23,544.00	$23,395.00	$80,624.00	$20,156.00
Maria	Southwest	$23,300.00	$24,600.00	$21,380.00	$15,937.00	$85,217.00	$21,304.25
Alana	Southwest	$31,200.00	$23,100.00	$17,700.00	$29,300.00	$101,300.00	$25,325.00
Leon	West	$30,900.00	$24,400.00	$16,800.00	$0.00	$72,100.00	$18,025.00
	Quarter Totals:	242641	224597	219356	225188	911782	

d. Click **Trace Dependents** to display the next level of dependent tracer arrows and view all relationships in the cell.

e. Observe that there is a second level of dependents to the grand totals of all quarters and to the average of all average sales per quarter.

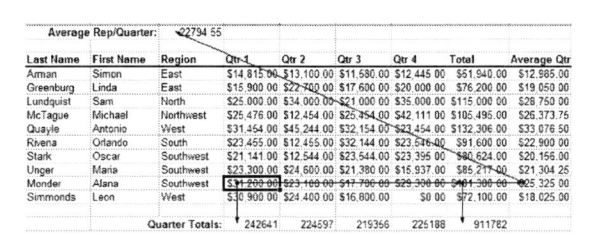

f. Click **Remove Arrows** to remove all dependent arrows.

g. Close the file without saving.

TOPIC B

Troubleshoot Invalid Data and Formula Errors

You used cell precedents and dependents to verify data results in a formula. Often, invalid data and formula in a worksheet play havoc in your analyses. In this topic, you will locate and fix invalid data and formula errors.

When working with an Excel workbook, you come to know that some invalid parameters are mixed with the data or formula. Excel's error checking options help you to quickly locate invalid data and formula errors, so that they can be fixed.

Invalid Data

Invalid data is any data in a worksheet that fits in a cell as an odd value and that does not conform to the cell's data validation scheme. Invalid data either stops the calculation process from proceeding to the next step or results in incorrect answers.

The Error Checking Command

The *Error Checking* command in the **Formula Auditing** group on the **Formulas** tab has options to check for errors in formulas. Cells with formula errors have an icon next to them.

There are various error checking options available.

Option	Description
Error Checking	Used to display an icon next to a cell that has an error. It also displays a green triangle at the upper-left corner of the cell.
Trace Error	Used for checking formula errors in a worksheet and indicating them with colored arrows. A blue arrow indicates cells that have no errors, a red arrow indicates cells that cause the error, and a black arrow indicates cells that are referenced by cells in a different workbook.
Circular References	Used when a formula refers to its own cell, either directly or indirectly.

Error Types

Though there are many types of errors affecting the quality of a worksheet, all formula errors begin with the pound sign (#).

Error Type	Occurs When
#DIV/0!	The numerical value in a cell is divided by 0.
#N/A	A function or formula does not have a value.
#NAME?	Text is not recognized in a formula.
#NULL!	You specify an intersection for values that cannot be intersected.
#NUM!	There are invalid numeric values in a formula.
#REF!	The reference to a cell is considered invalid.
#VALUE!	An improper type of argument is used.
#####	The cell contains a number, date, or time that is wider than the cell, or when the cell contains a date and/or time formula that produces a negative result.

How to Troubleshoot Invalid Data and Formula Errors

Procedure Reference: Troubleshoot Invalid Data

To troubleshoot invalid data:

1. On the **Data** tab, in the **Data Tools** group, from the **Data Validation** drop-down list, choose **Circle Invalid Data** to circle the invalid data on the worksheet.

2. If necessary, in the **Data Validation** dialog box, on the **Settings** tab, select the type of data a cell can accept, and click **OK.**

3. Repair the data in the circled cell or cells so that it matches the data validation criteria.

Procedure Reference: Troubleshoot Invalid Formulas

To troubleshoot invalid formulas:

1. On the **Home** tab, in the **Editing** group, click the **Find & Select** drop down list and select **Find** to open the **Find and Replace** dialog box.

2. On the **Find** tab, in the **Find what** text box, type # to search for cells with invalid formulas.

3. Expand **Find Options** by clicking the **Options** button.

4. From the **Look in** drop-down list, select **Values.**

5. Click **Find All** to list all cells that contain a pound sign (#) as hyperlinks at the bottom of the **Find and Replace** dialog box.

6. Click the hyperlink to a cell with the error you want to repair. Excel automatically advances to the cell.

7. In the worksheet, click the selected cell to activate the worksheet.

8. From the **Error Checking** drop-down list that appears next to the cell, choose **Edit in Formula Bar.**

9. In the **Formula Bar,** correct the formula.

10. In the **Find and Replace** dialog box, click the link to repair the next formula or click **Close.**

Procedure Reference: Troubleshoot Errors in Formulas

To troubleshoot errors in formulas:

1. Click the cell that contains the formula error.

2. On the **Formulas** tab, in the **Formula Auditing** group, from the **Error Checking** drop-down list, choose **Trace Error** to trace errors in the file.

3. If desired, remove all trace arrows.

4. Fix the errors in the formula.

5. If necessary, trace more errors and fix them.

6. Save and close the file.

ACTIVITY 3-2
Troubleshooting Invalid Data and Formula Errors

Data Files:

C:\084678Data\Auditing Worksheets\Quarter Totals.xlsx

Before You Begin:
The Excel application is open.

Scenario:
As the sales manager at OGC Bookstore, you combined worksheets that track the total sales of your sales representatives for the past two years. Before sending it to the vice president, you decide to verify that all entries in the file are valid. During the review, you find that the ID number for Leonard Simmonds is invalid. His actual ID number is 184533. You also need to check for invalid formulas in the worksheet and fix them.

---

1. Correct the invalid data in the worksheet.

   a. Display the **Open** dialog box, navigate to the C:\084678Data\Auditing Worksheets folder, and open the Quarter Totals.xlsx file.

   b. On the **Data** tab, in the **Data Tools** group, from the **Data Validation** drop-down list, select **Circle Invalid Data** to circle the invalid data in the worksheet.

   c. Observe that a red circle appears in cell **A9** indicating invalid data.

	IDNumber	Last Name	First Initial	Year 1
1	Average Rep/Year		$190,084.58	
2				
3	IDNumber	Last Name	First Initial	Year 1
4	105480	Arman	S	$214,815.00
5	105608	Greenburg	L	$215,900.00
6	110018	Lundquist	S	$125,000.00
7	147060	Unger	M	$123,300.00
8	161975	Monder	A	$231,200.00
9	Leonard	Simmonds	L	$230,900.00
10				
11			Totals	$1,141,115.00

   d. Select cell **A9**.

   e. In the **Data Tools** group, click **Data Validation**.

   f. In the **Data Validation** dialog box, on the **Settings** tab, verify that the minimum value is set to 100000 and the maximum to 999999, and click **OK**.

   g. In cell **A9**, change the value to *184533* and press **Enter**.

     h.   Observe that entering valid data in the cell automatically removes the circle.

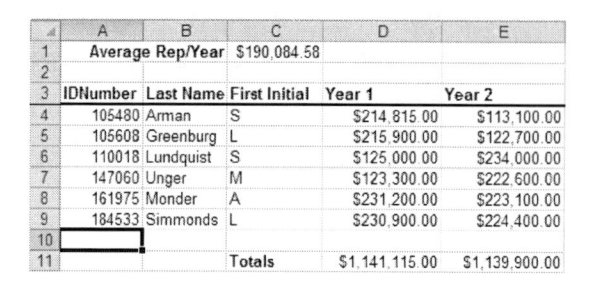

	A	B	C	D	E
1	Average Rep/Year		$190,084.58		
2					
3	IDNumber	Last Name	First Initial	Year 1	Year 2
4	105480	Arman	S	$214,815.00	$113,100.00
5	105608	Greenburg	L	$215,900.00	$122,700.00
6	110018	Lundquist	S	$125,000.00	$234,000.00
7	147060	Unger	M	$123,300.00	$222,600.00
8	161975	Monder	A	$231,200.00	$223,100.00
9	184533	Simmonds	L	$230,900.00	$224,400.00
10					
11			Totals	$1,141,115.00	$1,139,900.00

2.   Correct the invalid formulas.

     a.   Verify that the values in cells F6 and F11 are displayed as errors.

     b.   Select cell **F6.**

     c.   In the worksheet, hover the mouse pointer over the Error Checking icon, and click the drop-down arrow. From the displayed drop-down list, select **Edit in Formula Bar.**

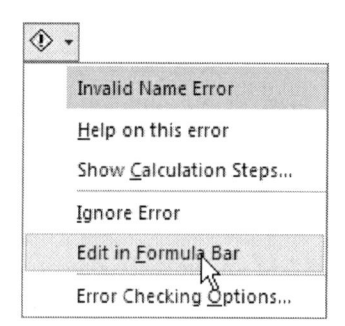

     d.   In the **Formula Bar,** observe that the data range is not specified properly.

     e.   Edit the formula to read *=SUM(D6:E6)*

     f.   Verify that the value in F11 is automatically corrected.

     g.   Save the file as *My Quarter Totals* and close it.

ACTIVITY 3-3
Troubleshooting Formula Errors

Data Files:

C:\084678Data\Auditing Worksheets\Auditing Error.xlsx

Before You Begin:
The Excel application is open.

Scenario:
In the Auditing Error workbook, the formula used to calculate the average sales made by each sales executive for the second quarter is not displaying correct values. You need to locate the error and fix it.

---

1. Trace the error in the formula.

   a. Display the **Open** dialog box, navigate to the C:\084678Data\Auditing Worksheets folder, and open the Auditing Error.xlsx file.

   b. Verify that cell E18 is selected, and observe that the Error Checking icon indicating the presence of an error is displayed next to the cell.

   c. On the **Formulas** tab, in the **Formula Auditing** group, from the **Error Checking** drop-down list, select **Trace Error** to trace the error in the selected cell.

   d. In the **Formula Bar,** observe that you have entered the formula as **=AVG(E4+E13)** in cell E18.

fx	=AVG(E4+E13)		
C	**D**	**E**	**F**
Region	**Qtr 1**	**Qtr 2**	**Qtr 3**
East	14815	• 13100	11580
East	15900	22700	17600
North	25000	34000	21000
Northwest	41414	45242	21444
West	24544	14545	21445
South	21212	14544	11244
Southwest	32111	32121	21345
Southwest	23300	24600	21380
Southwest	31200	23100	17700
West	30900	• 24400	16800
Quarter Totals:	260396	248352	181538
Average:	26 ◇ .6	#NAME?	18153.8

2. Correct the formula.

---

a. In the **Formula Auditing** group, click **Remove Arrows** to remove the trace arrow.

b. Edit the formula in cell E18 to read *=AVERAGE(E4:E13)*

c. Verify that there are no error checking icons on the worksheet.

d. Save the file as ***My Auditing Error*** and close it.

TOPIC C
Watch and Evaluate Formulas

You located invalid data and formulas in your workbook. Some formulas require continuous monitoring. In this topic, you will watch and evaluate formulas.

Imagine a worksheet that contains complex formulas, many of which are off the viewable portion of your screen. You want to know how certain formulas react to changes in data, and verify that they are returning the expected values. Evaluating formulas during the development process helps you to ensure that they are functioning the way you want them to.

The Watch Window Dialog Box

The *Watch Window* dialog box allows you to view the contents of a cell while the cell itself is off the viewable portion of your screen. The **Watch Window** dialog box identifies the name of the workbook in which the cell appears, the name of the worksheet on which the cell lives, the cell reference, the value stored in the cell, and the formula, if any, that the cell contains.

Formula Evaluation

The **Evaluate Formula** dialog box displays the formula to be evaluated for the selected cell. The **Evaluate** button in the dialog box evaluates complex nested formulas one step at a time. The most recent results are displayed in italics.

How to Evaluate Formulas
Procedure Reference: Watch Formulas

To watch formulas:

1. On the **Formulas** tab, in the **Formula Auditing** group, click **Watch Window.**
2. In the **Watch Window** dialog box, click **Add Watch** to display the **Add Watch** dialog box.
3. In the worksheet, select the cell or cells you want to watch.
4. In the **Add Watch** dialog box, click **Add.**
5. Make the necessary changes in the worksheet to update the data. In the **Watch Window** dialog box, observe the corresponding change to data in cells you want to watch.

Procedure Reference: Evaluate Formulas

To evaluate formulas:

1. On a worksheet, select a cell that contains the formula you want to evaluate.
2. On the **Formulas** tab, in the **Formula Auditing** group, click **Evaluate Formula.**
3. Click **Evaluate** to evaluate each portion of the formula in the same order in which the formula is calculated. Repeat this step as often as needed to evaluate each step of the formula.
4. Close the **Evaluate Formula** dialog box.

ACTIVITY 3-4
Watching and Evaluating Formulas

Data Files:

C:\084678Data\Auditing Worksheets\Loan Schedule.xlsx

Before You Begin:
The Excel application is open.

Scenario:
The Loan Schedule workbook tracks the amortization for loans that can be paid off in 60 months. You want to see the total interest that would be paid for payment terms of 24 months. Instead of scrolling down to the bottom of the worksheet every time you change the value in the Term in Months field, you decide to watch the cell that calculates the total interest paid. Additionally, you want to check whether the formula that calculates the remaining principal amount works properly.

---

1. Add the cell with the total interest paid data to the Watch Window.

    a. Display the **Open** dialog box, navigate to the C:\084678Data\Auditing Worksheets folder, and open the Loan Schedule.xlsx file.

    b. Select cell **D72**, and on the **Formulas** tab, in the **Formula Auditing** group, click **Watch Window.**

    c. In the **Watch Window** dialog box, click **Add Watch.**

    d. In the **Add Watch** dialog box, click **Add** to add cell D72 to the **Watch Window** dialog box.

    e. Observe that the data in the **Value** column is 4,697.16.

---

2. View the results for loans with a repayment period of 24 months.

    a. Press **Ctrl+Home** to scroll up to the top of the worksheet.

    b. In cell D5, enter *24* to change the term to 24 months.

    c. In the **Watch Window** dialog box, observe that the data in the **Value** column is displayed as 3,114.32 for loans with a repayment period of 24 months.

    d. In cell D5, type *36* and press **Enter.**

    e. In the **Watch Window** dialog box, observe that the data in the **Value** column is reverted to 4,697.16.

    f. Close the **Watch Window** dialog box.

---

3. Evaluate the formula for the first instance of the remaining principal amount.

    a. Select cell **F11.**

    b. In the **Formula Auditing** group, click **Evaluate Formula.**

---

c. In the **Evaluate Formula** dialog box, in the **Evaluation** text box, observe that cells B11, D5, C11, and E11 are included in the formula and B11 is underlined indicating that it will be evaluated next.

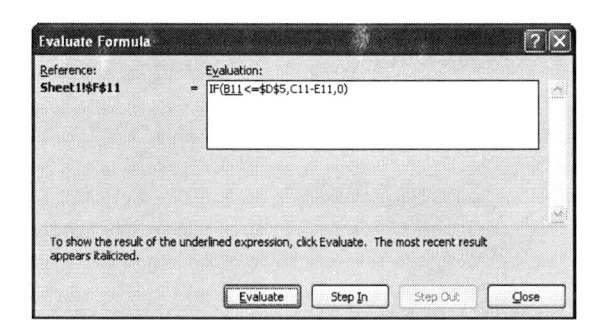

d. In the worksheet, observe that the value of cell B11 is 1, which will be substituted in the evaluation formula. In the **Evaluate Formula** dialog box, click **Evaluate.**

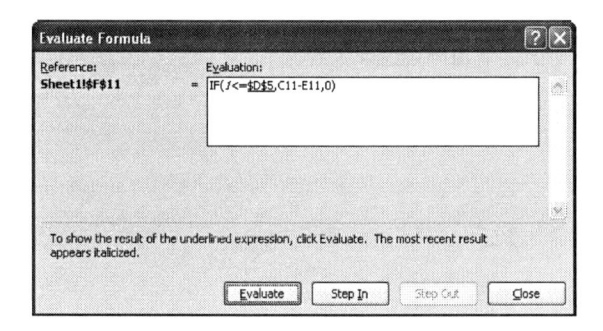

e. Click **Evaluate** to substitute the value in cell D5, which is underlined in the **Evaluation** text box.

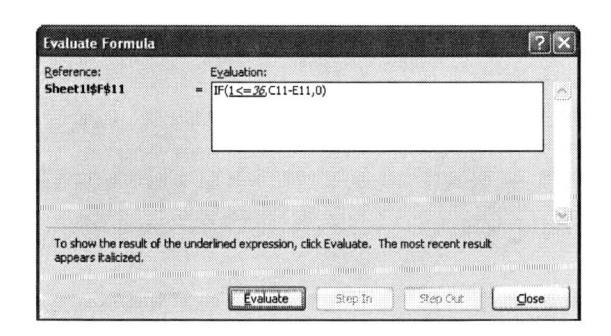

f. Click **Evaluate** to evaluate the expression 1<=36.

g. Observe that the condition less-than-or-equal-to is TRUE, and click **Evaluate** to substitute the value in cell C11.

h. Click **Evaluate** to show the result of the underlined expression.

i. Observe that the value of the underlined expression is substituted in order to make it clear how the formula is operating.

j. Continue to click **Evaluate** until the formula calculates the result 23,442.86, and then click **Close.**

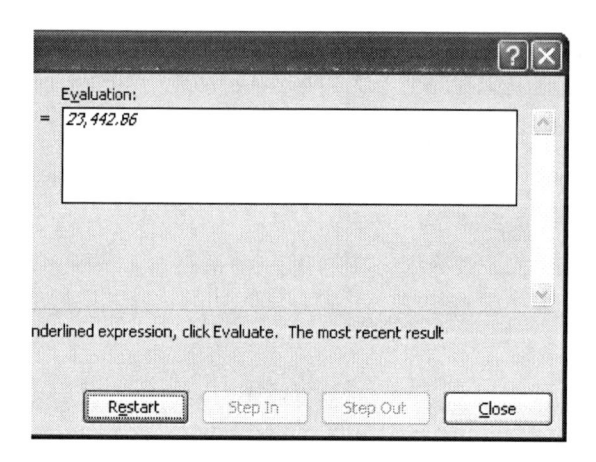

k. Save the file as ***My Loan Schedule*** and close it.

TOPIC D
Create a Data List Outline

You watched and evaluated formulas in order to closely monitor the data that was not within the view area. You have both individual data and data lists in your worksheet, and now you want to view only the data lists by themselves. In this topic, you will create a data list outline.

Viewing the data lists in a clear format can be a very effective means of analyzing and comparing a subset of data to the entire worksheet or workbook. But what if you want to view several data lists side by side and compare them? Data list outlines allow you to view multiple data lists at the same time.

Outlines

Definition:

An *outline* is a data organizing method in which a set of data is combined to form a group. Data in a worksheet must be sorted before it can be outlined. By outlining the data, users will be able to hide the cluttered data without removing them from the worksheet. Once outlines are created, they can be expanded or collapsed as necessary.

Example:

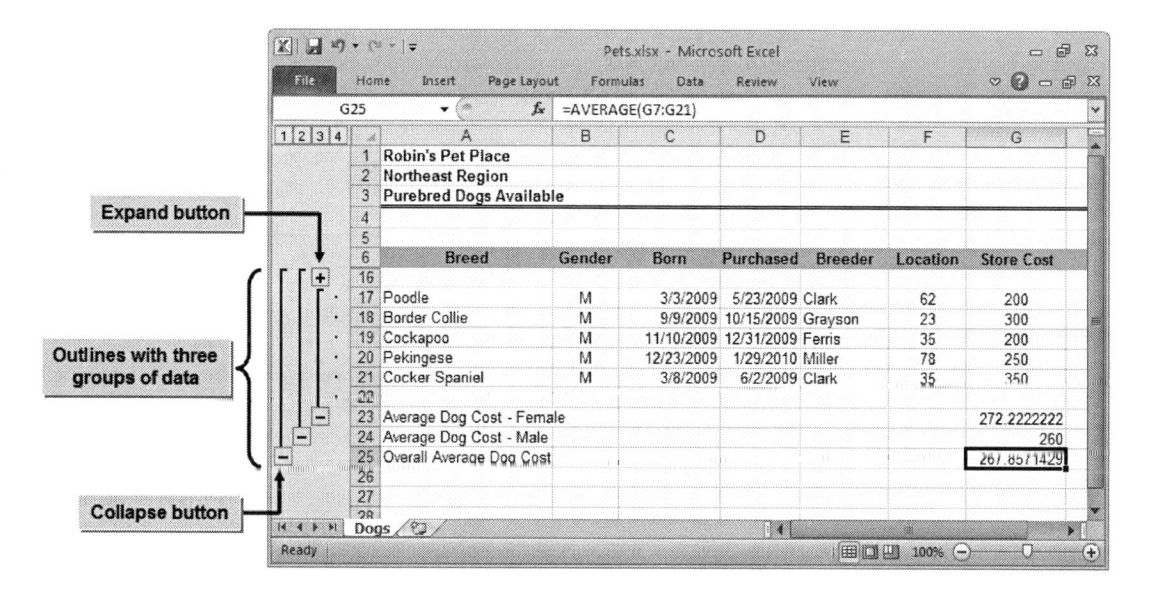

Figure 3-4: Outlines sort data according to a particular category.

Group Data

The group data feature will group the data based on certain criteria and displays an outline of the rows and columns of the grouped data. The outline is displayed as a bar above the column letters and row numbers.

The Outline Group

The **Outline** group on the **Data** tab contains options to group, ungroup, and subtotal data in a worksheet.

Option		Description
Group	Group	Combines a range of cells so that it is possible to collapse or expand them. The **Group** drop-down list has two options: **Group** and **Auto Outline.** The **Group** option groups the data by either row or column, and the **Auto Outline** option groups the data automatically based on type.
Ungroup	Ungroup	Ungroups the grouped range of cells.
Subtotal	Subtotal	Totals data between rows by inserting subtotals and grand totals for the selected cells automatically.

How to Create a Data List Outline

Procedure Reference: Group and Outline Data Using Auto Outline

To group and outline data using Auto Outline:

1. In the desired file, sort the list by a criterion of your choice.

2. Select a range of cells that need to be outlined.

3. On the **Data** tab, in the **Outline** group, from the **Group** drop-down list, select **Auto Outline** to automatically group and outline data.

4. If necessary, collapse the details.

Procedure Reference: Group and Outline Data Using the Group Option

To group and outline data using the Group option:

1. In the desired file, sort the list by a criterion of your choice.

2. Select rows or columns you want to group.

3. On the **Data** tab, in the **Outline** group, from the **Group** drop-down list, select **Group** to manually group and outline data.

4. If necessary, collapse the details.

Procedure Reference: Add Subtotals to Grouped Data Using the Subtotal Option

To add subtotals to grouped data using the Subtotal option:

1. Open the file with data that has been grouped.

2. Select a range of cells that has to be totaled.

3. On the **Data** tab, in the **Outline** group, click **Subtotal** to calculate the subtotal and add it to the grouped data.

ACTIVITY 3-5
Creating a Data List Outline

Data Files:

C:\084678Data\Auditing Worksheets\Pets.xlsx

Before You Begin:
The Excel application is open.

Scenario:

While working with a pet shop account, you would like to compare the average store cost by the gender of dogs to the total average. Your senior manager wants you to put the information in the workbook as an outline, so that he can easily see the averages.

---

1. Create individual groups.

    a. Display the **Open** dialog box, navigate to the C:\084678Data\Auditing Worksheets folder, and open the Pets.xlsx file.

    b. Verify that cell **A7** is selected.

    c. On the **Data** tab, in the **Outline** group, click the **Group** drop-down arrow, and select **Auto Outline** to automatically group the cells.

    d. On the left side of the worksheet, observe that separate outlines are created for the average cost of male and female dogs and also for the overall average cost of a dog.

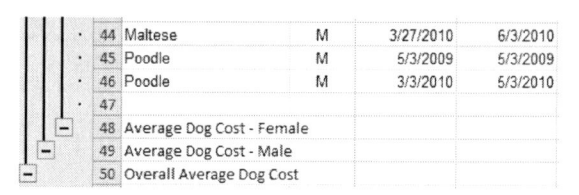

44	Maltese	M	3/27/2010	6/3/2010
45	Poodle	M	5/3/2009	5/3/2009
46	Poodle	M	3/3/2010	5/3/2010
47				
48	Average Dog Cost - Female			
49	Average Dog Cost - Male			
50	Overall Average Dog Cost			

    e. Select the range **A7:H27**.

    f. In the **Outline** group, click **Group**.

    g. In the **Group** dialog box, verify that **Rows** is selected and click **OK**.

---

2. Collapse the details so that only the averages by gender and the overall costs are shown.

    a. To the left of row heading 28, click the minus sign to collapse the list.

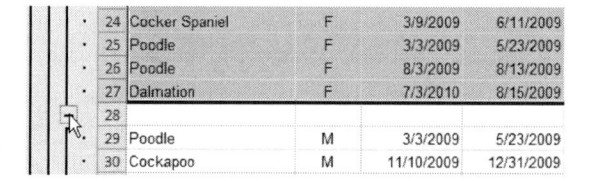

24	Cocker Spaniel	F	3/9/2009	6/11/2009
25	Poodle	F	3/3/2009	5/23/2009
26	Poodle	F	8/3/2009	8/13/2009
27	Dalmation	F	7/3/2010	8/15/2009
28				
29	Poodle	M	3/3/2009	5/23/2009
30	Cockapoo	M	11/10/2009	12/31/2009

b. To the left of row heading 48, click the **minus sign** to collapse the list.

	45	Poodle	M	5/3/2009	5/3/2009
	46	Poodle	M	3/3/2010	5/3/2010
	47				
	48	Average Dog Cost - Female			
	49	Average Dog Cost - Male			
	50	Overall Average Dog Cost			

c. Observe that the gender-wise average cost and the overall cost is displayed.

d. Save the file as *My Pets* and close the workbook.

ACTIVITY 3-6
Adding Subtotals to Grouped Data

Data Files:

C:\084678Data\Auditing Worksheets\Grouped Pets.xlsx

Before You Begin:

The Excel application is open.

Scenario:

You have created an outline of all dogs in the store. Now, you are required to subtotal dogs by each breed so that it is easier to maintain a report of the cost of each breed in that particular store.

1. Display the **Subtotal** dialog box.

   a. Display the **Open** dialog box, navigate to the C:\084678Data\Auditing Worksheets folder, and open the Grouped Pets.xlsx file.

   b. Select any cell in the table.

   c. On the **Data** tab, in the **Outline** group, click **Subtotal**.

2. Subtotal the store cost by the gender of dogs.

   a. In the **Subtotal** dialog box, in the **At each change in** drop-down list, verify that **Breed** is selected.

   b. In the **Add subtotal to** list box, uncheck **Price**.

   c. Check **Store Cost** and click **OK**.

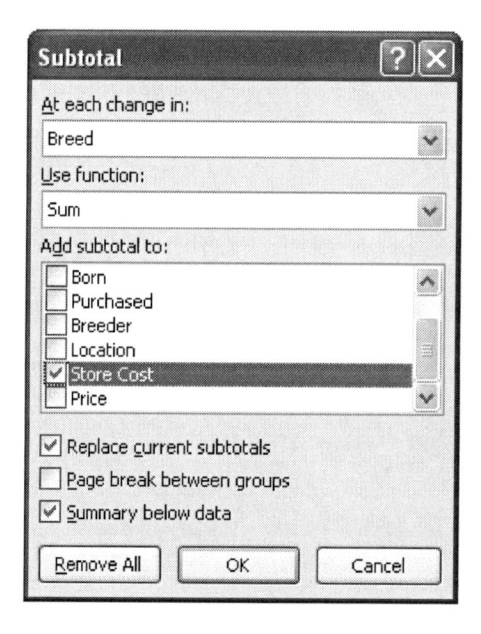

d.   Verify that the subtotals are calculated for the store cost.

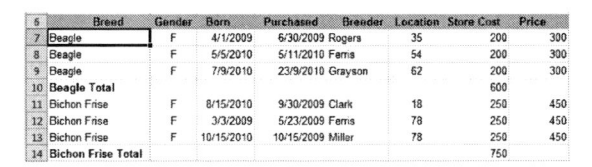

3.   Collapse details revealing only the subtotal.

a.   To the left of row 10, click the minus sign to collapse the subtotal of Beagle.

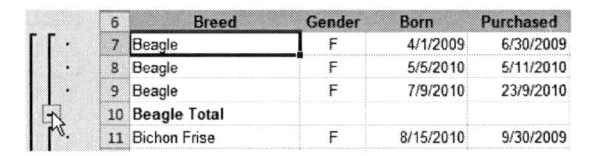

b.   To the left of row 14, click the minus sign to collapse the subtotal of Bichon Frise.

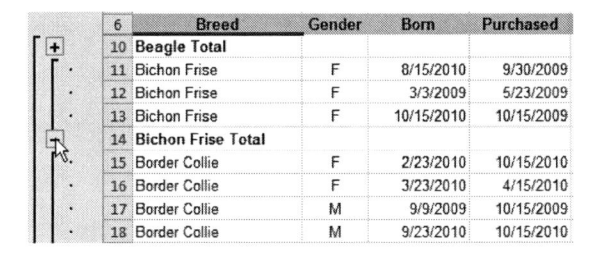

c.   Observe the subtotals of each breed and the total of breeds in the store.

d.   Click the minus signs to the left of the rows 20,23,28,34,41,47,54 to collapse the subtotals.

e.   Save the file as **My Grouped Pets** and close it.

Lesson 3 Follow-up

In this lesson, you audited worksheets. Auditing worksheets helps you to validate data and ensure that formulas, functions, and data work as intended.

1. **What auditing features will you use in your workbooks?**

2. **How will you use the auditing features when you encounter an error in your workbook?**

4 | Analyzing Data

Lesson Time: 1 hour(s)

Lesson Objectives:

In this lesson, you will analyze data.

You will:

- Create a trendline.
- Create sparklines for data.
- Create scenarios.
- Perform a what-if analysis.
- Perform a statistical analysis with the Analysis ToolPak.

Introduction

You audited worksheets and ensured that formulas, functions, and data all work together in the way you intended. Now you need to make use of the data to make business decisions. In this lesson, you will analyze data.

In any organization, business decisions are made after exhaustively analyzing data. The decision-making process can be made more productive if data is presented in an effective manner. Tools in Excel allow you to display data in formats that are easy to comprehend.

TOPIC A

Create a Trendline

You are familiar with the use of PivotTables and PivotCharts for analyzing data. In addition, Excel provides tools for forecasting values based on the current chart data. In this topic, you will create a trendline.

Predicting future trends is important in any business plan. Instead of using worksheets, you can make use of trendlines to graphically forecast possibilities that help in making good business decisions.

Trendlines

Definition:

A *trendline* is a graphical representation of trends in a data series that allows you to make informed decisions. Usually represented as a line, a trendline can be particularly useful in depicting current or future trends. Trendlines can be added to the data series in a column, line, bar, area, stock, or bubble chart. They can be created using default or user-defined settings.

Example:

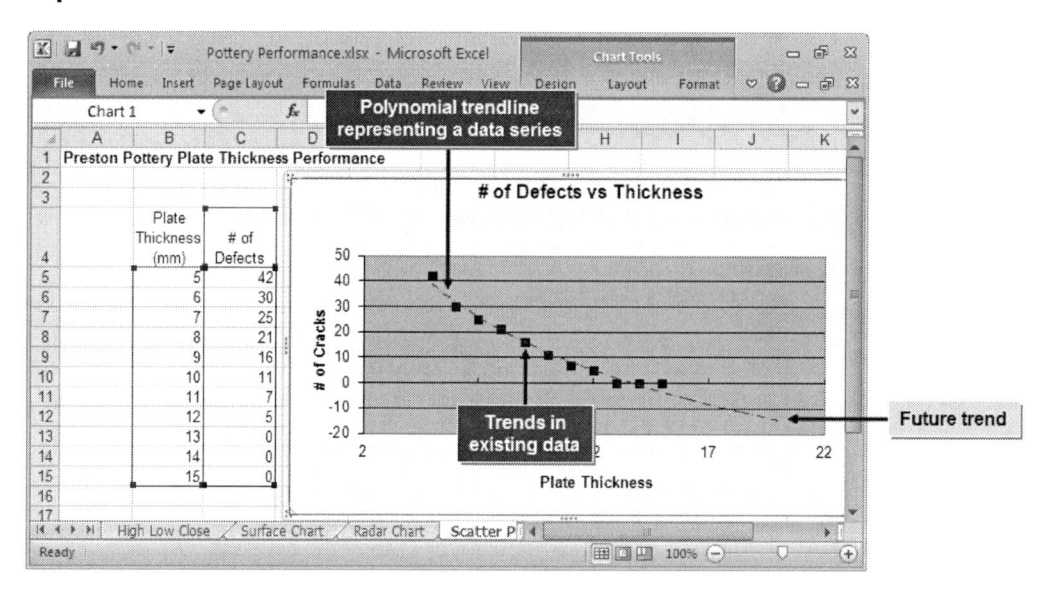

Figure 4-1: Trendlines are useful in depicting current or future trends.

Types of Trendlines

Six types of trendlines are used for studying data patterns.

Trendline Type	Description
Exponential	Curved lines that are best used when data values rise or fall at increasingly higher rates.
Linear	Straight lines that are best used with linear data sets.
Logarithmic	Curved lines that are best used when the rate of change in the data increases or decreases quickly and finally levels out.
Polynomial	Curved lines that are best used when the data fluctuates with ups and downs.
Power	Curved lines that are best used with data sets, which compare measurements that increase at a specified rate.
Moving Average	Curved lines that are used to smooth out any fluctuations in data, thereby displaying a pattern in the data.

The Format Trendline Dialog Box

The **Format Trendline** dialog box contains options for customizing trendlines. Using this dialog box, you can choose the type of trendline and parameters such as the forward and backward periods up to which a trendline can be generated. You can also set the parameters for the trendline color, style, and visual effects.

How to Create a Trendline

Procedure Reference: Create a Trendline with Default Settings

To create a trendline with default settings:

1. In a chart, select the series of data you want to plot along a trendline.
2. On the **Chart Tools Layout** contextual tab, in the **Analysis** group, from the **Trendline** drop-down list, select a trendline type.

Procedure Reference: Create a Trendline with User-Defined Settings

To create a trendline with user-defined settings:

1. In a chart, select the series of data you want to plot along a trendline.
2. Display the **Format Trendline** dialog box.
   - On the **Chart Tools Layout** contextual tab, in the **Analysis** group, from the **Trendline** drop-down list, select **More Trendline Options.**
   - Or, right-click the data series, and choose **Add Trendline.**
3. In the **Format Trendline** dialog box, in the **Trend/Regression Type** section, select the type of trendline you want.
4. If necessary, in the **Trendline Name** section, specify a name for the trendline.
   - Select the **Automatic** option to give the trendline an automatic name.
   - Or, select the **Custom** option, and in the **Custom** text box, type a name for the trendline.

5. In the **Forecast** section, specify the desired settings.

- In the **Forward** text box, type the desired value to determine how far ahead you want to forecast.

- In the **Backward** text box, type the desired value to determine how far behind you want to estimate.

6. If necessary, in the left pane of the **Format Trendline** dialog box, choose the required options to make changes to the line color, line style, or apply shadow styles and glow effects to the trendline.

7. Click **Close** to close the **Format Trendline** dialog box and view the trendline.

ACTIVITY 4-1
Creating a Trendline

Data Files:

C:\084678Data\Analyzing Data\Pottery Performance.xlsx

Before You Begin:
The Excel application is open.

Scenario:
You need to forecast the thickness of plates which, when manufactured, will be of company standard quality and will have a few cracks. You have a scatter plot chart to use for your reports. You find in the chart that there is a sudden decrease in the plate thickness values and then they level out. You decide to begin your forecasting by applying a line color and style to the trendline.

---

1. Add a trendline with the default settings to forecast the plate thickness by five units.

   a. Display the **Open** dialog box, navigate to the C:\084678Data\Analyzing Data folder, and open the Pottery Performance.xlsx file.

   b. In the scatter plot chart, click the first value at the intersection of (5,42) to select the data series.

   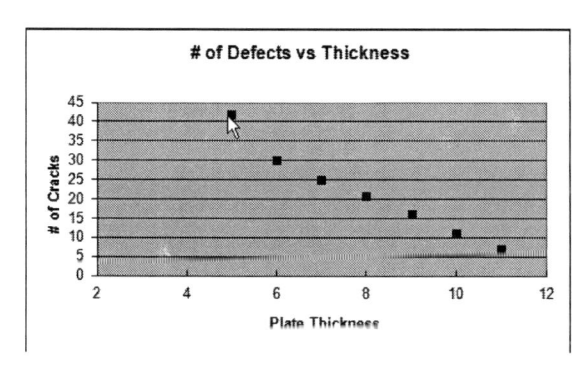

   c. On the **Chart Tools Layout** contextual tab, in the **Analysis** group, from the **Trendline** drop-down list, select **More Trendline Options.**

   d. In the **Format Trendline** dialog box, in the **Trend/Regression Type** section, select **Logarithmic.**

   e. In the **Forecast** section, in the **Forward** text box, type *5*

   f. Click **Close** to close the **Format Trendline** dialog box.

---

g. Observe that, according to the trendline, a plate thickness of 13 or greater will result in 0 (zero) cracks.

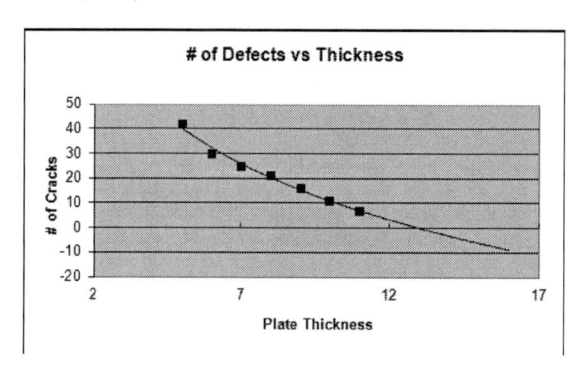

2. Customize the trendline by applying a line color and style.

a. Display the **Format Trendline** dialog box.

b. In the left pane, select **Line Color,** and in the right pane, select the **Solid line** option.

c. From the **Color** gallery, in the **Standard Colors** section, select **Dark Red.**

d. In the left pane, select **Line Style.**

e. In the right pane, from the **Dash type** gallery, select **Long Dash Dot,** and click **Close.**

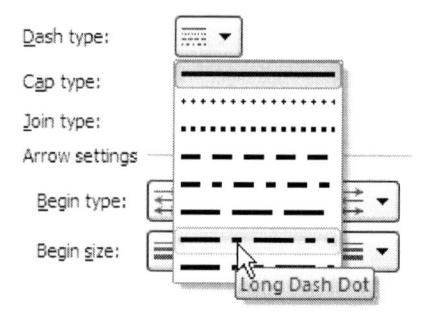

f. Observe that the chart displays a trendline with the specified settings.

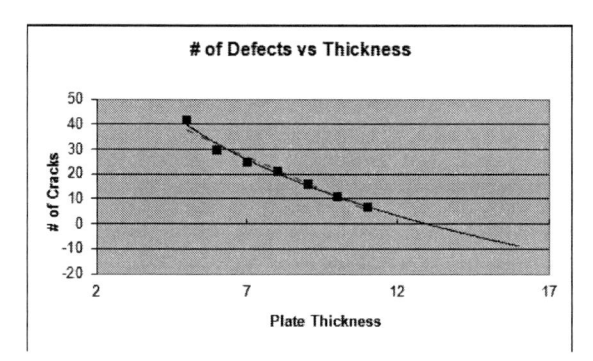

g. Save the file as **My Pottery Performance** and close it.

TOPIC B

Create Sparklines

You used charts to display trends in data. Excel 2010 comes with an added feature known as sparklines that provides a much simpler means of displaying data trends. In this topic, you will create sparklines.

Using regular charts may sometimes hide the worksheet data, making it difficult to view both the data and graphical representation on the same sheet. Sparklines provide the simplest way to represent trends in a cell on a worksheet.

Sparklines

Definition:

A *sparkline* is a tiny chart embedded in a cell to represent the trend for a given range, which can be a row or column. Unlike a chart, a sparkline can be used as a cell background. Moreover, you can create a sparkline for a single range and then extend it to multiple ranges using the fill handle.

Example:

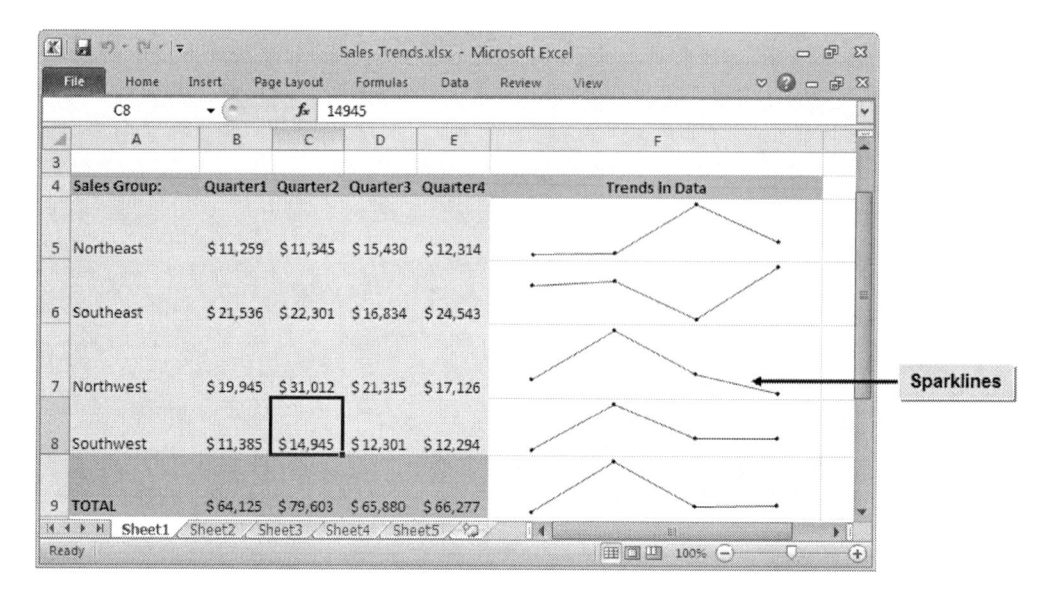

Figure 4-2: Sparklines displaying data trends.

Placement of Sparklines

Though sparklines can be placed anywhere on the worksheet, it is good practice to display them as close to the source as possible to make them more relevant. This is necessary because sparklines fit within a cell, and displaying them away from source data would make them seem irrelevant.

Types of Sparklines

You can choose any of the three types of sparklines in Excel.

Sparkline Type	Description
Line	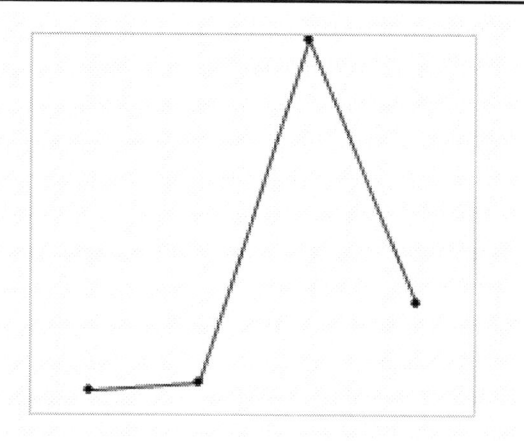 Data trends are displayed in the form of a straight or zigzag line.
Column	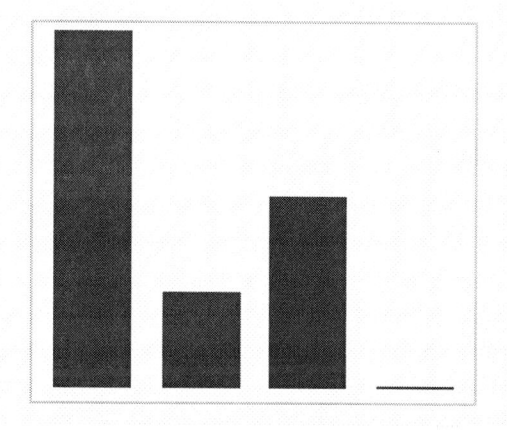 Data trends are displayed in the form of columns. Each data value is represented by a column whose size is proportional to the data value.

Sparkline Type	Description
Win\Loss	
	Data trends are displayed through the high points, the median point, and the low points.

Markers

Markers are used to highlight a point where the orientation of the trendline changes. Markers can be applied only to line sparklines.

The Sparkline Tool Design Tab

The **Sparkline Tools Design** contextual tab is activated when a cell or range containing sparklines is selected. This tab includes five groups containing formatting options for sparklines.

Group	Description
Edit Data	Contains options for editing the source data of sparklines and modifying the location of a sparkline.
Type	Allows you to choose any of the three types of sparklines: **Line, Column,** and **Win\Loss.**
Show	Contains check boxes for displaying or hiding high points, low points, negative points, first point, last point, and markers. The **Marker** check box is disabled for column and **Win\Loss** type sparklines.
Style	Contains the styles gallery for sparklines. Also contains drop-downs that launch galleries for sparkline and marker colors.
Group	Contains options for grouping or ungrouping sparklines so that they can share similar formatting. Grouping sparklines is similar to the grouping of graphical objects. Any formatting applied to a sparkline will be automatically applied to other sparklines of the group.

How to Create Sparklines

Procedure Reference: Create a Sparkline

To create a sparkline:

1. Select the data range for which you want to create a sparkline.

2. On the **Insert** tab, in the **Sparklines** group, select the sparkline type you want to create.

3. In the **Create Sparklines** dialog box, in the **Location Range** text box, enter the location where you want the sparkline to appear, and then click **OK.**

4. If necessary, select the sparkline, and on the **Sparkline Tools Design** contextual tab, in the **Type** group, select the required type of sparkline to change the sparkline type.

Procedure Reference: Group Sparklines

To group a set of sparklines:

1. Select the individual sparklines to be grouped.

2. On the **Sparklines Tools Design** contextual tab, in the **Group** group, click **Group** to group the sparklines.

3. If necessary, select any one sparkline from the group, and on the **Sparklines Tools Design** contextual tab, in the **Groups** group, click **Ungroup** to ungroup a set of sparklines.

Procedure Reference: Format Sparklines

To format a sparkline:

1. Select a sparkline or group of sparklines that you want to format.

2. On the **Sparkline Tools Design** contextual tab, in the **Show** group, check or uncheck the required check boxes.

   - Check or uncheck the **High Point** or **Low Point** check box to show or hide the highest or the lowest value.

   - Check or uncheck the **First Point** or **Last Point** check box to show or hide the first or the last value.

   - Check or uncheck the **Negative Points** check box to show or hide the negative values.

   - Check or uncheck the **Markers** check box to show or hide all data markers for a line sparkline.

3. On the **Sparkline Tools Design** contextual tab, in the **Style** group, choose the required style, sparkline color, and marker color to be applied.

Procedure Reference: Customize Sparklines

To customize sparklines:

1. Select a sparkline or a group of sparklines.

2. On the **Sparkline Tools Design** contextual tab, in the **Group** group, from the **Axis** drop-down list, select an option to change the scaling and visibility of the sparkline's horizontal and vertical axis.

- Select **General Axis Type** to display the sparkline as a general horizontal axis type.

- Select **Date Axis Type** if your data includes date, to use the date axis type for arranging the data on data points to reflect any irregular time period.

- Select **Show Axis** to show the sparkline horizontal axis.

- Select **Plot Data Right-to-Left** to change the direction in which data is plotted in a sparkline.

- Select **Automatic for Each Sparkline** to specify the automatic minimum and maximum values for all sparklines.

- Select **Same for All Sparklines** to specify the same minimum and maximum values for all sparklines.

- Select **Custom Value** to specify custom minimum and maximum values for the sparklines.

Removing Sparklines

To remove a sparkline, select the cell containing the sparkline, and on the **Sparkline Tools Design** contextual tab, in the **Group** group, click **Clear.** To delete multiple groups of sparklines, you must select all the groups and, from the **Clear** drop-down list, select **Clear selected Sparkline Groups.** You can also use the shortcut menu to remove the sparklines.

Handling Empty Cells or Zero Values

You can choose how a sparkline handles empty cells in a range by using the **Hidden and Empty Cell Settings** dialog box. The dialog box is available in the **Edit Data** drop-down list in the **Sparkline** group on the **Sparkline Tools Design** contextual tab. You can choose to display empty cells through gaps or zeros, or simply connect the existing data series.

Increasing the Size of Sparklines

If a sparkline does not appear clear due to the large amount of data present, you can increase the width of the column or row to make the cell bigger. You can also merge two cells to make the sparkline graphic bigger.

ACTIVITY 4-2
Creating Sparklines

Data Files:

C:\084678Data\Analyzing Data\Sales Trends.xlsx

Before You Begin:
The Excel application is open.

Scenario:
You have to present a report on the sales trend for the last fiscal. You want to display the sales trend for each region in a cell closest to data. Because you do not want any data on the worksheet to be hidden, you decide to use sparklines instead of charts to depict the trends in each of the regions throughout the year.

---

1. Display the last year's sales trends for each region.

   a. Display the **Open** dialog box, navigate to the C:\084678Data\Analyzing Data folder, and open the Sales Trends.xlsx file.

   b. Select the range **B5:E5.**

   c. On the **Insert** tab, in the **Sparklines** group, click **Line.**

   d. In the **Create Sparklines** dialog box, in the **Choose where you want the sparklines to be placed** section, in the **Location Range** text box, type *F5* and click **OK.**

   e. Observe that a line sparkline is added in cell F5.

   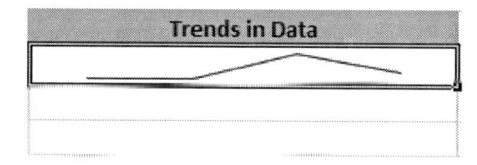

   f. Drag the fill handle from cell F5 to cell F9 to create sparklines for all regions and the total.

   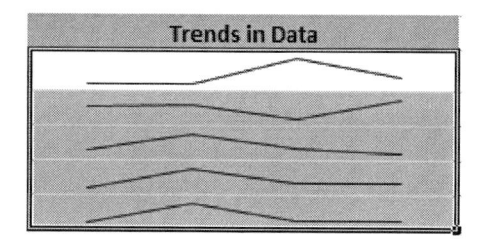

---

2. Enhance the sparklines by adding markers and styles and increasing the height of the rows.

---

a. With the range F5:F9 selected, on the **Sparkline Tools Design** contextual tab, in the **Show** group, check **Markers.**

b. Observe that the markers highlighting the trend for each quarter are added to all sparklines.

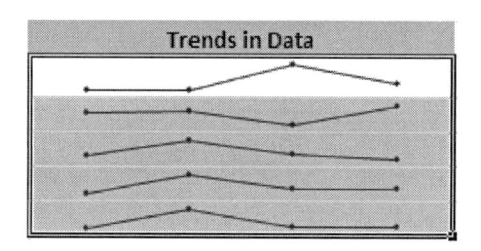

c. On the **Sparkline Tools Design** contextual tab, in the **Style** group, click the **More** button, and from the gallery, select **Sparkline Style Dark #6,** which is the last option in the fifth row.

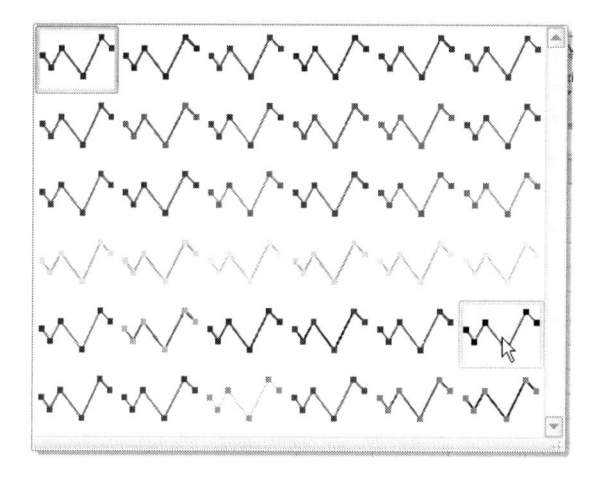

d. Change the row height of rows 5 through 9 to 40.

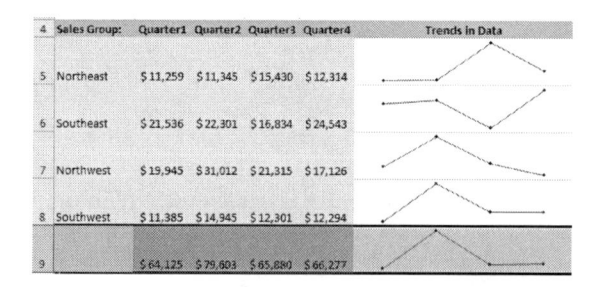

e. Save the file as *My Sales Trends* and close it.

TOPIC C

Create Scenarios

You analyzed data using trendlines and sparklines. You are now ready to use data to help in forecasting based on the criteria set. In this topic, you will create scenarios and analyze their outcomes.

Business meetings often include discussions on the outcomes of implementing different plans. As different scenarios may result in different outcomes, it is necessary to analyze the outcome before implementing any plan. Excel allows you to create and test multiple scenarios to help you choose a particular outcome and plan accordingly.

Scenarios

Definition:

A *scenario* is a set of input values substituted for the primary data in a worksheet. These input values are used to forecast outcomes based on the data that represents the scenario in your worksheet. You can create any number of scenarios in a worksheet and switch between them to view their results.

Example:

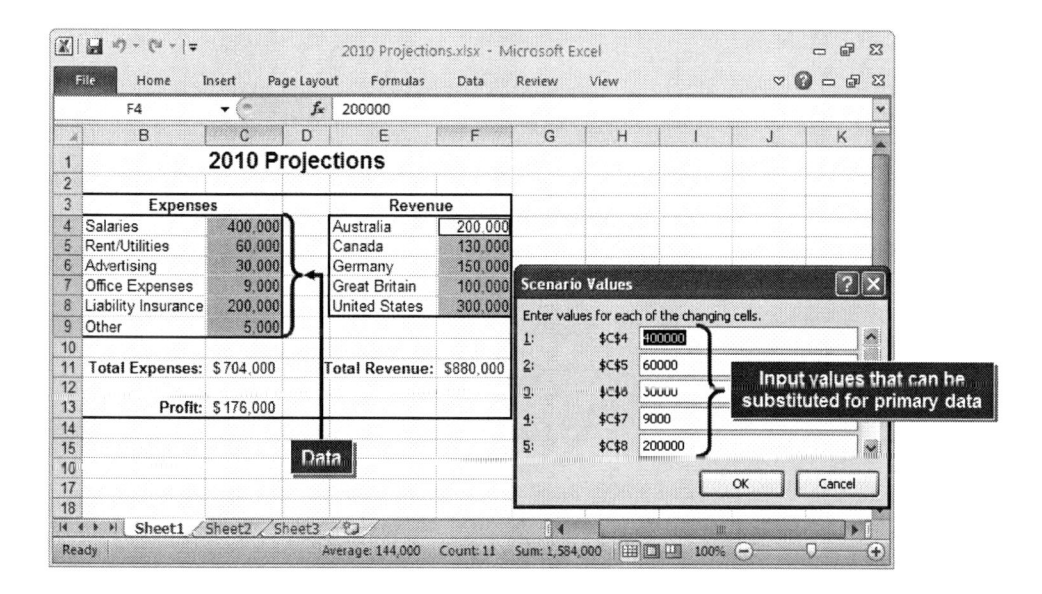

Figure 4-3: *The scenario displays the outcome for a set of values.*

The What-If Analysis Option

The **What-If Analysis** option is used for performing analysis using the **Scenario Manager**, **Goal Seek**, and **Data Table** options.

Option	Used To
Scenario Manager	Create scenarios.
Goal Seek	Set the value stored in a single cell to a specific value, thereby changing the value stored in another cell.
Data Table	Display the varying results of formulas based on different values given as input.

The Scenario Manager Dialog Box

The options in the **Scenario Manager** dialog box allow you to create, edit, delete, and merge scenarios.

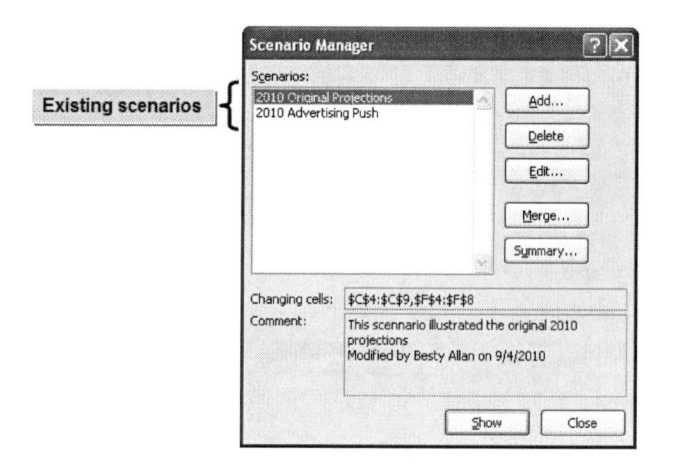

Figure 4-4: *The options in the Scenario Manager dialog box enable you to alter existing data and project new possibilities.*

Option	Description
Scenarios	Lists all scenarios you have created in the worksheet.
Add	Invokes the **Add Scenario** dialog box that allows you to create a new scenario.
Delete	Deletes the selected scenario.
Edit	Invokes the **Edit Scenario** dialog box that allows you to edit a scenario.
Merge	Allows you to merge scenarios from other worksheets.
Summary	Displays a summary of the scenario in the **Scenario Summary** dialog box.
Changing Cells	Displays the cell reference for changing cells.

Option	*Description*
Comment	Displays the comments entered in the **Add Scenario** dialog box.
Show	Displays the result of the selected scenario on a worksheet.

How to Create Scenarios

Procedure Reference: Create a Scenario

To create a scenario:

1. Select a range for which you want to create a scenario.

2. On the **Data** tab, in the **Data Tools** group, from the **What-If Analysis** drop-down list, select **Scenario Manager.**

3. In the **Scenario Manager** dialog box, click **Add.**

4. In the **Add Scenario** dialog box, in the **Scenario Name** text box, type a name for the scenario.

5. In the **Changing cell** text box, enter the range of cells whose values will be updated to change the scenario.

6. If necessary, add a comment in the **Comment** text box, and then click **OK.**

7. If necessary, create as many scenarios as required by repeating steps 3 through 6.

8. If necessary, in the **Scenario Manager** dialog box, select a scenario, and click **Show** to display the scenario.

ACTIVITY 4-3
Creating Scenarios

Data Files:

C:\084678Data\Analyzing Data\Projections.xlsx

Before You Begin:
The Excel application is open.

Scenario:
You would like to analyze the expense and revenue data of the previous year and then forecast a particular outcome and plan accordingly for the current year. You would like to retain the value of the existing data and compare this with a situation where the advertising budget is increased by $40,000 and each country's revenue by 10 percent.

---

1. Create a scenario that maintains the original projection numbers.

   a. Display the **Open** dialog box, navigate to the C:\084678Data\Analyzing Data folder, and open the Projections.xlsx file.

   b. Select the ranges **C4:C9** and **F4:F8**.

   c. On the **Data** tab, in the **Data Tools** group, from the **What-If Analysis** drop-down list, select **Scenario Manager**.

   d. In the **Scenario Manager** dialog box, click **Add.**

   e. In the **Add Scenario** dialog box, in the **Scenario name** text box, type *Original Projections*

   f. In the **Changing cells** text box, observe that the value **C4:C9,F4:F8** is already entered as the range was selected in the first step.

   g. Select the content in the **Comment** text box.

   h. Replace the text with *This scenario illustrates the original projections* and click **OK.**

   i. In the **Scenario Values** dialog box, click **OK** to accept the current values and to return to the **Scenario Manager** dialog box.

---

2. Create another scenario to specify the new value for the advertising budget.

   a. In the **Scenario Manager** dialog box, click **Add.**

   b. In the **Add Scenario** dialog box, in the **Scenario name** text box, type *Advertising Push*

   c. Select the content in the **Comment** text box.

   d. Replace the text with *This scenario increases the advertising budget to $40,000 and each country's revenue by 10%* and then click **OK.**

e. In the **Scenario Values** dialog box displaying the values for the first range of cells, in the **$C$6** text box, double-click and type *40000*

3. Specify the incremental values for the range of cells displaying data related to revenues generated in a country.

   a. In the dialog box, scroll down to view the values in the second range **F4:F8.**

   b. Select the value in the **$F$4** text box, and type *220000*

   c. Change the remaining values in the **Scenario Values** dialog box as follows:

   $F$5: 143000

   $F$6: 165000

   $F$7: 110000

   $F$8: 330000

   d. Click **OK.**

4. Display the scenarios.

   a. Position the **Scenario Manager** dialog box such that the data on the worksheet is not hidden.

   b. In the **Scenario Manager** dialog box, verify that **Advertising Push** is selected, and click **Show.**

   c. Observe that the values in the ranges **C4:C9** and **F4:F8** change as specified in the scenario and the workbook displays new results for the total expenses, total revenue, and profit.

Total Expenses:	$	714,000	Total Revenue:	$	968,000
Profit:	$	254,000			

   d. In the **Scenario Manager** dialog box, in the **Scenarios** list box, select **Original Projections,** and click **Show.**

   e. Observe that the values in the workbook revert to the original values.

Total Expenses:	$	704,000	Total Revenue:	$	880,000
Profit:	$	176,000			

   f. In the **Scenario Manager** dialog box, click **Close.**

   g. Save the file as *My Projections* and close it.

TOPIC D
Perform a What-If Analysis

You analyzed data using trendlines and scenarios. You now want to forecast potential values by changing variables in formulas without affecting the original data. In this topic, you will perform a what-if analysis.

You use a worksheet to calculate the monthly payments on a mortgage. You want to change the monthly payment value from $700 to $800 per month to see how the increased payment will affect the overall tenure of the loan term. By performing a what-if analysis, you can make this type of projection without rewriting formulas.

Add-Ins

Add-ins are modules that provide additional features and commands for Excel. Some add-ins such as Solver and Analysis ToolPak are built into Excel, while others have to be downloaded and installed from the Download Center at Office.com. Add-ins can be classified into three categories.

Add-ins	*Description*
Excel add-ins	Add-ins that are available by default when you install Excel.
Downloadable add-ins	Add-ins that need to be downloaded and installed for using them. Once you install these add-ins, they can be accessed from the Ribbon.
Custom add-ins	Add-ins that are developed by Excel users, which have to be installed for using them.

Goal Seek

The Goal Seek feature enables you to fix the result of a calculation and determine the inputs for a formula to arrive at the desired result. To use the Goal Seek feature, you must enter a formula in a cell and then specify the value that is to be calculated in this cell. You must also specify the cell reference, which contains the input value that Excel must adjust to arrive at the result.

The Solver Tool

The *Solver* tool is used for setting the value of a cell with formula by changing the values in multiple other cells. This option allows you to either retain the Solver solution or restore the original values.

Example of Using the Solver Tool

You have planned to borrow money and purchase an all-terrain vehicle. You are sure that you can afford a monthly payment of $400 as long as the interest rate is 12 percent or less. Using Solver, you can calculate the amount you can borrow for the specified constraints.

The Solver Parameters Dialog Box

The **Solver Parameters** dialog box has various options and sections for setting parameters.

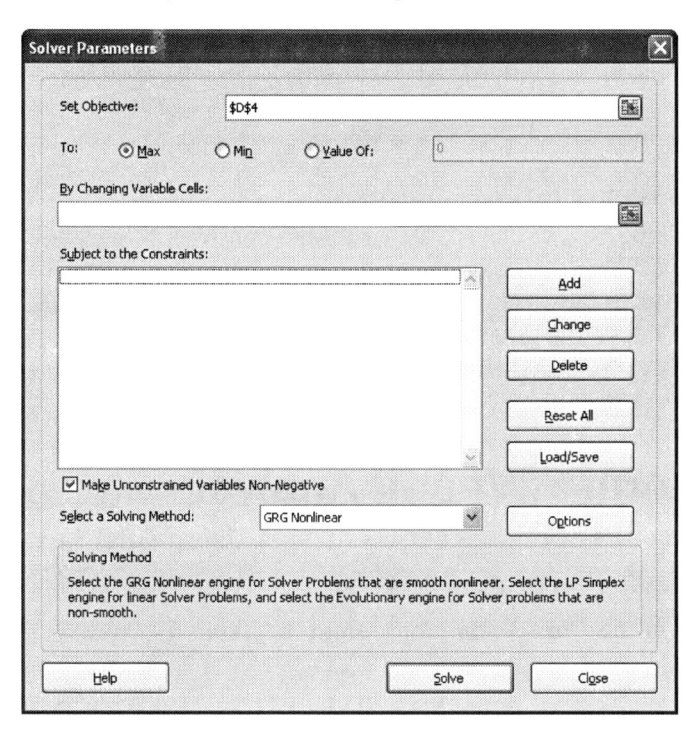

Figure 4-5: The various options in the Solver Parameters dialog box.

Item	Used To
Set Objective	Enter the cell reference or name for the objective or target cell. The objective cell is a cell that will contain the target result.
To	Choose the required option to display the maximum, minimum, or fixed value in the objective cell.
By Changing Variable Cells	Enter the reference or name of variable cells. Variable cells are cells with values that will change based on the value of the objective cell.
Subject to the Constraints	View the constraints that have been created. Constrained cells are cells that meet a specified criterion, and they can be a number, a cell reference, or a formula. The five types of constraints that can be applied are less than or equal to, equal to, greater than or equal to, integer, and binary.
Add	Display the **Add Constraints** dialog box to create a constraint.
Change	Display the **Change Constraints** dialog box to modify the selected constraint.
Delete	Delete the selected constraint.
Reset All	Reset all Solver options and cell values.
Select a Solving Method	Allow users to select a solving technique. The description of the technique is displayed in the **Solving Method** section.
Load/Save	Load and save problem models.

Item	Used To
Options	Display the **Solver Options** dialog box where you can set up advanced features such as time limits for solving a problem and the precision of constraints. Advanced features of the solution process can also be controlled by using this dialog box.

The Solver Results Dialog Box

The **Solver Results** dialog box displays whether all the constraints specified have been satisfied after running Solver. This dialog box provides you options to add the values that have been produced by Solver to the worksheet or retain the existing values in the worksheet. You can also return to the **Solver Parameters** dialog box by checking the **Return to Solver Parameters Dialog** check box or if needed, you can also save the values as a scenario to compare them later.

How to Perform a What-If Analysis

Procedure Reference: Perform a What-If Analysis Using Goal Seek

To perform a what-if analysis using Goal Seek:

1. On the **Data** tab, in the **Data Tools** group, from the **What-If Analysis** drop-down list, select **Goal Seek.**

2. In the **Goal Seek** dialog box, in the **Set cell** text box, enter the cell reference whose value should remain unchanged.

3. In the **To value** text box, type the value for the set cell.

4. In the **By changing cell** text box, enter the cell reference for which you need to change the value and click **OK.**

5. In the **Goal Seek Status** dialog box, click **OK** to accept the solution.

Procedure Reference: Load the Solver Add-In

To load the Solver Add-In feature on Data tab of the Ribbon:

1. Display the **Excel Options** dialog box.

2. In the left pane, select **Add-Ins.**

3. If necessary, in the right pane, from the **Manage** drop-down list, select **Excel Add-Ins,** and then click **Go.**

4. In the **Add-Ins** dialog box, in the **Add-Ins Available** list box, check **Solver Add-In,** and click **OK.**

5. Click **Yes** to install the **Solver Add-In.**

Procedure Reference: Perform a What-If Analysis Using Solver

To perform a what-if analysis using Solver:

1. Open an existing worksheet.

2. On the **Data** tab, in the **Analysis** group, click **Solver.**

3. In the **Solver Parameters** dialog box, in the **Set Objective** text box, enter the cell reference of the target cell for which the value should remain unchanged.

4. In the **To** section, select an option and specify the value for the target cell.

5. In the **By Changing Variable Cells** text box, enter the cell references that Solver can change to produce the desired outcome.

6. In the **Subject to the constraints** section, click **Add.**

7. In the **Add Constraint** dialog box, add the constraints or conditions that need to be applied to the changing cells.

8. Add the constraint to the **Subject to the constraints** section.

   ● Click **Add** to add the current constraint and to proceed with the steps to add another.

   ● Or, click **OK** to add the constraint and to return to the **Solver Parameters** dialog box.

9. In the **Solver Parameters** dialog box, click **Solve.**

10. In the **Solver Results** dialog box, click **OK.**

ACTIVITY 4-4
Using Goal Seek to Analyze Data

Data Files:

C:\084678Data\Analyzing Data\Loan Schedule.xlsx

Before You Begin:
The Excel application is open.

Scenario:
You have developed a worksheet named Loan Schedule that amortizes a car loan. The worksheet currently amortizes a $24,000 loan over 60 months with a 12 percent interest rate. However, after reviewing some of your other monthly expenses, you have come to realize that you can only afford a $17,500 loan with a monthly payment set at $350.00. You need to determine the term of the loan based on this new data.

---

1. Decrease the value of the principal loan amount.

    a. Display the **Open** dialog box, navigate to the C:\084678Data\Analyzing Data folder, and open the Loan Schedule.xlsx file.

    b. In cell D3, replace the existing value with **17500**

Principal Amount:	17500	Monthly Payment	
Interest Rate:	12%	$389.28	
Term in Months:	60		
	Beginning		Remaining
Month	Principal	Interest	Principal	Principal
	Balance	Paid	Paid	Amount

    c. Observe that the data in cell **F4** changes to **$389.28** based on the current values of principal amount, interest rate, and term.

---

2. Calculate the new loan term for the defined principal amount and a monthly payment of $350.

    a. Observe the data in cell **D5**.

    b. On the **Data** tab, in the **Data Tools** group, from the **What-If Analysis** drop-down list, select **Goal Seek.**

    c. In the **Goal Seek** dialog box, in the **Set cell** text box, type **F4** and press **Tab.**

    d. In the **To value** text box, type **350** to set the monthly payment amount and press **Tab.**

    e.

In the **By changing cell** text box, type *D5* and click **OK.**

f.   Observe that the new loan term displayed in cell **D5** is **69.66** months.

Term in Months:	69.66			
Month	Beginning Principal Balance	Interest Paid	Principal Paid	Remaining Principal Amount
1	17,500.00	175.00	175.00	17,325.00
2	17,325.00	173.25	176.75	17,148.25
3	17,148.25	171.48	178.52	16,969.73
4	16,969.73	169.70	180.30	16,789.43
5	16,789.43	167.89	182.11	16,607.32
6	16,607.32	166.07	183.93	16,423.39
7	16,423.39	164.23	185.77	16,237.63
8	16,237.63	162.38	187.62	16,050.00

g.   In the **Goal Seek Status** dialog box, click **OK.**

h.   Save the file as *My Loan Schedule*

ACTIVITY 4-5
Using Solver to Analyze Data

Before You Begin:

The My Loan Schedule.xlsx file is open.

Scenario:

A windfall has come your way and you can make higher monthly payments on your new car. Based on other expenses in your long-term budget, you have decided that you can now afford a $500 monthly payment as long as the interest rate stays between 10 and 15 percent, and your payments are up to 36 months. Now, you want to find out how much you can borrow.

---

1. Load the Solver Add-In.

   a. Display the **Excel Options** dialog box.

   b. In the left pane, select the **Add-Ins** category.

   c. At the bottom of the right pane, verify that **Excel Add-ins** is selected in the **Manage** drop-down list.

   d. To the right of the **Manage** drop-down list, click **Go.**

   e. In the **Add-Ins** dialog box, check **Solver Add-in,** and click **OK.**

   f. If necessary, click **Yes** to install the **Solver Add-In.**

---

2. Set the monthly payment objective to $500 in Solver.

   a. In the worksheet, click cell **F4.**

   b. On the **Data** tab, in the **Analysis** group, click **Solver.**

   c. In the **Solver Parameters** dialog box, in the **Set Objective** text box, observe that the cell **$F$4** is displayed.

   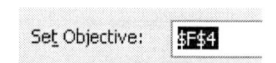

   d. In the **To** section, select **Value Of.**

   e. In the **Value Of** text box, double-click and type *500*

---

3. Specify the cells for the principal amount value, interest rate, and term in months.

   a. Click in the **By Changing Variable Cells** text box.

   b. Type *D3, D4, D5* to include them as variable cells.

---

4. Add constraints to set the interest rate between 10 to 15 percent and the term to be less than or equal to 36 months.

---

a. In the **Subject to the Constraints** section, click **Add.**

b. In the **Add Constraint** dialog box, in the **Cell Reference** text box, type *D4*

c. From the drop-down list, to the right of the **Cell Reference** text box, select >=.

d. In the **Constraint** text box, type *10%* and click **Add** to add the next constraint.

e. In the **Cell Reference** text box, type *D4*

f. Verify that <= is selected in the drop-down list box and, in the **Constraint** text box, type *15%* and click **Add** to add the third constraint.

g. In the **Cell Reference** text box, type *D5*

h. Verify that <= is selected in the drop-down list box and, in the **Constraint** text box, type *36*

i. In the **Add Constraint** dialog box, click **OK.**

j. In the **Solver Parameters** dialog box, in the **Subject to the Constraints** list box, notice that the specified constraints are listed.

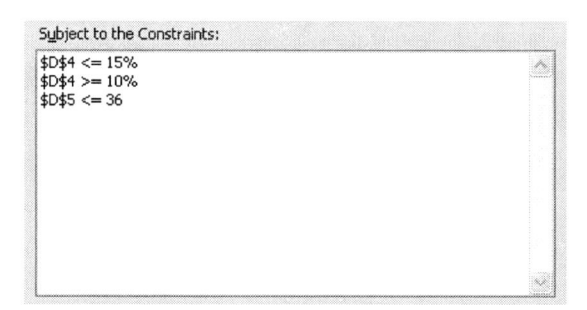

5. Calculate the new principal amount.

a. In the **Solver Parameters** dialog box, click **Solve** to run the Solver.

b. In the **Solver Results** dialog box, click **OK** to retain the Solver solution.

c. On the worksheet, observe that the principal amount is changed to **15115.01.**

d. Save the file as *My Solved Loan Schedule* and close the file.

TOPIC E

Perform a Statistical Analysis with the Analysis ToolPak

You performed a what-if analysis to make projections based on existing data. Now you need to analyze complex data to provide new insights into data that could not have been derived from Excel's standard functions. In this topic, you will perform a statistical analysis with the Analysis ToolPak.

Analyzing complex data may involve a lot of steps and is prone to errors. Performing a statistical analysis using the tools available in the Analysis ToolPak simplifies the task of obtaining the desired value from complex data sets.

The Analysis ToolPak

The **Analysis ToolPak** is an add-in that contains a variety of tools that help you perform sophisticated statistical analyses. It includes tools to create histograms, derive random samples, and perform regression analyses.

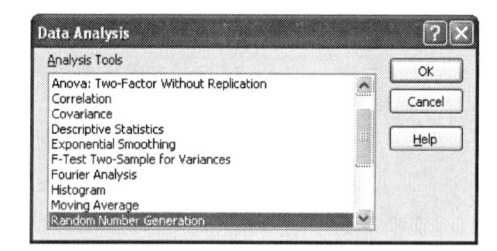

Figure 4-6: The Analysis ToolPak contains a variety of tools for performing sophisticated statistical analyses.

The Analysis ToolPak – VBA Add-In

The Analysis ToolPak – VBA contains VBA functions that can be used along with the tools provided in the Analysis ToolPak add-in. These functions are primarily used by software programmers and developers.

How to Perform a Statistical Analysis with the Analysis ToolPak

Procedure Reference: Load the Analysis ToolPak

To load the Analysis ToolPak:

1. In the **Excel Options** dialog box, in the left pane, select **Add-Ins.**

2. If necessary, in the right pane, from the **Manage** drop-down list, select **Excel Add-ins** and then click **Go.**

3. In the **Add-Ins** dialog box, check **Analysis ToolPak** and click **OK.**

Procedure Reference: Perform a Statistical Analysis with the Analysis ToolPak

To perform a statistical analysis with the Analysis ToolPak:

1. On the **Data** tab, in the **Analysis** group, click **Data Analysis.**

2. In the **Data Analysis** dialog box, select the desired data analysis tool and click **OK.**

3. In the dialog box that opens for the tool you selected, set the values and options you want and click **OK.**

Procedure Reference: Use the Sampling Analysis Tool for Performing an Analysis

To use the Sampling analysis tool for performing an analysis:

1. On the **Data** tab, in the **Analysis** group, click **Data Analysis.**

2. In the **Data Analysis** dialog box, in the **Analysis Tools** list box, select **Sampling** and click **OK.**

3. In the **Sampling** dialog box, in the **Input** section, in the **Input Range** text box, enter the cell reference for the range of data for which you want to perform the analysis.

4. If necessary, check **Labels** to include the first row or column of input range as labels in the sample.

5. In the **Sampling Method** section, select the desired option.

   - Select **Periodic** and enter a value in the **Period** text box to indicate the periodic interval at which you want sampling to happen.

   - Or, select the **Random** option and enter a value in the **Number of samples** text box that you want to display in the output column.

6. In the **Output options** section, select the desired option.

   - Select **Output Range**, and in the **Output Range** text box, enter the cell reference for the output.

   - Or, select **New Worksheet Ply** in order to insert and display the results in a new worksheet beginning at cell A1. If necessary, in the **New Worksheet Ply** text box, type the desired name for the sheet.

   - Or, select **New Workbook** in order to display the results in a new workbook.

7. Click **OK.**

ACTIVITY 4-6

Performing a Statistical Analysis with the Analysis ToolPak

Data Files:

C:\084678Data\Analyzing Data\Randomize.xlsx

Before You Begin:

The Excel application is open.

Scenario:

Your company has collected the names of 60 people who are willing to participate in a focus group to help refine its flagship product. However, you can only have ten people in the focus group. The team overseeing the focus group needs a way to randomly select people from a list of 60. The random list needs to include the focus group candidates' ID number and last name.

1. Load the Analysis ToolPak add-in.

   a. Display the **Open** dialog box, navigate to the C:\084678Data\Analyzing Data folder, and open the Randomize.xlsx file.

   b. In the **Excel Options** dialog box, in the left pane, select **Add-Ins.**

   c. In the right pane, verify that **Excel Add-ins** is selected in the **Manage** drop-down list.

   d. To the right of the **Manage** drop-down list, click **Go.**

   e. In the **Add-Ins** dialog box, in the **Add-Ins available** section, check **Analysis ToolPak,** and click **OK.**

   f. If necessary, click **Yes** to install the Analysis ToolPak add-in.

2. Open the Sampling analysis tool.

   a. On the **Data** tab, in the **Analysis** group, click **Data Analysis.**

   b. In the **Data Analysis** dialog box, in the **Analysis Tools** list box, scroll down and select **Sampling,** and click **OK.**

3. In a new worksheet, create a random sample of ten people.

   a. In the **Sampling** dialog box, in the **Input** section, in the **Input Range** text box, type *A2:A61* to specify the range of people.

   b. In the **Sampling Method** section, in the **Number of Samples** text box, type *10*

c.   In the **Output options** section, in the **New Worksheet Ply** text box, type *Focus Group Sample* and click **OK** to display a randomly generated sample on the new worksheet named **Focus Group Sample.**

	A
1	495129
2	452786
3	241191
4	476393
5	110018
6	388620
7	821802
8	917325
9	883703
10	456377

> Because the sample is randomly generated, the data shown in the sample screenshot may be different from the data that appears on the screen.

4.   In the worksheet, look up the last name under each unique ID.

a.   On the **Focus Group Sample** worksheet, select cell **B1.**

b.   On the **Formulas** tab, in the **Function Library** group, from the **Lookup & Reference** drop-down list, select **VLOOKUP.**

c.   In the **Function Arguments** dialog box, in the **Lookup_value** text box, type *A1* to return the value in the first column of the table.

d.   In the **Table_array** text box, specify the cell range *'Focus Group Candidates'!$A$2:$C$61* to include the data from the range A2:C61 in the **Focus Group Candidates** worksheet.

e.   In the **Col_index_num** text box, type *3* to display the last name corresponding to the ID from the **Focus Group Candidates** worksheet, and click **OK.**

f.   Notice that the last name of the first unique ID is displayed.

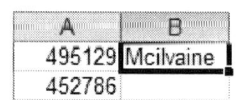

A	B
495129	Mcilvaine
452786	

g. Drag the fill handle from cell **B1** to cell **B10** to display the last name of all other candidates.

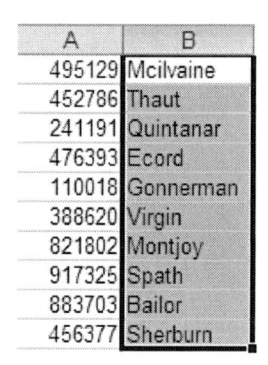

A	B
495129	Mcilvaine
452786	Thaut
241191	Quintanar
476393	Ecord
110018	Gonnerman
388620	Virgin
821802	Montjoy
917325	Spath
883703	Bailor
456377	Sherburn

h. Save the workbook as *My Randomize* and then close the file.

Lesson 4 Follow-up

In this lesson, you used some of the data analysis tools in Excel. Analyzing data helps you to make prudent business decisions.

1. **What are the various scenarios for which an organization would use trendlines?**

2. **What are the various types of sparklines available in Excel? Which one would you prefer?**

5 | Working with Multiple Workbooks

Lesson Time: 35 minutes

Lesson Objectives:

In this lesson, you will work with multiple workbooks.

You will:

- Create a workspace.
- Consolidate data.
- Link cells in different workbooks.
- Edit links.

Introduction

You stored data in a workbook and analyzed it. Multiple workbooks are also used for interpreting data. Excel includes some advanced features that enable you to work with data in more than one workbook and link all workbook data. In this lesson, you will work with multiple workbooks.

Using multiple workbooks or windows to refer to a particular data is a troublesome affair. But when workbooks share the same set of data, you can consolidate and link the data. You can use an Excel 2010 file as a repository for data from multiple workbooks.

TOPIC A

Create a Workspace

You analyzed data in a workbook. It would be convenient if you could open a set of workbooks with the size and position intact whenever you require them in your calculations. In this topic, you will create a workspace to manage data across multiple workbooks.

When you have multiple workbooks that share data, it would be easier to manage if you could consolidate all of the workbooks into a single source file. By creating a workspace that includes all related data, you can avoid switching between windows and have everything you need in one location.

Workspaces

Definition:

A *workspace* is an Excel file that contains information on the location, screen size, and screen position of multiple workbooks. Workspace files are saved with the .xlw extension. A single workspace file can open multiple workbook files at a time.

Example:

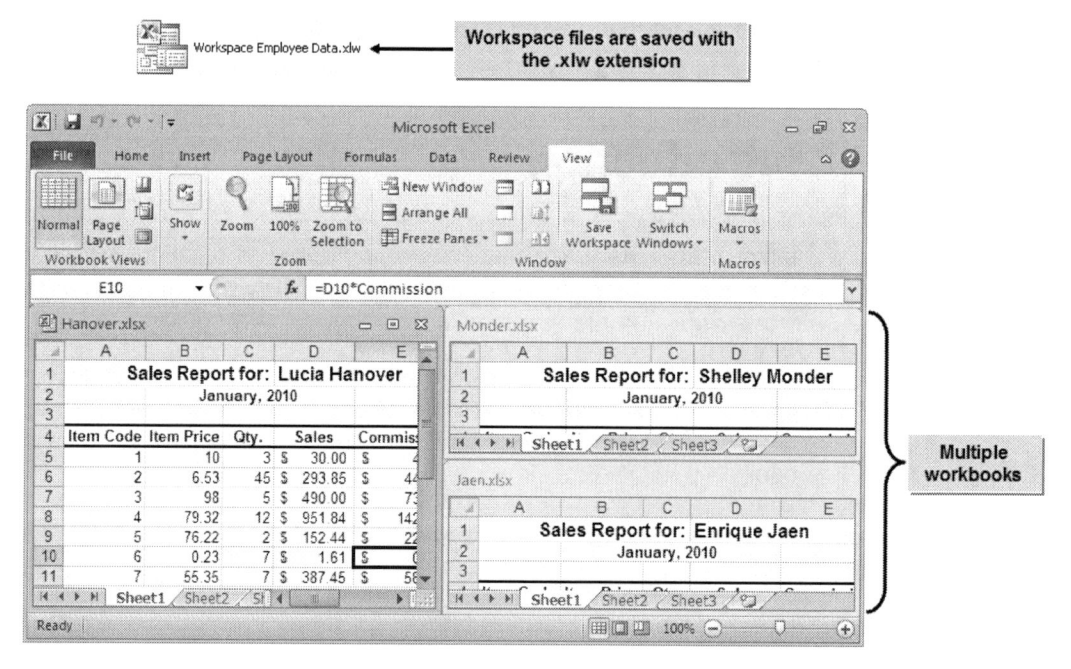

Figure 5-1: A workspace is a collection of multiple workbooks.

How to Create a Workspace

Procedure Reference: Create a Workspace

To create a workspace:

1. Open all files that you want to include in a workbook.
2. Size and position the windows as you would like them to appear.
3. Arrange the windows.
4. On the **View** tab, in the **Window** group, click **Save Workspace.**
5. In the **Save Workspace** dialog box, in the **File name** text box, type the desired name.
6. Click **Save.**

ACTIVITY 5-1
Creating a Workspace

Data Files:

C:\084678Data\Working with Multiple Workbooks\Hanover.xlsx, C:\084678Data\Working with Multiple Workbooks\Monder.xlsx, C:\084678Data\Working with Multiple Workbooks\Jaen.xlsx, C:\084678Data\Working with Multiple Workbooks\Consolidation.xlsx

Before You Begin:

The Excel application is open.

Scenario:

You are in charge of updating the sales of each employee at OGC Bookstores. The information is stored in three different workbooks, which you are using all the time. You want to create a single source that can open all three workbooks, whenever required, at the same time with intact display.

---

1. Tile all the open windows.

   a. Display the **Open** dialog box, navigate to the C:\084678Data\Working with Multiple Workbooks folder, and open the Hanover.xlsx, Monder.xlsx, Jaen.xlsx, and Consolidation.xlsx files.

   b. On the **View** tab, in the **Window** group, click **Arrange All.**

   c. In the **Arrange Windows** dialog box, in the **Arrange** section, verify that the **Tiled** option is selected, and click **OK.**

---

2. Create a workspace.

   a. In the **Window** group, click **Save Workspace.**

   b. In the **Save Workspace** dialog box, if necessary, navigate to the C:\084678Data\ Working with Multiple Workbooks folder.

   c. In the **Save Workspace** dialog box, in the **File name** text box, type **Workspace Sales Reports**

   d. Observe that the file type displayed in the **Save as type** drop-down list is **Workspaces (*.xlw),** and click **Save.**

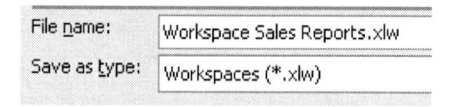

---

3. Test the created workspace.

   a. Close all open workbooks.

   b. Display the **Open** dialog box.

---

c.   Select the **Workspace Sales Reports.xlw** file, and click **Open.**

d.   Observe that the Hanover.xlsx, Monder.xlsx, Jaen.xlsx, and Consolidation.xlsx files are arranged in windows of the same sequence, position, and size they were saved in.

TOPIC B
Consolidate Data

You created a workspace that includes multiple workbooks sharing data. You may now want to summarize data from multiple workbooks into a single workbook. In this topic, you will consolidate data.

It can be time consuming to open all workbooks and read their summaries. Consolidating data from multiple workbooks makes the analysis process more efficient.

Data Consolidation

Definition:

Data consolidation is the method of summarizing data from several ranges into a single range. The data range can be in the same worksheet or workbook, or in different workbooks. You can consolidate data by position if it has an identical structure, or by category if the data is similar but in different locations.

Example:

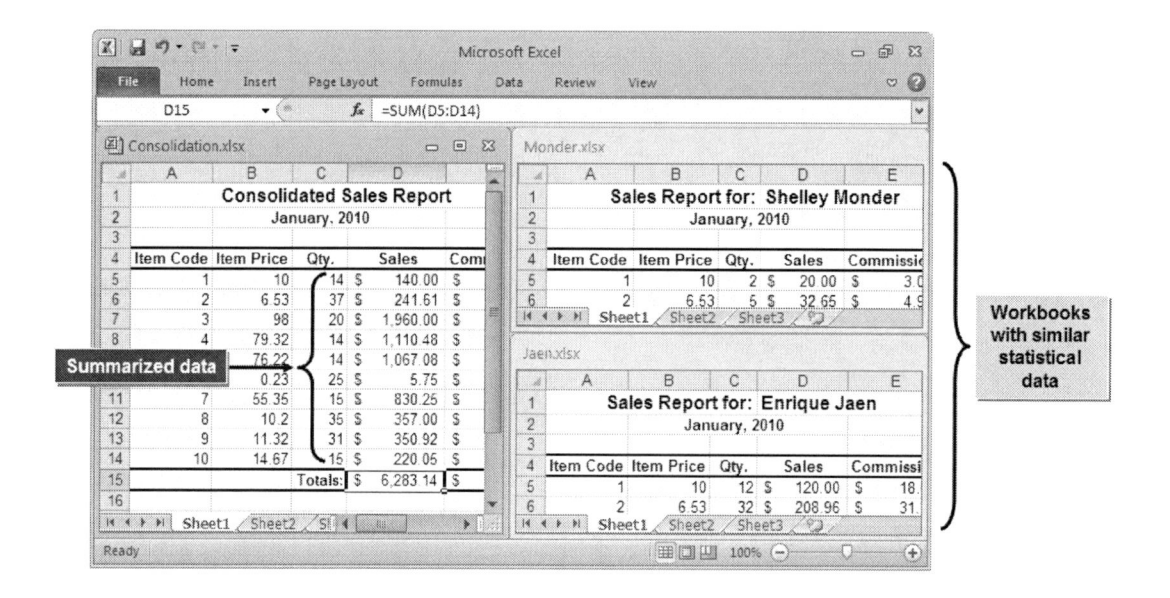

Figure 5-2: *Consolidated data from different workbooks.*

The Consolidate Dialog Box

The **Consolidate** dialog box has a number of options that can be used to consolidate data.

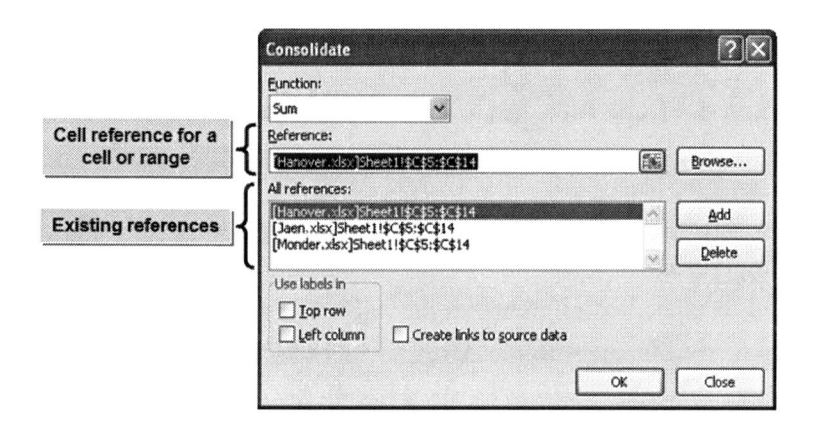

Figure 5-3: The Consolidate dialog box consolidates data from different cells.

Option	Description
Function	A drop-down list that includes all the available built-in functions.
Reference	A text box that can be used to enter the cell reference for the cell or range.
Browse	A button that can be used to browse, if data is present in another workbook.
All references	A list box where all existing references are listed.
Add	A button that can be used to add a reference, which has been entered in the **References** text box, to the **All references** list box.
Delete	A button that can be used to delete a cell reference that has been added to the **All references** list box.
Top row	A check box that is used to specify the location of the labels in the source range in the top row.
Left column	A check box that is used to specify the location of the labels in the source range in the left column.
Create links to source data	A check box that can be used to create a link to source data.

How to Consolidate Data

Procedure Reference: Consolidate Data

To consolidate data:

1. Open all workbooks from which you want to consolidate data.

2. Arrange the windows in the desired position and size.

3. Select the worksheet and the cell or range of cells where you want the consolidated data to be placed.

4. On the **Data** tab, in the **Data Tools** group, click **Consolidate.**

5. In the **Consolidate** dialog box, from the **Function** drop-down list, select a built-in function to consolidate data, if desired.

6. In the **Reference** text box, enter the cell reference for the range of data you want to consolidate from other worksheets.

7. Click **Add** to add the specified reference to the **All references** section.

8. If necessary, add more references to the **All references** section.

9. Check **Create links to source data** to create a link to the source data, and click **OK** to complete the consolidation.

ACTIVITY 5-2

Consolidating Data

Before You Begin:

The Hanover.xlsx, Monder.xlsx, Jaen.xlsx, and Consolidation.xlsx files are open.

Scenario:

You have three sales reports (Hanover, Monder, and Jaen) that need to be summarized and consolidated in the Consolidation workbook. You begin by consolidating the range that contains the quantity data in each of the worksheets.

---

1. In the Consolidation workbook, select the range where you want the consolidated data to be placed.

    a. Double-click the title bar of the Consolidation.xlsx window to maximize it.

    b. Observe the cells in column C which are blank, and the cells in columns D and E which have formulas.

    c. Select the range **C5:C14** to select the cells that will hold the quantity data.

---

2. In the Monder workbook, reference the range that has the quantity data.

    a. On the **Data** tab, in the **Data Tools** group, click **Consolidate.**

    b. In the **Consolidate** dialog box, next to the **Reference** text box, click the **Collapse dialog** button.

    c. Switch to the Monder.xlsx window.

    d. Select the range **C5:C14** to select the quantity data, and press **Enter.**

    e. In the **Consolidate** dialog box, click **Add** to add the specified reference to the **All references** list box.

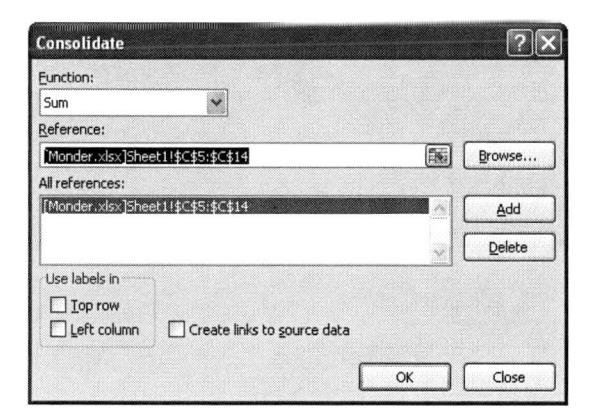

The default view in the **Reference** and **All references** fields should be [File name]Sheet1![Range Reference]. If it does not appear as mentioned, then the students need to navigate to C:\084678Data\Working with Multiple Workbooks and select the respective file once.

3. In the Jaen and Hanover workbooks, reference the range that has the quantity data.

    a. In the **Consolidate** dialog box, click the **Collapse** dialog button.

    b. Switch to the Jaen.xlsx window.

    c. Select the range **C5:C14** to select the quantity data, and press **Enter.**

    d. In the **Consolidate** dialog box, click **Add** to add the specified reference to the **All references** list box.

    e. Reference the range that has the quantity data from Hanover.xlsx.

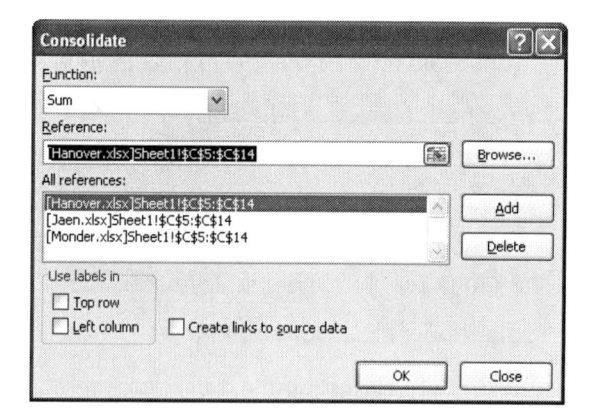

4. Create links to the source data.

    a. Check **Create links to source data,** and click **OK** to complete the consolidation.

    b. In the consolidated workbook, observe that the quantity data from all the workbooks have been consolidated.

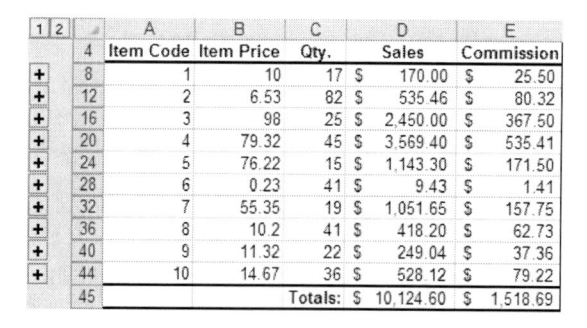

5. View the referenced data in the consolidated workbook.

a. Below the **Name Box,** click **2** to expand all of the referenced data.

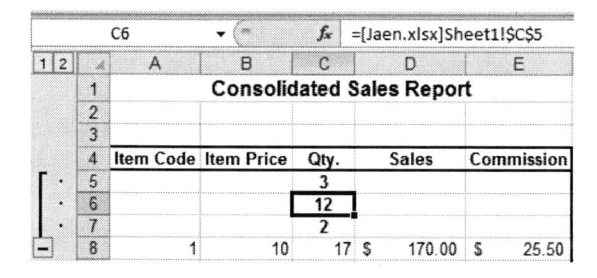

b. Select cell **C5.**

c. In the **Formula Bar,** observe that the data is from Hanover.xlsx.

d. Select cell **C6.**

e. In the **Formula Bar,** observe that the data is from Jaen.xlsx.

f. Select cell **C7.**

g. In tho **Formula Bar,** observe that data is from Monder.xlsx.

---

6. Verify the changes made in the Monder workbook.

a. Switch to the Monder.xlsx window.

b. In cell C5, enter **5**

---

c. Switch to the Consolidation.xlsx window.

d. Observe that the value in C7 has changed to **5.**

e. Save the Consolidation.xlsx file as ***My Consolidation***

f. Close all open files and leave Excel open.

TOPIC C
Link Cells in Different Workbooks

You consolidated data into a single worksheet. Now you would like to link the data in one workbook with the data in other workbooks. In this topic, you will link cells in different workbooks.

When you have different but related workbooks, it would be best to create a direct link from one cell in one workbook to related cells in other workbooks. Linking cells in different workbooks allows you to streamline your workflow by removing the need to open workbooks containing related data.

How to Link Cells in Different Workbooks
Procedure Reference: Link Cells in Different Workbooks

To link cells in different workbooks:

1. Open the source workbook that will contain the links and the target workbook.
2. In the source workbook, select the cell where you want to place the formula and then begin creating a formula.
3. Select the cells in the target workbooks using operators as needed for creating the formula.
4. Press **Enter** when you have finished creating the formula.

External References

An *external reference* is a reference to another workbook or a defined name in another workbook.

Source and Dependent Workbooks

A *source workbook* is the workbook to which a formula refers, and a *dependent workbook* is a workbook that contains a link to another workbook.

ACTIVITY 5-3
Linking Cells in Different Workbooks

Data Files:

C:\084678Data\Working with Multiple Workbooks\Finch.xlsx, C:\084678Data\Working with Multiple Workbooks\Decker.xlsx, C:\084678Data\Working with Multiple Workbooks\ Weckl.xlsx, C:\084678Data\Working with Multiple Workbooks\Summary.xlsx

Before You Begin:
The Excel application is open.

Scenario:
You need to calculate the total sales and total commissions for the three sales representatives whose data is stored in the Finch, Decker, and Weckl workbooks, respectively. You have already begun developing the Summary workbook that will summarize and calculate the total for each of the files. Any update to the sales data in any of the files should be reflected in the Summary workbook.

---

1. Create a formula that sums the sales totals from each of the sales representatives' worksheets.

   a. Display the **Open** dialog box, navigate to the C:\084678Data\Working with Multiple Workbooks folder, and open the Finch.xlsx, Decker.xlsx, Weckl.xlsx, and Summary.xlsx files.

   b. In the Summary.xlsx window, in cell A5, type = to begin creating the formula.

   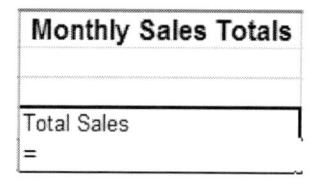

   c. Activate the Finch.xlsx window.

   d. In the Finch.xlsx window, select cell **D15.**

   e. Type **+** to continue keying in the formula.

   f. Activate the Decker.xlsx window.

   g. In the Decker.xlsx window, select cell **D15,** and type **+**

   h. Activate the Weckl.xlsx window.

   i. In the Weckl.xlsx window, select cell **D15,** and press **Enter.**

j.   Observe that the value of Total Sales displayed in cell **A5** of Summary.xlsx is $10,124.60.

Monthly Sales Totals

Total Sales	
$	10,124.60

---

2.   Update the sales data for Item 3 in Finch.xlsx.

a.   Activate the Finch.xlsx window.

b.   In the Finch.xlsx window, in cell C7, enter *6*

c.   On the **View** tab, in the **Window** group, from the **Switch Windows** drop-down list, select **Summary.xlsx**.

d.   Observe that the **Total Sales** value in Summary.xlsx has changed to $9,536.60.

Monthly Sales Totals

Total Sales	
$	9,536.60

e.   Save the file as *My Summary*

f.   Activate the Finch.xlsx window and save the file as *My Finch*

g.   Close all windows.

TOPIC D

Edit Links

You created links in different workbooks. You now need to change the reference to a linked cell in a source workbook. In this topic, you will edit links.

When working on a workbook that contains links to cells in another workbook, there are chances that the linked cells in the source workbook might have changed or moved. Creating links from scratch will be tedious and time-consuming. Editing links can minimize the upkeep time because you don't have to create a new link from scratch.

How to Edit Links

Procedure Reference: Edit Links

To edit links:

1. Open the file that contains the links you want to edit.

2. In the **Microsoft Security Options** message bar, select **Enable Content.**

3. In the **Microsoft Excel** warning box, click **Edit Links.**

4. In the **Edit Links** dialog box, select the name of the workbook with the link to be redirected.

5. Click **Change Source.**

6. In the **Change Source: [Filename]** dialog box, select the name of the workbook to which you want to establish a new link, and click **OK** to change the source file.

7. In the **Edit Links** dialog box, click **Close.**

ACTIVITY 5-4
Editing Links

Data Files:

Weckl.xlsx, My Summary.xlsx

Before You Begin:
The Excel application is open.

Scenario:
Janet Weckl changed her surname to Covington. Her workbook has to be edited and renamed to reflect this change. Additionally, you need to ensure that the link in the My Summary workbook that currently addresses the Weckl workbook will point to the new Covington workbook that you will create.

1. Edit the Weckl workbook to reflect Ms. Covington's name change.

   a. Display the **Open** dialog box, navigate to the C:\084678Data\Working with Multiple Workbooks folder, and open the Weckl.xlsx file.

   b. In cell **D1,** enter *Janet Covington*

   c. Save and close the file.

   d. In Windows Explorer, navigate to the C:\084678Data\Working with Multiple Workbooks folder, and rename the Weckl file to *Covington.xlsx*

   e. Close Windows Explorer.

2. Edit the My Summary workbook so that it points to the Covington workbook.

   a. Open the My Summary.xlsx file.

   b. On the message bar below the **Ribbon**, click **Enable Content.**

   c. In the **Microsoft Excel** warning box, click **Edit Links.**

   d. In the **Edit Links** dialog box, observe that the status of Weckl.xlsx is displayed as **Error: Source not found.**

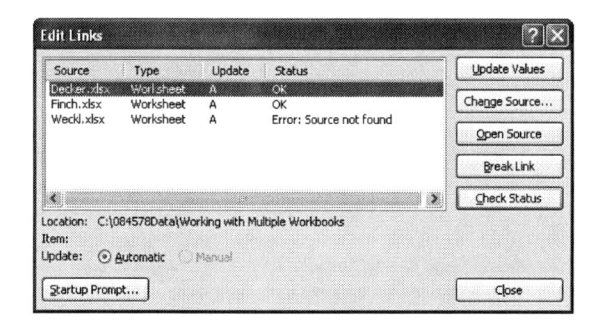

   e. In the list box, select **Weckl.xlsx.**

f. Click **Change Source.**

g. In the **Change Source: Weckl.xlsx** dialog box, select **Covington.xlsx,** and click **OK** to change the source file.

h. In the **Edit Links** dialog box, observe that the status of the file has changed to **OK.**

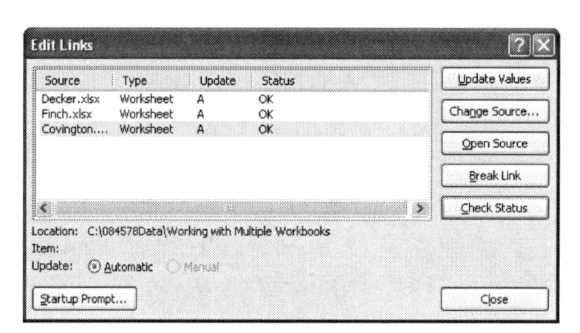

i. In the **Edit Links** dialog box, click **Close.**

j. Save the file as *My Updated Summary* and close it.

Lesson 5 Follow-up

In this lesson, you worked with multiple workbooks. Using an Excel file as a repository for data helps reduce the trouble of using multiple workbooks.

1. Which Excel features would you use when dealing with multiple workbooks?

2. How will you manage your workbooks when frequently updating data?

6 | Importing and Exporting Data

Lesson Time: 30 minutes

Lesson Objectives:

In this lesson, you will import and export data.

You will:

- Export Excel data.
- Import a delimited text file.
- Import and export XML data.

Introduction

You shared data between different worksheets and workbooks. You would now like to begin sharing Excel data with other applications, while meeting emerging standards for data storage and distribution. In this lesson, you will import and export data from Excel to other applications.

Re-creating data in one application when you already have that data in another is a redundant and time-consuming task. Importing and exporting data allows you to use data from other applications in Excel and vice versa, without having to re-create it from scratch. Also, by structuring workbooks with XML, you can exchange data with other XML-compliant applications on multiple platforms.

TOPIC A
Export Excel Data

Now that you have consolidated your workbooks and created workbooks that link to other workbooks, you are ready to take the next step. You can use some of the data stored in an Excel file in other applications. In this topic, you will export Excel worksheet data.

Imagine you have created a worksheet that contains useful information that can be shared within your organization. Excel allows you to export data from a worksheet to external applications, saving you from the need to re-create data. Exporting data from Excel to other applications not only minimizes your effort and saves time, but it also reduces the chance of error or data omission.

Exporting

Exporting is the process of sending data that is created in one application to a different application. When data is exported, a copy of the data is formatted specifically for the application it will be used in, and the original data stays the same. The data exported can be manipulated in the new application. Excel can export a range of data, a worksheet, or an entire workbook.

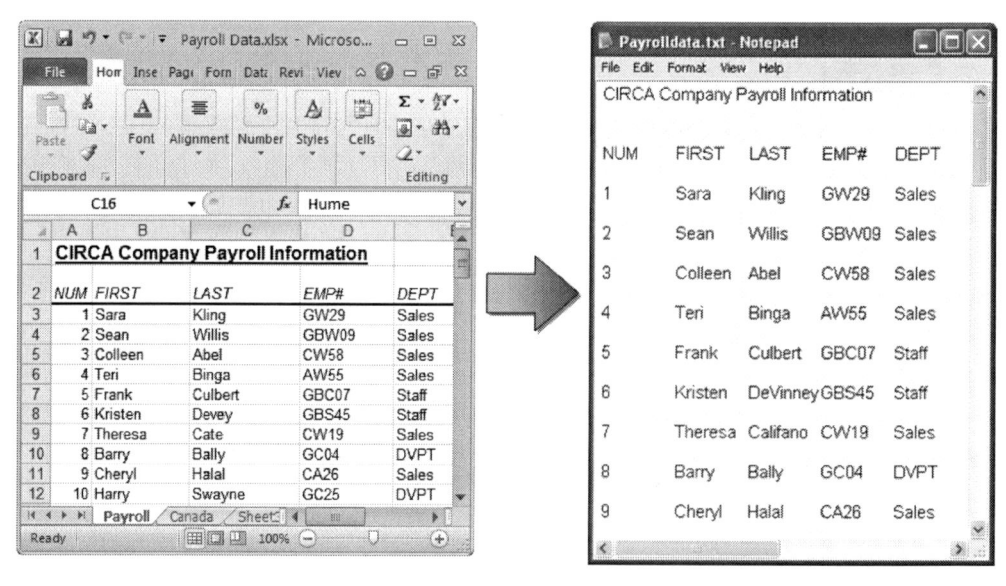

Data in Excel   Data after exporting to Notepad

Figure 6-1: Exporting Excel data to a text file.

File Types for Exporting Excel Data

Data stored in Excel can be exported in a variety of file types. The file type is determined by the application to which you are exporting the data.

File Type	Description
XML	Saves a workbook as an eXtensible Markup Language file. Primarily, web-based applications make use of this format.
HTML	Saves a workbook as a HyperText Markup Language file. Data that is used on the web or viewed in a web browser is saved in this format. By using this file type, you can save either the entire workbook or only the active worksheet.
TXT	Saves a workbook as a tab-delimited text file for word processing. Unlike the HTML file type, the TXT file type does not allow you to save multiple sheets. It can only be used to save the active sheet in the workbook.
CSV	Saves a workbook as a comma-delimited text file.
PDF	Saves a workbook as a Portable Document Format file. This file type can be used for easy printing and distribution.
XPS	Saves a workbook as a XML Paper Specification file, which can be opened and printed from a number of applications.

Exporting Excel Files to Word

In Excel 2010, there is no option for exporting an Excel file as a Word document directly. Therefore, you will save Excel files in the TXT file format and then process them in Word.

How to Export Excel Data

Procedure Reference: Save Excel Data in a Different File Format

To save Excel data in a different file format:

1. With a workbook open, display the **Save As** dialog box.
2. If necessary, from the **Save in** drop-down list, select the location to save the file.
3. In the **File name** text box, enter the name of the file.
4. From the **Save as type** drop-down list, select the desired file format, and click **Save.**

Procedure Reference: Export Excel Data to Microsoft Word

To export Excel data to Microsoft Word:

1. Open the worksheet that needs to be exported to Microsoft Word.
2. Display the **Save As** dialog box.
3. From the **Save in** drop-down list, select the location for the new file.
4. In the **File name** text box, enter a desired name.
5. From the **Save as type** drop-down list, select **Text (Tab Delimited)(*.txt).**
6. In the **Microsoft Excel** warning box, click **Save** to save only the active worksheet.
7. In the **Microsoft Excel** information box, click **Yes** to leave out any incompatible features.
8. Open the TXT file in Microsoft Word.

ACTIVITY 6-1
Exporting Excel Data to Microsoft Word

Data Files:

C:\084678Data\Importing and Exporting Data\Payroll Data.xlsx

Before You Begin:
The Excel application is open.

Scenario:
Your manager has signed off on the final data included in the Payroll Data workbook. In doing so, he has requested that you also make this data available in Word so that he can use the data for a mail merge to distribute the payroll information to appropriate managers.

1. Save the Payroll worksheet as a tab-delimited text file.

   a. Display the **Open** dialog box, navigate to the C:\084678Data\Importing and Exporting Data folder, and open the Payroll Data.xlsx file.

   b. Verify that the Payroll worksheet is displayed, and display the **Save As** dialog box.

   c. In the **File name** text box, type *My Payroll Data*

   d. From the **Save as type** drop-down list, select **Text (Tab delimited) (*.txt)**.

   ```
   Excel Workbook (*.xlsx)
   Excel Macro-Enabled Template (*.xltm)
   Excel 97-2003 Template (*.xlt)
   Text (Tab delimited) (*.txt)
   Unicode Text (*.txt)
   XML Spreadsheet 2003 (*.xml)
   Microsoft Excel 5.0/95 Workbook (*.xls)
   ```

   e. Click **Save**.

   f. In the **Microsoft Excel** warning box, click **OK** to save only the active worksheet.

   g. In the **Microsoft Excel** message box, click **Yes** to retain the existing format and leave out any incompatible features.

   h. Close the workbook without saving it.

2. View the contents of the text file in Microsoft Word.

   a. Open Microsoft Word 2010.

   b. On the **File** tab, choose **Open,** and navigate to the C:\084678Data\Importing and Exporting Data folder.

c.   From the **Files of type** drop-down list, select **All Files (*.*).**

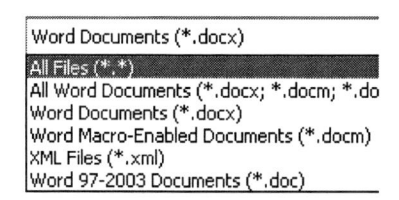

d.   Select **My Payroll Data.txt,** and click **Open.**

e.   Notice that the data exported from Excel is displayed in the Word document.

```
CIRCA Company Payroll Information

NUM   FIRST  LAST   EMP#   DEPT   HRS   HOURLY RATE GROSS PAY
1     Sara   Kling  GW29   Sales  35.5  $12.50      $443.75
2     Sean   Willis        GBW09  Sales 35.5  $13.30      $472.15
3     Colleen       Abel   CW58   Sales 42    $16.75      $703.50
4     Teri   Binga  AW55   Sales  40    $8.75 $350.00
5     Frank  Culbert       GBC07  Staff 40    $12.60      $504.00
6     Kristen       Devey  GBS45  Staff 35    $24.00      $840.00
7     Theresa       Cate   CW19   Sales 35    $12.10      $423.50
8     Barry  Bally  GC04   DVPT   40    $21.50      $860.00
9     Cheryl        Halal  CA26   Sales 35.5  $13.30      $472.15
10    Harry  Swayne        GC25   DVPT  40    $21.50      $860.00
11    Shing  Chen   GBC05  DVPT   35.5  $13.30      $472.15
12    Seth   Rose   CC76   DVPT   32    $5.50 $176.00
13    Bob    Ambrose       GW14   Sales 35.5  $12.50      $443.75
```

f.   Close the Word application without saving the file.

TOPIC B
Import a Delimited Text File

In the previous topic, you exported Excel data to Microsoft Word. Similarly, you can also import data into Excel and use the application functions to customize the data. In this topic, you will import data from a delimited text file to Excel.

Text files containing numerical data separated by tabs or commas require formatting. Working with such files is feasible if data is split into columns. Excel gives you the flexibility to format and manipulate data imported from delimited text files.

Importing

Importing is the process of capturing data from one application for use in another application. Excel can import all data or only a set of data from a file. Importing changes the format so that the data can be manipulated within a worksheet. The imported data appears no different from the data that was created directly in Excel and can be manipulated in the same manner. Data can also be imported from other spreadsheet applications, databases, text documents, or the web.

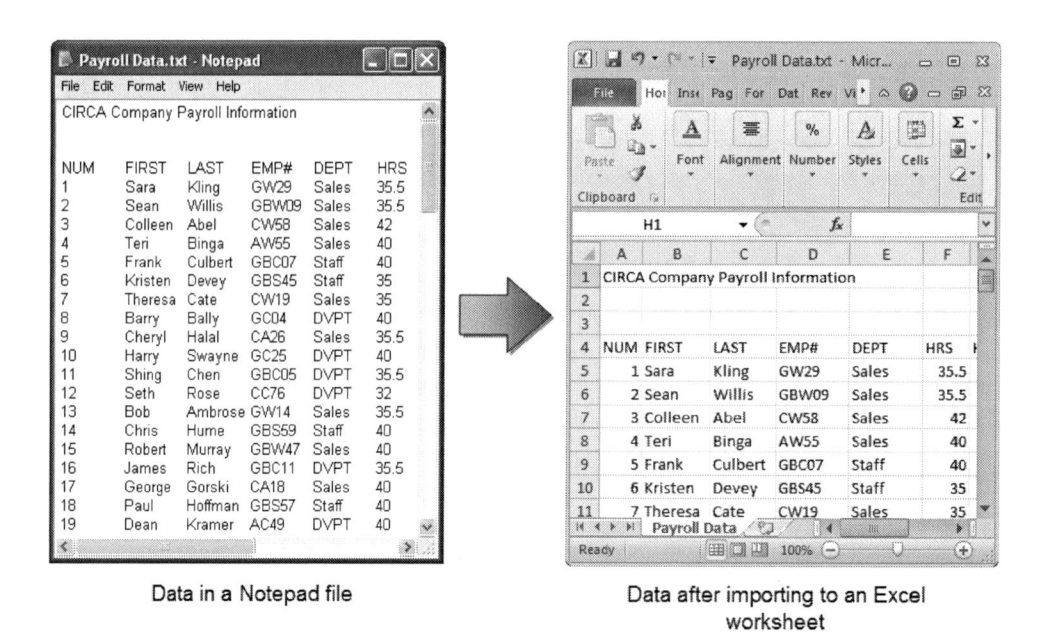

Data in a Notepad file   Data after importing to an Excel worksheet

Figure 6-2: *Importing a text file to Excel.*

The Get External Data Group

The **Get External Data** group on the **Data** tab contains options that allow you to import data from other applications into Excel.

Command	Description
From Access	Imports external data from an Access database.
From Web	Imports external data from the web.
From Text	Imports external data from a text file.
From Other Sources ▾	Imports data from other sources such as SQL Server, Analysis Services, XML Data Import, Data Connection Wizard, and Microsoft Query.
Existing Connections	Imports external data from an existing connection. This command opens the **Existing Connections** dialog box, which allows you to select a data source from the list of commonly used data sources.

Delimited Text Files

Definition:

A *delimited text file* is a TXT file that contains data fields separated or delimited by certain characters. Tab is the default character to delimit data in TXT files, but this character can also be changed to commas, quotation marks, or spaces. Delimited text files can be created in most word processing applications.

Example:

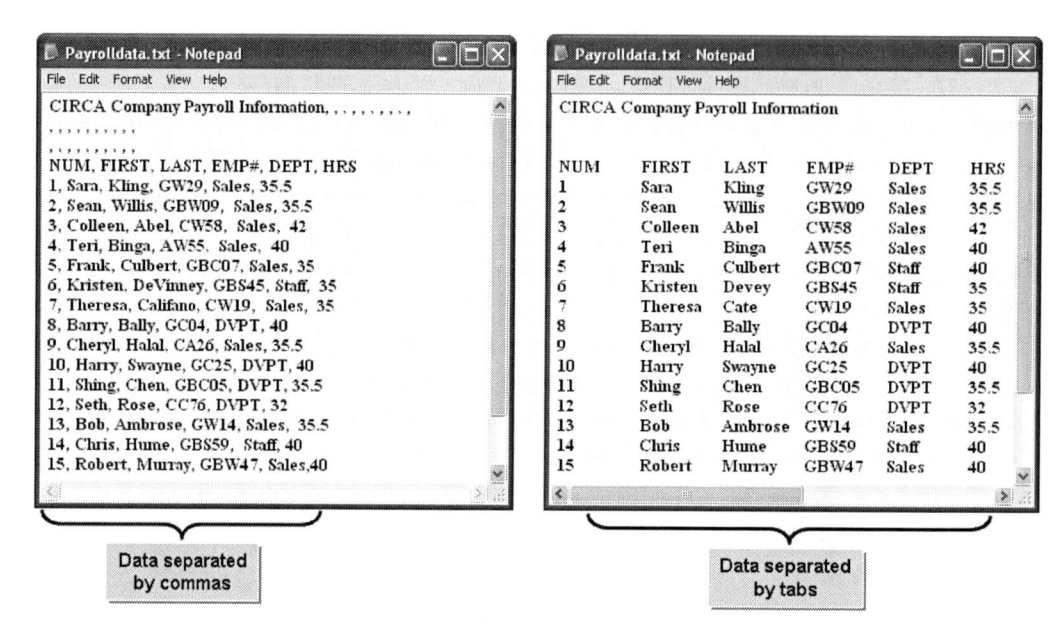

Figure 6-3: Tab is the default character for delimiting data.

Methods of Importing Text Files

In Excel, you can import data from a text file in two different ways. The text file can either be opened directly in Excel or imported as an external data range. When directly opening in Excel, you do not establish a connection to the text file, whereas by specifying the data in the text file as external data to import, you will establish a connection to the text file. Any changes made to the original text file will be reflected in the corresponding data in the worksheet whenever it is refreshed.

How to Import a Delimited Text File

Procedure Reference: Import a Delimited Text File by Opening It

To import a delimited text file by opening it:

1. Open a new or an existing Excel worksheet into which you want to import the text file and select the first cell in which to import the text file.

2. Display the **Open** dialog box.

3. Select the delimited text file you want to import into Excel and click **Open.**

4. On the **Text Import Wizard - Step 1 of 3** page, in the **Preview of file** section, set the desired options, preview the selected data to split, and click **Next.**

5. On the **Text Import Wizard - Step 2 of 3** page, in the **Delimiters** section, check or uncheck the desired delimiter check boxes.

6. If necessary, check the **Treat consecutive delimiters as one** check box to avoid the creation of an extra column if there are two subsequent delimiters.

7. If necessary, from the **Text qualifier** drop-down list, select the desired option.

- Select **" (quotation mark)** to specify that the delimiter within any text between quotation marks should be ignored or;

- Select **' (apostrophe)** to specify that the delimiter within any text that follows an apostrophe should be ignored or;

- Select **{none}** to ignore text qualifiers.

8. In the **Data preview** section, preview the split contents, and click **Next.**

9. On the **Text Import Wizard - Step 3 of 3** page, in the **Data preview** section, select the desired column, and then select a column data format option to specify the data type.

- Select the **General** option to convert all currency characters to the Excel currency format or;

- Select the **Text** option to convert all number characters to the Excel text format or;

- Select the **Date** option, and from the **Date** drop-down list, select the desired date format to convert all date characters to the Excel date format or;

- Select the **Do not import column (skip)** option to avoid splitting and moving the column selected in the preview section.

 You need to choose the data format that closely matches the preview data.

10. If necessary, click **Advanced,** and in the **Advanced Text Import Settings** dialog box, specify the settings used to recognize numeric data, and click **OK.**

11. Click **Finish.**

Procedure Reference: Import a Text File by Connecting to It

To import a text file by connecting to it:

1. Open a new or an existing Excel worksheet into which you want to import the text file.

2. On the **Data** tab, in the **Get External Data** group, click **From Text.**

3. In the **Import Text File** dialog box, navigate to the delimited text file, and click **Import.**

4. In the **Text Import Wizard,** specify the settings to import the delimited file.

5. Click **Finish.**

6. If necessary, in the **Import Data** dialog box, specify the location for the import.

- Select **Existing worksheet** and specify the location in the text box to place the import in the active worksheet or;

- Select **New worksheet** to place the import in a new worksheet, starting at cell A1.

7. In the **Import Data** dialog box, click **Properties.**

8. In the **External Data Range** dialog box, in the **Refresh control** section, set the refresh properties.

- Check **Prompt for file name on refresh** to prompt for the file name on every refresh or;

- Check **Refresh every** and specify the time period in the minutes list box in which to refresh the data in the imported file or;

- Check **Refresh data when opening the file** to refresh data whenever the file is opened.

9. In the **Import Data** dialog box, click **OK.**

10. If necessary, format the worksheet as required.

ACTIVITY 6-2
Importing a Delimited Text File

Data Files:

C:\084678Data\Importing and Exporting Data\Payroll.txt

Before You Begin:

The Excel application is open.

Scenario:

Some department managers within your organization still use a comma-delimited text file to update their payroll information. To accommodate all the managers in the organization, you are tasked with converting the comma-delimited file into an Excel file so that the employee payroll data can, going forward, be stored in Excel and can reflect all the changes made to the file every time the text file is updated.

---

1. Select the **Payroll** text file to import.

   a. Create a new workbook in Excel.

   b. On the **Data** tab, in the **Get External Data** group, click **From Text.**

   c. If necessary, in the **Import Text File** dialog box, navigate to the C:\084678Data\ Importing and Exporting Data folder.

   d. In the **Import Text File** dialog box, select **Payroll.txt,** and click **Import.**

---

2. Specify the delimiter settings for the text to be imported.

   a. On the **Text Import Wizard - Step 1 of 3** page, click **Next** to accept delimited as the data file type and to start the import at row 1.

   b. On the **Text Import Wizard - Step 2 of 3** page, in the **Delimiters** section, uncheck **Tab,** check **Comma,** and click **Next.**

   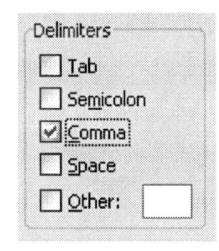

   c. On the **Text Import Wizard - Step 3 of 3** page, verify that **General** is selected as the **Column data format** for the first column.

   d.

Click **Finish** to display the **Import Data** dialog box.

3. Set the import properties for the delimited text.

    a. In the **Import Data** dialog box, click **Properties.**

    b. In the **External Data Range Properties** dialog box, in the **Refresh control** section, check the **Refresh data when opening the file** check box, and click **OK** to refresh data in the imported file whenever it is opened.

    c. In the **Import Data** dialog box, click **OK** to import data to the existing worksheet.

    d. Notice that the delimited text is imported to the Excel worksheet.

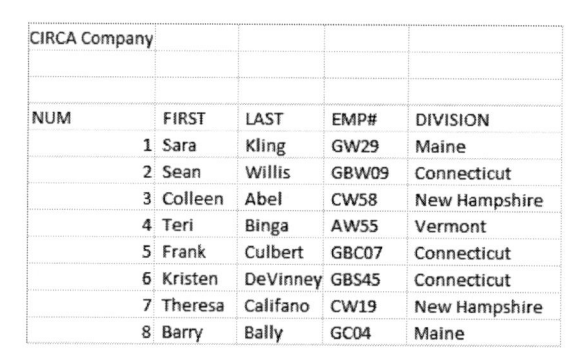

CIRCA Company				
NUM	FIRST	LAST	EMP#	DIVISION
1	Sara	Kling	GW29	Maine
2	Sean	Willis	GBW09	Connecticut
3	Colleen	Abel	CW58	New Hampshire
4	Teri	Binga	AW55	Vermont
5	Frank	Culbert	GBC07	Connecticut
6	Kristen	DeVinney	GBS45	Connecticut
7	Theresa	Califano	CW19	New Hampshire
8	Barry	Bally	GC04	Maine

    e. Save the file as ***My Payroll Import*** and close it.

TOPIC C
Import and Export XML Data

So far you have imported and exported static data to edit data in a suitable application. Next, you will manipulate XML data in Excel. In this topic, you will import and export XML data in Excel.

When you have data stored in an XML file that you want to manipulate using the Excel user interface, you must access that data in such a way that it is displayed in Excel in an easily readable and familiar format. Not being proficient in XML is not a cause for concern. If you receive an XML file, you can access and manipulate data by importing or exporting it to Excel.

XML

Definition:

XML, or eXtensible Markup Language, is a language that describes data by creating structured text files that are readable and easy to interpret. XML elements contain tags to hold data. Once an XML file is defined, data can be exchanged between different systems or programs. XML files are saved with the .xml file extension. XML can be processed by a variety of databases and applications.

Example:

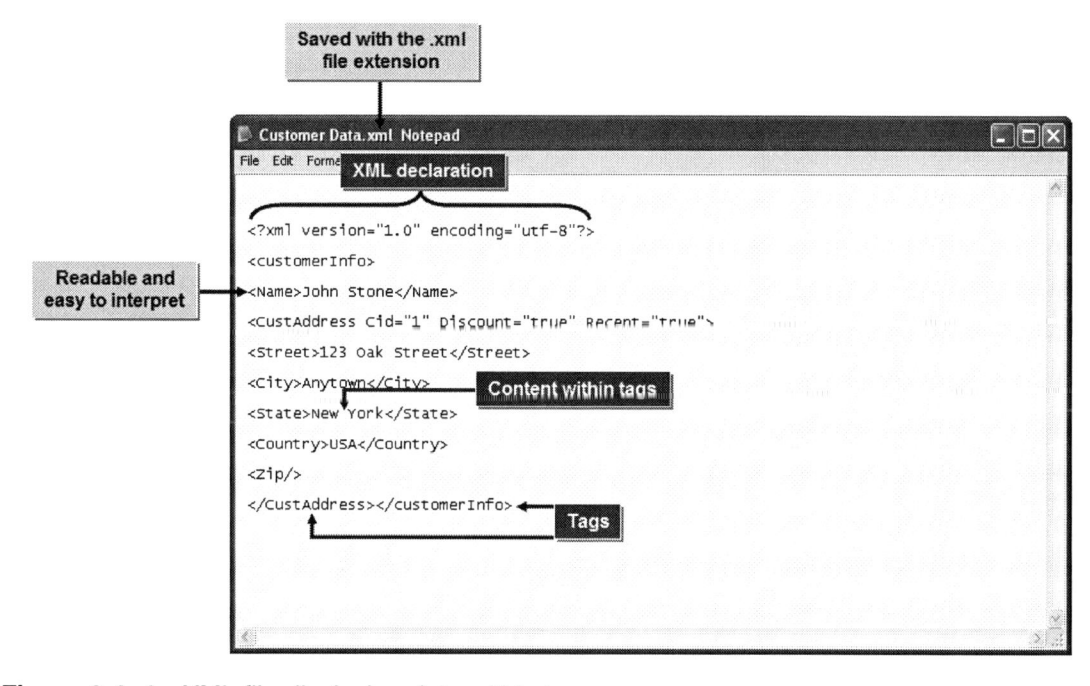

Figure 6-4: An XML file displaying data within tags.

XML Components

An XML file contains various components.

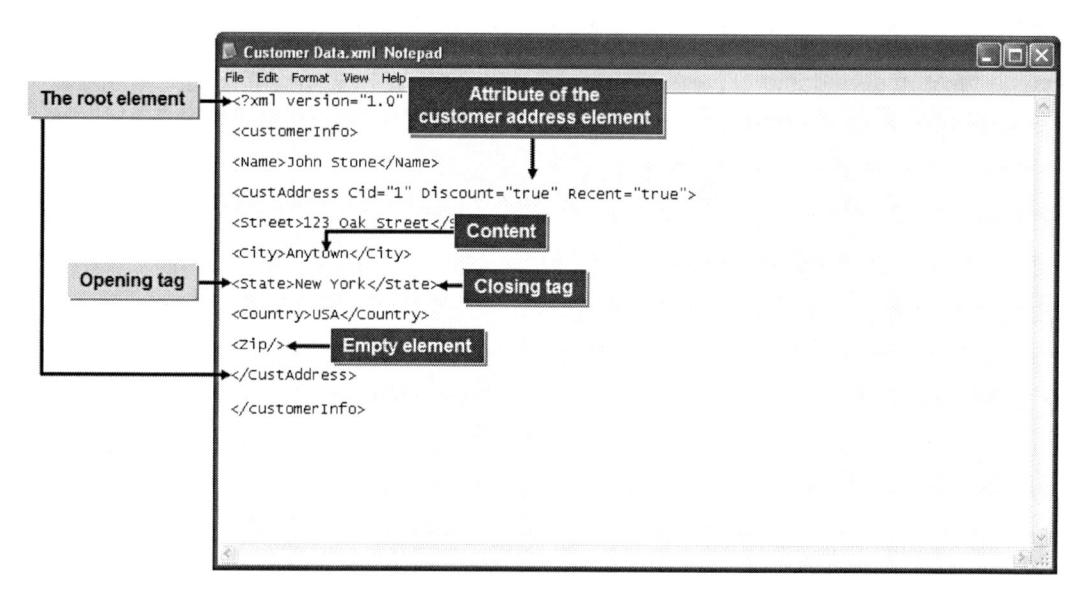

Figure 6-5: The components of an XML file.

Component	Description
Opening tag	Begins with a less-than symbol, followed by the tag name, and then a greater than symbol.
Closing tag	Begins with a less-than symbol, followed by a forward slash, the tag name, and then a greater-than symbol.
Content	Everything that appears between the opening tag and the closing tag in an XML file.
Empty element	Begins with a less-than symbol, followed by the tag name and a space, and then a forward slash followed by a greater-than symbol.
Root element	Primary element in any XML file into which all other elements are nested.
Attribute	Additional data to describe the element included in the opening tag, after the element name.

Characteristics of XML Elements

There are specific characteristics of XML elements.

- Elements that contain content begin with an opening tag and end with a closing tag.

- Elements that do not contain content can use either both opening and closing tags, or a single tag that defines the element as empty.

- Elements within other elements are called nested elements.

- Anything between the opening and closing tags of any given element is part of that element.

- Some elements can have attributes, which provide additional data to describe the element.

XML files must be well formed. A well-formed document is the minimum structural requirement for XML documents to conform to. A well-formed XML document must have the following properties:

- Contain an XML declaration that identifies the file as an XML document.
- Contain a minimum of one element, the root element.
- Properly nest all elements within the root element.
- Properly nest all tags.
- Properly match start tags to corresponding end tags.
- Properly match tag names and the case of the tag name text for start tags and their corresponding end tags.

XML Schemas

Definition:

An *XML schema* is an XML file that sets the rules and defines the structure of other XML files of a particular type. Schemas define the data type for the elements and attributes in XML files. Multiple XML files of the same type can use the same schema to validate their structure. XML schemas are saved with the .xsd file extension.

Example:

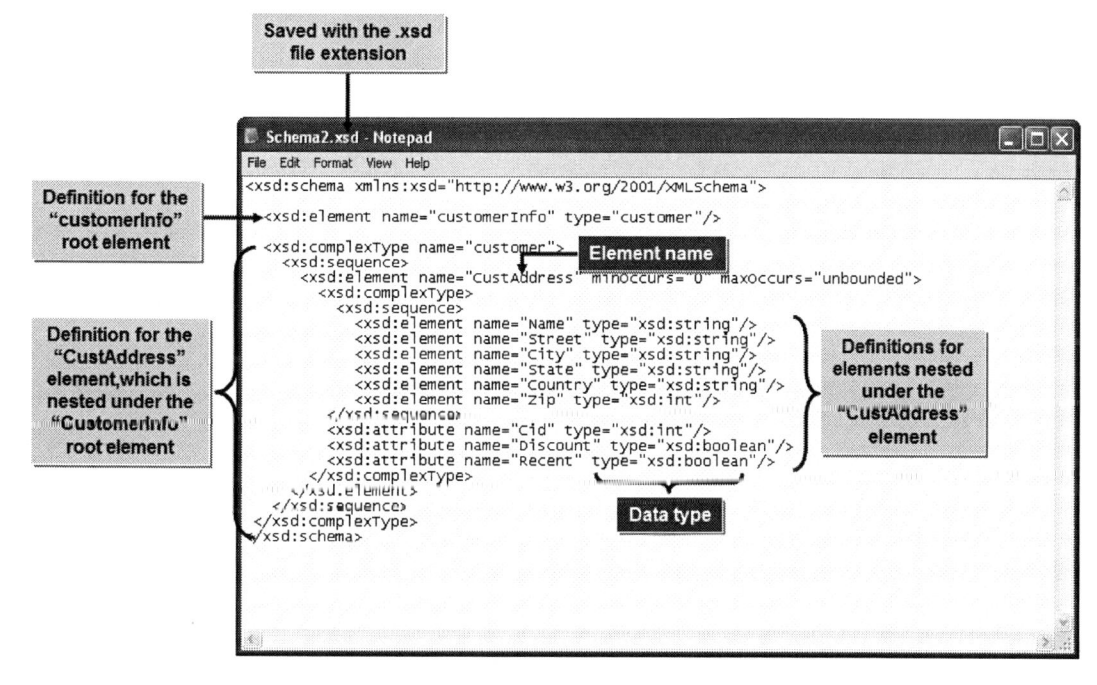

Figure 6-6: An XML schema file.

XML Maps

Definition:

An *XML map* is an Excel component that maps the contents of an Excel workbook to the corresponding elements and structure of a specified XML schema. After importing the necessary data, XML maps enable the export of the contents of the Excel workbook to any XML file that is of the type defined by the mapped XML schema. An XML map can apply some or all of the elements of a schema to a worksheet.

Example:

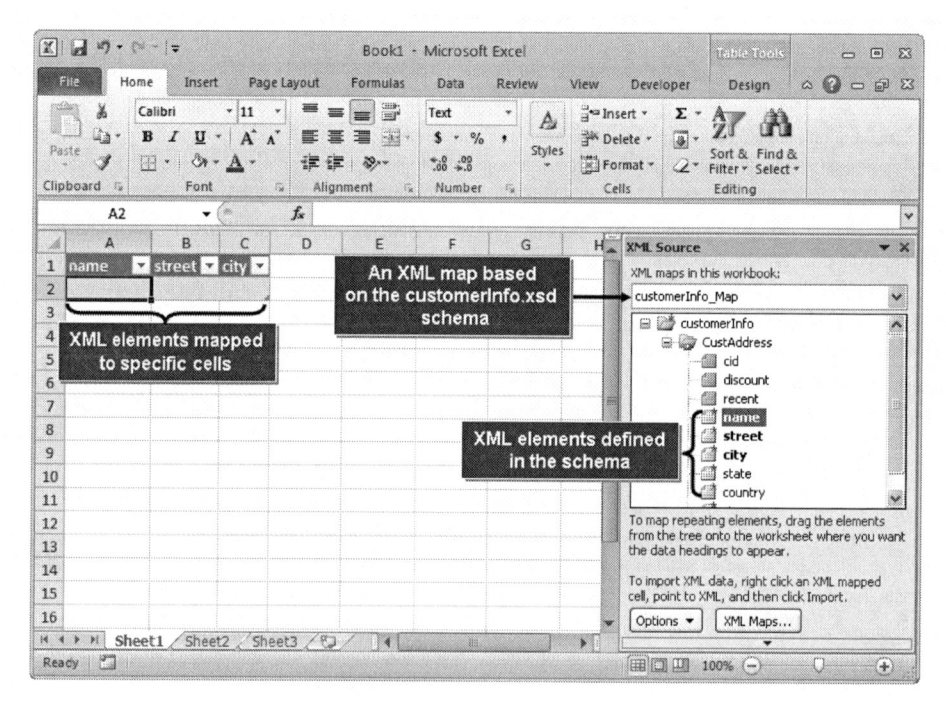

Figure 6-7: *An XML map shown in Excel.*

The XML Source Task Pane

The **XML Source** task pane contains various options for managing XML maps.

Option	Description
The **XML maps in this workbook** drop-down list	Displays a drop-down list that lists all XML maps added to a workbook. You can select the desired XML map from this list.
The **XML maps in this workbook** list box	Lists the XML map and its elements selected from the **XML maps in this workbook** drop-down list.
The **Options** button	Displays various options that will help you manage XML data.
The **XML Maps** button	Opens the **XML Maps** dialog box, which allows you to add, delete, or rename XML maps.

The XML Group

The **XML** group on the **Developer** tab has various commands that allow you to work with XML files in Excel, by mapping, importing, or exporting them.

Command	Allows You To
Source	Display the **XML Source** task pane, which will allow you to manage XML maps.
Map Properties	Modify or view XML map properties.
Expansion Packs	Create or manage XML expansion packs, the groups of files that are created using an XML schema.
Refresh Data	Refresh the imported XML data in the workbook.
Import	Import an XML file.
Export	Export an XML file.

How to Import and Export XML Data

Procedure Reference: Change the Location of XML Mapped Elements

To change the location of XML mapped elements:

1. Open the file that contains the XML map you want to modify.
2. On the worksheet, select the cell having a mapped element.
3. Change the location of the selected element.
   - Cut and paste the selected cell to a new position in the workbook or;
   - Change the location using the **XML Source** task pane.
     a. In the **XML Source** task pane, right-click the highlighted XML element, and choose **Remove element.**
     b. In the **XML Source** task pane, right-click the highlighted XML element again, and choose **Map element.**
     c. In the **Map XML** dialog box, in the **Where do you want to map the XML elements** text box, specify the new location for the selected mapped element.

Procedure Reference: Delete an XML Map

To delete an XML map:

1. If necessary, open the file that contains the XML map you need to delete, and then open the **XML Source** task pane.
2. In the **XML Source** task pane, click **XML Maps.**
3. In the **XML Maps** dialog box, select the name of the map to be deleted, and click **Delete.**
4. In the **Microsoft Excel** warning box, click **OK** so that you will no longer be able to import or export XML data using this map.
5. In the **XML Maps** dialog box, click **OK.**

Procedure Reference: Import XML Data

To import XML data:

1. Open an existing workbook that has an XML map, or create a new workbook.
2. Display the **Developer** tab on the Ribbon.
    1. On the **File** tab, select **Options**, and in the **Excel Options** dialog box, select **Customize Ribbon.**
    2. In the **Main** tabs list, check **Developer** to display the **Developer** tab, and click **OK.**
3. If necessary, map the elements of an XML schema to the workbook.
4. On the **Developer** tab, in the **XML** group, click **Import.**
5. In the **Import XML** dialog box, navigate to and select the file to be imported.
6. Click **Import.**

XML Import

If you are importing XML data into an Excel workbook and it is not already mapped to Excel through a schema, then Microsoft Office Excel will create a schema based on the XML data source. When data is imported as an XML table into the worksheet, the schema of the XML data file will be displayed in the **XML Source** task pane.

Procedure Reference: Import XML Data as an External Data

To import XML data as an external data:

1. Open a new Excel workbook.
2. On the **Data** tab, in the **Get External Data** group, click **From Other Sources,** and select **From XML Data Import.**
3. In the **Select Data Source** dialog box, navigate to the desired folder, select the desired XML file to be imported, and click **Open.**
4. In the **Microsoft Excel** information box, click **OK** to create a schema based on the XML data source.
5. In the **Import Data** dialog box, specify the location for the import.
    - Choose **XML table in existing worksheet** and specify the location in the text box to place the import into an XML table in the active worksheet or;
    - Choose **Existing worksheet** and specify the location in the text box to place the import as flattened XML data or;

 A flattened XML table consists of a two-dimensional table that contains columns and rows. The column headings will be the XML tags and the rows below the column headings will contain the appropriate data. In cases where XML data is flattened, Excel will not infer a schema, and the XML map will not be available in the **XML Source** task pane.

    - Choose **New worksheet** to place the import in a new worksheet, and place the data at the upper-left corner of the worksheet.
6. If necessary, in the **Import Data** dialog box, click **Properties,** and set the import properties.
7. Click **OK.**

Procedure Reference: Export XML Data

To export XML data:

1. Open the file that contains the data you want to export.

2. On the **Developer** tab, in the **XML** group, click **Export.**

3. In the **Export XML** dialog box, navigate to the folder where you want to store the exported XML file.

4. In the **File name** text box, type a name for the file to be exported.

5. Click **Export.**

Managing XML Workbooks

The data in an XML-based workbook can be edited, deleted, cut, pasted, and sorted just like any other data in an Excel sheet.

Layout Limitations

When you want to import data into an XML-mapped worksheet, you have to add new data to that worksheet and then export all of the data so that your XML map appears as a contiguous list. This means that your mapped XML elements must appear as column headings in adjacent columns and they cannot be separated from one another. To force XML elements to remain contiguous across adjacent cells, you can map them from left to right, across column headings.

ACTIVITY 6-3
Developing XML Maps

Data Files:

C:\084678Data\Importing and Exporting Data\Schema1.xsd, C:\084678Data\Importing and Exporting Data\Schema2.xsd

Before You Begin:

The Excel application is open.

Scenario:

Your manager has sent you two XML schemas, Schema1 and Schema2. According to him, one of these files handles customer contact information; however, he does not know how to tell which file contains this information. Once you figure out which schema handles customer contact information, the other map can be deleted. You decide to view both schemas in Excel and then delete the map you are not going to use. You will then map the contents of the correct schema to an Excel sheet and name the workbook My New Customer Data.

---

1. Display the **Developer** tab on the Ribbon.

   a. Open a blank workbook in Excel.

   b. Display the **Excel Options** dialog box, and select **Customize Ribbon.**

   c. In the **Customize the Ribbon** section, in the **Main Tabs** list box, check the **Developer** check box, and then click **OK** to display the **Developer** tab on the Ribbon.

---

2. Add Schema1.xsd and Schema2.xsd to a blank workbook.

   a. On the **Developer** tab, in the **XML** group, click **Source.**

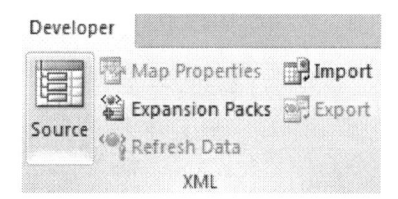

b.   In the **XML Source** task pane, click **XML Maps.**

c.   In the **XML Maps** dialog box, click **Add.**

d.   In the **Select XML Source** dialog box, navigate to the C:\084678Data\Importing and Exporting Data folder.

e.   Select **Schema1.xsd** and click **Open.**

f.   In the **XML Maps** dialog box, click **Add.**

g.   In the **Select XML Source** dialog box, double-click **Schema2.xsd** to add the schema to the **XML Maps** dialog box.

h.   In the **XML Maps** dialog box, click **OK.**

i.   Observe that **customerInfo_Map** listing the customer contact details is displayed in the **XML Source** task pane.

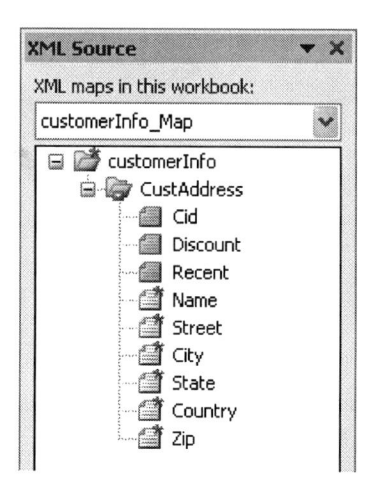

> j. In the **XML Source** task pane, from the **XML maps in this workbook** drop-down list, select **Listing_Map.**
>
> k. Verify that this data is from the schema that is not needed.
>
> l. From the **XML maps in this workbook** drop-down list, select **customerInfo_Map.**

3. Map customer contact information from the **XML Source** task pane to the worksheet.

> a. From the **XML Source** task pane, drag the **Name** element to cell A1.
>
> b. From the **XML Source** task pane, drag the **Street** element to cell B1.
>
> c. Similarly, drag the **City** element to cell C1, the **State** element to cell D1, the **Country** element to cell E1, and the **Zip** element to cell F1.

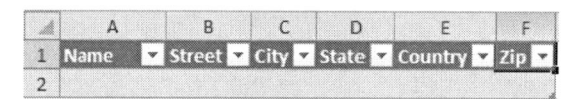

4. Delete the map that does not track customer contact information.

> a. In the **XML Source** task pane, click **XML Maps.**
>
> b. In the **XML Maps** dialog box, select **Listing_Map,** and click **Delete.**
>
> c. In the **Microsoft Excel** message box, click **OK** so that you will no longer be able to export or import data using this XML map.
>
> d. In the **XML Maps** dialog box, click **OK.**
>
> e. Save the file as *My New Customer Data.xlsx*

ACTIVITY 6-4
Importing and Exporting XML Data

Before You Begin:
The My New Customer Data.xlsx file is open.

Scenario:
Your manager has sent you an XML file that contains customer contact data. You decide to import the XML data into your workbook, which uses the Schema2 schema. In addition, you want to create an XML version of the file because your manager needs to send it to another department that does not use Excel.

---

1. Import data for the specified field from the Customer Data.xml file.

   a. On the **Developer** tab, in the **XML** group, click **Import.**

   b. In the **Import XML** dialog box, select **Customer Data.xml,** and click **Import.**

   c. Notice that the XML data is imported into the mapped cells in the worksheet.

   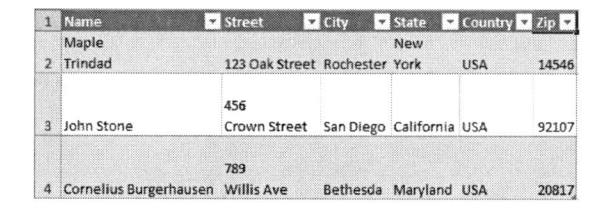

---

2. Export the data to a new XML file.

   a. On the **Developer** tab, in the **XML** group, click **Export.**

   b. If necessary, in the **Export XML** dialog box, navigate to the folder where you would like to store the exported file.

   c. In the **File name** text box, type *My Customer Data Update* and click **Export.**

   d. Close the **XML Source** task pane.

   e. Save the file as *My Customer Data Update* and close it.

---

3. Check whether the XML file is generated.

   a. Display the **Open** dialog box, navigate to the location where you saved the exported XML file, and open it in Excel.

   b. In the **Open XML** dialog box, click **OK.**

   c. In the **Microsoft Excel** dialog box, click **OK.**

   d. Verify that the customer information is exported and then close the file without saving it.

---

    e.   In Windows Explorer, navigate to the location where you saved the exported XML file and open it with Internet Explorer.

    f.   Observe the customer information is exported and then close the Internet Explorer and Windows Explorer windows.

Lesson 6 Follow-up

In this lesson, you imported and exported data between Excel and other applications. By importing and exporting data, you can use data from other applications in Excel and Excel data in other applications without having to re-create it from scratch.

1. **Which of the data in your documents could be converted to an XML-based workbook?**

2. **In terms of data layout and structure, what are the advantages of exporting an Excel file to Word?**

7 | Integrating Excel Data with the Web

Lesson Time: 20 minutes

Lesson Objectives:

In this lesson, you will integrate Excel data with the web.

You will:

- Publish a worksheet to the web.
- Import data from the web.
- Create a web query to import dynamic data from the web.

Introduction

In the last lesson, you worked with the import and export functions in Excel to share data with other applications. Similarly, you can share data on the web. In this lesson, you will import data from the web into a workbook and export your workbooks to the web.

Publishing an Excel file to the web enables you to access the data from any location. You can also import all or portions of the data from the web whenever required. More-over, any changes made to the published file will be dynamically updated so that the information available on the Internet is always current.

TOPIC A

Publish a Worksheet to the Web

The first step in sharing Excel information on the web is publishing a worksheet to the web. You have exported and imported Excel worksheets to and from other applications. Now, you want to access and manipulate a worksheet from another computer over the Internet by publishing it to the web. In this topic, you will publish an Excel worksheet to the web.

Wouldn't it be convenient if you could view, manipulate, and make changes to your workbooks from anywhere and any system? Excel allows you to do just that. By publishing worksheets to the web, you can expand the reach of your worksheet and make it more accessible.

File Publish

Definition:

File publish is a method of publishing data to a web page. Excel can publish a range of data, a worksheet, or an entire workbook to the web.

Example:

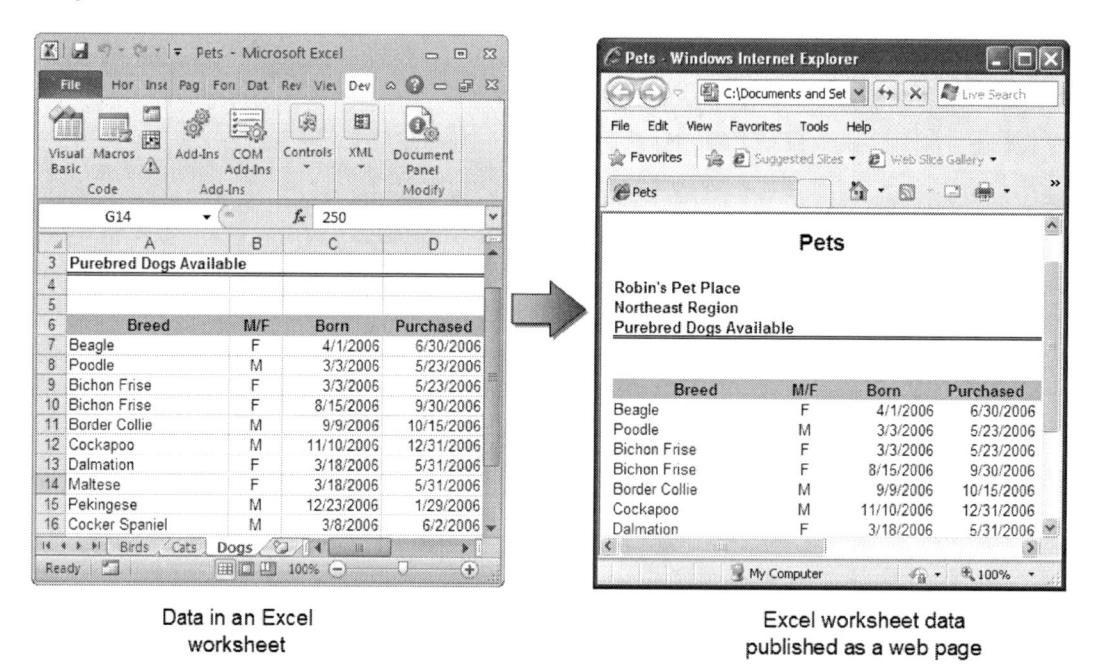

Data in an Excel
worksheet

Excel worksheet data
published as a web page

Figure 7-1: *A file published from Excel.*

The Publish As Web Page Dialog Box

The **Publish as Web Page** dialog box allows you to transform Excel data into a web page that can then be uploaded to a web server.

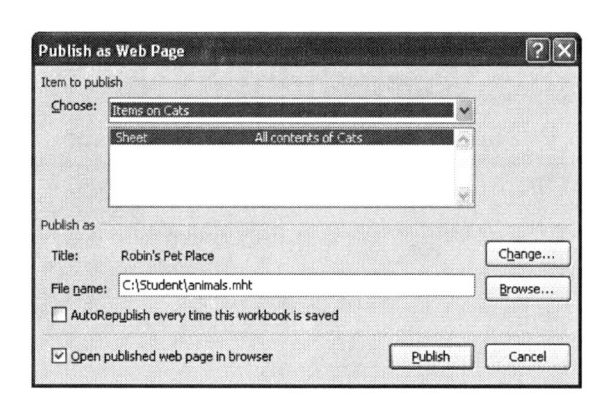

Figure 7-2: Options available in the Publish as Web Page dialog box.

Option	Description
Choose	Allows you to specify whether it is the entire workbook, a single worksheet, a range of cells, or items from each worksheet that need to be published as a web page. The previously published items in the workbook, and all the worksheet tabs will be listed in the list box.
Title	Displays the title of the web page.
Change	Launches the **Set Title** dialog box where you can specify a name for the web page.
File name	Displays the location specified for the web page and also allows you to type a new location for the web page.
Browse	Launches the **Publish as** dialog box to browse through the computer and specify the location and name for your web page.
AutoRepublish every time this workbook is saved	Allows you to autorepublish your workbook every time it is saved.
Open published web page in browser	Allows you to open the published web page in a browser.
Publish	Publishes the selected Excel data as a web page.

Publishing a Range of Cells

When you have to publish a range of cells as a web page, you can specify the desired range in the list box below the **Choose** drop-down list in the **Publish as Web Page** dialog box.

Publishing a Web Page

Publishing is one way to generate the HTML format that is required to display information on the web. When you publish a web page, you have more options than when you simply export the data in an HTML format. While the data that is published as a web page can be manipulated through any web browser, exported HTML data cannot be manipulated.

How to Publish a Worksheet to the Web

Procedure Reference: Publish a Worksheet as a Web Page

To publish a worksheet to the web:

1. In the **Save As** dialog box, select a location in which you need to save the web page.
2. In the **File name** text box, type a file name.
3. From the **Save as type** drop-down list, select an option to save the worksheet as a web page.
   - Select **Single File Web Page (*.mht; *.mhtml)** to save the worksheet as a web page that includes all the supporting information or;
   - Select **Web Page (*.htm; *.html)** to save the worksheet as a web page, and to create a folder that contains all the supporting information.
4. If necessary, add a title to the web page.
   a. Click **Change Title.**
   b. In the **Set Page Title** dialog box, in the **Page title** text box, type a title for the page, and click **OK.**
5. In the **Save As** dialog box, click **Publish.**
6. In the **Publish as Web Page** dialog box, set publication properties.
   a. In the **Item to publish** section, from the **Choose** drop-down list, select the item to be published.
   b. If necessary, click **Change,** and in the **Set Title** dialog box, specify a different name for the page, and click **OK.**
   c. Click **Browse,** and in the **Publish As** dialog box, specify the desired location and a name to publish the web page.
   d. Check **AutoRepublish every time this workbook is saved** to autorepublish the workbook every time it is saved.
   e. If necessary, check the **Open published web page in browser** check box to open the published web page in a browser.
7. Click **Publish** to publish the worksheet as a web page.

ACTIVITY 7-1
Publishing a Worksheet to the Web

Data Files:

C:\084678Data\Integrating Excel Data with the Web\Animals.xlsx

Before You Begin:
You will need a live Internet connection to complete this activity.

Scenario:
At Robin's Pet Place, cats don't seem to be selling as fast as the other animals. The owner has decided to have the Cats worksheet in the Animals workbook available on the Internet to see if that will generate more sales. She also wants the web page to reflect any changes she makes in the Animals workbook every time she saves it, so that the latest information is always available on the Internet. She has decided to name the web page Robin's Pet Place – Purebred Cats Available, and name the file My Cats Page.

1. Specify the file name and type for the published page.

   a. Display the **Open** dialog box, navigate to the C:\084678Data\Integrating Excel Data with the Web folder, and open the Animals.xlsx file.

   b. Select the various tabs in the workbook and observe the data in the other worksheets and then activate the Cats worksheet.

   c. Display the **Save As** dialog box.

   d. Type the file name as *My Cats Page*

   e. From the **Save as type** drop-down list, select **Single File Web Page (*.mht; *.mhtml).**

2. Give a title and publish the Cats worksheet as a web page.

   a. In the **Save As** dialog box, click **Publish.**

   b. In the **Publish as Web Page** dialog box, in the **Item to publish** section, from the **Choose** drop-down list, verify that **Items on Cats** is selected as the worksheet for publishing to a web page.

   c. In the **Publish as** section, click **Change.**

   d. In the **Set Title** dialog box, in the **Title** text box, type *Robin's Pet Place - Purebred Cats Available* and click **OK.**

   e. Check **AutoRepublish every time this workbook is saved.**

   f. Check the **Open published web page in browser** check box and click **Publish.**

g. Notice that the worksheet opens in a browser window.

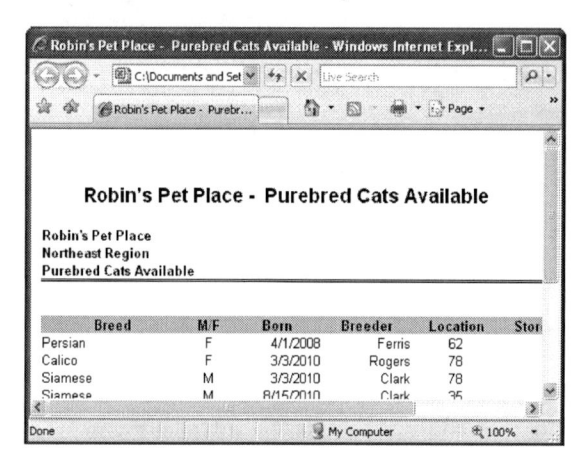

h. Close the browser window.

i. Close the workbook without saving.

TOPIC B

Import Data from the Web

You published your worksheet as a web page, thereby enhancing the reach of your worksheet. Now, you would like to use data that you found on the web in your workbook. In this topic, you will import data from the web to your workbook.

When you are browsing the web, you might find data that you would like to use in your workbook. You could cut and paste the data, but it would be a very tedious process and there is no guarantee that it would copy correctly. You might even miss some of the data altogether. To capture data from the web, you must import the data to your file.

How to Import Data from the Web

Procedure Reference: Import Data from the Web into Excel

To import data from the web:

1. With the desired worksheet open, on the **Data** tab, in the **Get External Data** group, click **Existing Connections.**

2. In the **Existing Connections** dialog box, from the **Show** drop-down list, select a connection option.

   - Select **All Connections** to display all the connection files available or;
   - Select **Connections in this workbook** to display all files that are connected to the active workbook or;
   - Select **Connection files on the network** to display all files that are connected to the network or;
   - Select **Connection files on this computer** to display all files that are connected to the computer.

3. In the **Select a Connection** list box, select the desired file connection, and click **Open.**

4. If necessary, in the **Import Data** dialog box, select where you would like to save the data.

5. If necessary, in the **Import Data** dialog box, click **Properties,** set the refresh properties, and click **OK.**

6. Click **OK** to import the data to the worksheet.

ACTIVITY 7-2
Importing Data from the Web

Data Files:

C:\084678Data\Integrating Excel Data with the Web\Currency Rates.xlsx

Before You Begin:

You will need a live Internet connection to complete this activity.

Scenario:

The President of Robin's Pet Place is considering franchising in other countries. She has asked you to download information on currency rates from the web to a new workbook so that she can review them.

---

1. Open the currency rate information to be imported.

    a. Display the **Open** dialog box, navigate to the C:\084678Data\Integrating Excel Data with the Web folder, and open the Currency Rates.xlsx file.

    b. On the **Data** tab, in the **Get External Data** group, click **Existing Connections.**

    c. In the **Existing Connections** dialog box, observe that **MSN MoneyCentral Investor Currency Rates** is selected by default, and click **Open.**

---

2. Import the currency rate information.

    a. In the **Import Data** dialog box, click **OK** to accept cell A3 as the default location in the existing worksheet, and start the import.

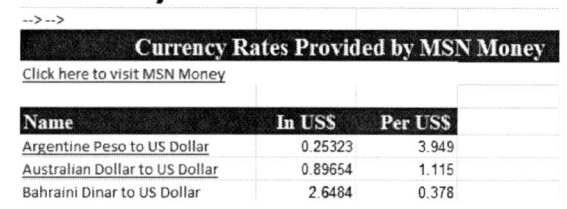

Currency Rates Information

Name	In US$	Per US$
Currency Rates Provided by MSN Money		
Click here to visit MSN Money		
Argentine Peso to US Dollar	0.25323	3.949
Australian Dollar to US Dollar	0.89654	1.115
Bahraini Dinar to US Dollar	2.6484	0.378

    b. Observe that the selected data is imported into the worksheet.

    c. Save the workbook as *My Currency Rates* and close it.

TOPIC C
Create a Web Query

In the previous topic, you imported static data from the web into your workbook. Now, you will focus on importing data that change on a regular basis into your workbook. In this topic, you will create a web query to import dynamic data from the web.

There is a large amount of data on the web that changes on a daily or sometimes on an hourly basis. Capturing this data by importing it would require repeating the import process over and over again, and you could never really be sure that the data is current. Fortunately, in Excel, you can create a web query that will update, in real time, the data you import.

Web Queries

A *web query* allows you to import data that changes frequently on the web. It determines what portions of the web page are available to import. A web query can be used to import a single table, multiple tables, or all of the text on a web page. Unlike other imported data, web query data is updated in the worksheet automatically each time the information on the website is updated. A connection to the Internet is necessary for the data to update.

The New Web Query Dialog Box

The **New Web Query** dialog box contains various options that allow you to import data from the web by creating a query.

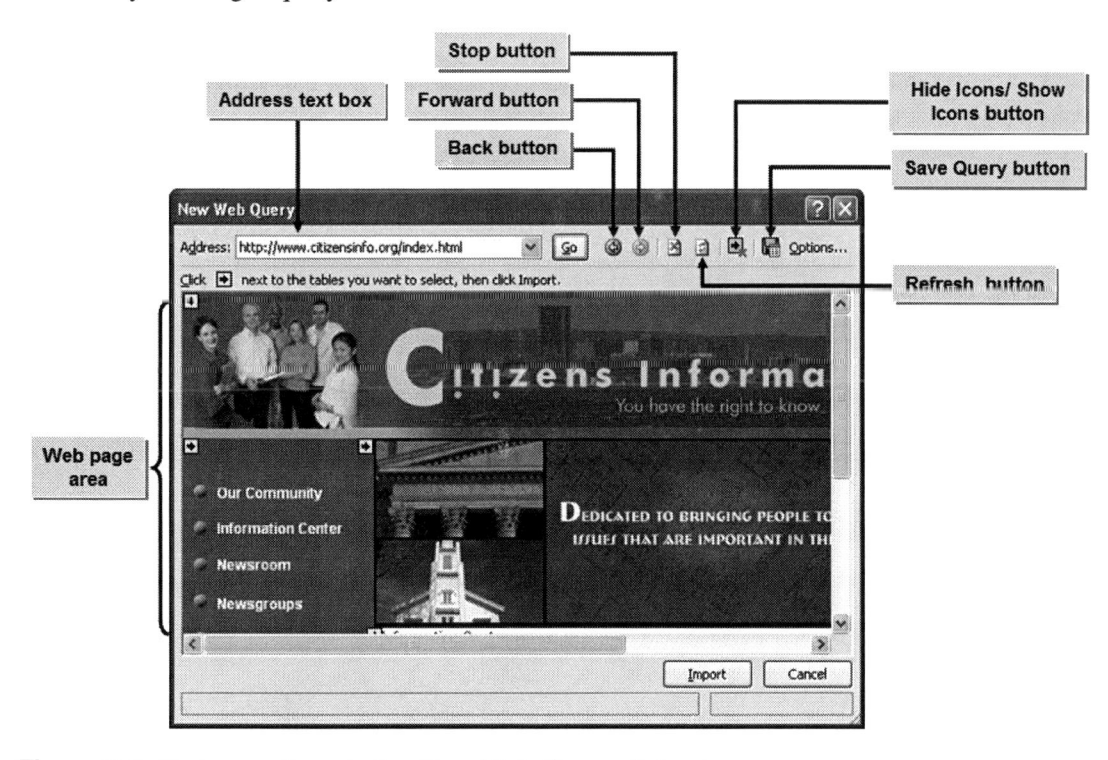

Figure 7-3: Various options in the New Web Query dialog box.

Option	Allows You To
Address	Enter the URL of the web page from where you need to import data.
Go	Go to the specified URL.
Back	Go to the previous page visited.
Forward	Go to the next page.
Stop	Stop the search for the web page specified in the **Address** text box.
Refresh	Refresh the active web page.
Hide Icons/Show Icons	Toggle between the hide and show options that allow you to select the tables to be imported from the web page.
Save Query	Open the **Save Query** dialog box, which will allow you to specify the location and name for the query, and save the query file.
Options	Open the **Web Query Options** dialog box, which will allow you to adjust the way Excel imports the data.
Web page area	Display the web page chosen. Breaks data into groups that are generally referred to as tables and are marked by small yellow boxes. You can select the table or tables and import them into Excel.
Import	Import the selected data from the web into Excel. This button will display the **Import Data** dialog box, where you can specify the location for the imported data.
Cancel	Cancel import.

Data in the New Web Query Dialog Box

In the **New Web Query** dialog box, you can navigate to the desired web page and select the table or tables of information that you want to import into Excel. Data on a web page is broken into groups that are generally referred to as tables. These groups are marked by small yellow boxes with arrows that appear at the top left of each table of information. You can select a table of information by clicking this box, and after selection, the box changes to green with a check mark. On clicking the box again, the table becomes deselected.

How to Create a Web Query

Procedure Reference: Create a Web Query

To create a web query:

1. Select the worksheet to which the data will be imported.

2. On the **Data** tab, in the **Get External data** group, click **From Web.**

3. In the **New Web Query** dialog box, navigate to the web page from where you want to import data.

   a. In the **Address** text box, type the URL of the web page from where you need to import data.

   b. Click **Go.**

4. On the web page displayed, in the **New Web Query** dialog box, select the table you want to import, and click **Import.**

5. In the **Import Data** dialog box, if necessary, select where you would like to put the data and set the refresh properties.

6. Click **OK.**

ACTIVITY 7-3
Creating a Web Query

Data Files:

C:\084678Data\Intergrating Excel Data with the Web\Price.html

Before You Begin:
You will need a live Internet connection to complete this activity.

Scenario:
Your manager has approached you about doing some work for an external client. This client would like to use Excel to keep track of information posted on the company's website. You need to use Excel to extract data from the Everything for Coffee's price list web page and create a workbook that can be delivered to the client.

---

1. Import the coffee maker information into the workbook.

   a. Open a new workbook in Excel.

   b. On the **Data** tab, in the **Get External Data** group, select **From Web.**

   c. In the **Address** text box, type *C:\084678Data\Integrating Excel Data with the Web\ Price.html* and click **Go.**

   d. In the web page pane, click the yellow arrow box next to **Percolators** to select the Percolators table.

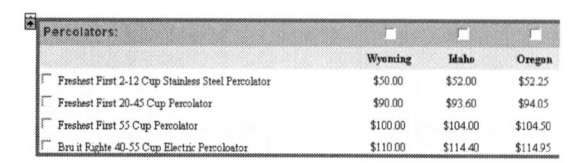

   e. Click each yellow arrow box next to **French Press, Automatic Drip, Espresso, Grind and Brew,** and **Gourmet Beans** to select the other tables.

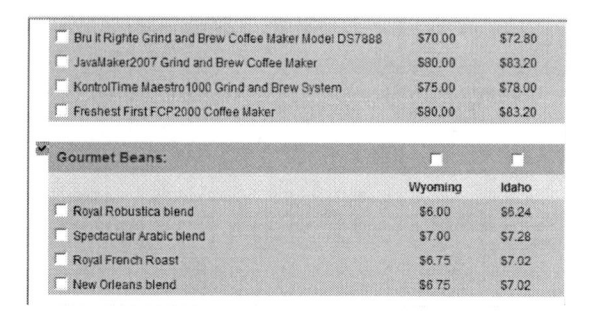

   f. Click **Import.**

---

2. Set the import properties.

a.   In the **Import Data** dialog box, click **Properties.**

b.   In the **External Data Range Properties** dialog box, in the **Refresh control** section, check **Refresh every.**

c.   Set the **Refresh every** option to *30* minutes, and click **OK.**

d.   Click **OK** to import the coffee maker price information.

e.   On the sheet tab bar, double-click **Sheet1** and rename it as *Coffee Makers*

---

3.   Import the coffee accessory information into a new sheet in the workbook.

a.   Select **Sheet2** of the workbook.

b.   On the **Data** tab, in the **Get External Data** group, select **From Web.**

c.   In the **Address** text box, type *C:\084678Data\Integrating Excel Data with the Web\ Price.html* and click **Go.**

d.   Scroll down to view the Filters and Cups product categories.

e.   Click each arrow box next to **Filters** and **Cups,** and then click **Import.**

f.   In the **Import Data** dialog box, click **OK.**

g.   Update the sheet name to *Accessories*

h.   Save the file as *Everything for Coffee Prices* and close it.

i.   Close the Excel application.

Lesson 7 Follow-up

In this lesson, you integrated data from the web and published Excel data to the web. Whether you need to transfer workbook data to the web for others to see, or import data from the web, working with data on the web offers flexibility and portability.

1.   **What type of data would you like to export to the web?**

2.   **What type of data will you import?**

Follow-up

In this course, you automated some common tasks, applied advanced analysis techniques to more complex data sets, shared workbooks with others, and shared Excel data with other applications. Advanced analysis techniques help you to extract more value from your static data by summarizing and forecasting values that are not readily apparent. Using collaboration techniques helps you to add value to your data and analysis by allowing you to incorporate feedback from others.

1. **What are the various tools provided by Excel to troubleshoot errors in formulas?**

2. **What are the various features of Excel that you might use when sharing a workbook with other users?**

3. **What are the various advanced data analysis tools provided by Excel?**

What's Next?

Microsoft® Office Excel® 2010: Level 4 is the next course in this series. In this course, you will learn to use more complex formulas, functions, arrays, and advanced editing and formatting options. You will also learn about exchanging data with other programs, command-line switches, and data organizing and cleansing.

 # Creating Excel Forms

A form is a document or interface that is used to collect data. Forms can be of two types—printed or online. Each form contains suitable elements for a user to input data. Printed forms may contain instructions, and blank spaces with labels for writing, typing, or printing data. Online forms contain controls that display information and also allow you to enter information interactively. Controls are objects that allow users to enter or edit data, perform an action, or make a selection. Excel provides various tools and options to create forms. You can use various types of controls in Excel forms.

Control	Description
Button	Allows users to initiate an action by clicking it.
Combo Box	Allows users to either type an entry or select an option from a list of options, which are displayed when an arrow is clicked.
Check Box	Allows users to check or uncheck the box to select or deselect an item or option.
Spin Button	Allows users to enter a value by typing a value, or by clicking arrows to increase or decrease the default value.
List Box	Allows users to make a selection from a list of options.
Option Button	Allows users to select a single option from a list of mutually exclusive choices.
Group Box	Groups related controls such as check boxes, and combo boxes into a single unit.
Label	Displays descriptive text such as titles, and captions.
Scroll Bar	Allows users to scroll through a range of values.

In Excel, you can insert any of the form controls in a form and set its properties. You can also set the properties of the form

Insert a Form Control in an Excel Worksheet:

1. Enable the **Developer** tab.
2. On the **Developer** tab, in the **Controls** group, from the **Insert** drop-down list, select a control and click on the worksheet to insert the control.
3. Change the properties of a control.
   a. Right-click a control, and choose **Format Control.**
   b. In the **Format Control** dialog box, specify the required options.

      c.   Click **OK.**

4.   If necessary, change the properties of the worksheet that you want to use as a form.

      a.   Select a cell on the worksheet.

      b.   On the **Developer** tab, in the **Controls** group, click **Properties.**

      c.   In the **Properties** pane, specify the settings for the worksheet.

      d.   If necessary, close the **Properties** pane.

B | Microsoft Office Excel 2010 Exam 77–882

Selected Element K courseware addresses Microsoft Office Specialist certification skills for Microsoft Office 2010. The following table indicates where Excel 2010 skills are covered. For example, 3-A indicates the lesson and topic number applicable to that skill, and 3-1 indicates the lesson and activity number.

Objective Domain	Level	Topic	Activity
1. Managing the Worksheet Environment			
1.1 Navigate through a worksheet			
1.1.1 Use hot keys	1	1-B	1-2
1.1.2 Use the name box	1	1-A, 3-B	3-2
1.2 Print a worksheet or workbook			
1.2.1 Print only selected worksheets	1	6-B	
1.2.2 Print an entire workbook	1	6-B	
1.2.3 Construct headers and footers	1	6-A	6-1
1.2.4 Apply printing options			
1.2.4.1 Scale	1	6-B	6-3
1.2.4.2 Print titles	1	6-A	6-2
1.2.4.3 Page setup	1	6-A	6-2, 6-3
1.2.4.4 Print area	1	6-B	6-3
1.2.4.5 Gridlincs	1	6-A	6-3
1.3 Personalize the environment by using Backstage			
1.3.1 Manipulate the Quick Access Toolbar	1	1-C	1–3
1.3.2 Customize the ribbon			
1.3.2.1 Tabs	1	1-C	
1.3.2.2 Groups	1	1-C	
1.3.3 Manipulate Excel default settings (Excel Options)	1	1-C	1-3
	2	6-A	6-1
1.3.4 Manipulate workbook properties (document panel)	3	1-A	
1.3.5 Manipulate workbook files and folders			

Objective Domain	Level	Topic	Activity
1.3.5.1 Manage versions	2	6-A	
1.3.5.2 AutoSave	2	6-A	
2. Creating Cell Data			
2.1 Construct cell data			
2.1.1 Use paste special			
2.1.1.1 Formats	1	2-C	
2.1.1.2 Formulas	1	2-C	
2.1.1.3 Values	1	2-C	
2.1.1.4 Preview icons	1	2-C	
2.1.1.5 Transpose rows	1	3-A	3-1
2.1.1.6 Transpose columns	1	3-A	
2.1.1.7 Operations			
2.1.1.7.1 Add	1	2-C	
2.1.1.7.2 Divide	1	2-C	
2.1.1.8 Comments	1	2-C	
2.1.1.9 Validation	1	2-C	
2.1.1.10 Paste as a link	1	2-C	
2.1.2 Cut	1	2-C	
2.1.3 Move	1	2-C,3-A	3-1
2.1.4 Select cell data	1	1-B	1-2
2.2 Apply AutoFill			
2.2.1 Copy data	1	3-A	
2.2.2 Fill a series	1	3-A	3-1
2.2.3 Preserve cell format	1	3-A	
2.3 Apply and manipulate hyperlinks			
2.3.1 Create a hyperlink in a cell	2	6-B	6-2
2.3.2 Modify hyperlinks	2	6-B	
2.3.3 Modify hyperlinked cell attributes	2	6-B	
2.3.4 Remove a hyperlink	2	6-B	
3. Formatting Cells and Worksheets			
3.1 Apply and modify cell formats			
3.1.1 Align cell content	1	4-C	4-3
3.1.2 Apply a number format	1	4-D	4-4
3.1.3 Wrapping text in a cell	1	4-C	4-3
3.1.4 Use Format Painter	1	4-A	4-2
3.2 Merge or split cells			
3.2.1 Use Merge & Center	1	4-C	4-3
3.2.2 Merge Across	1	4-C	
3.2.3 Merge cells	1	4-C	
3.2.4 Unmerge Cells	1	4-C	

Objective Domain	Level	Topic	Activity
3.3 Create row and column titles			
3.3.1 Print row and column headings	1	6-A	
3.3.2 Print rows to repeat with titles	1	6-A	6-2
3.3.3 Print columns to repeat with titles	1	6-A	
3.3.4 Configure titles to print only on odd or even pages	1	6-A	
3.3.5 Configure titles to skip the first worksheet page	1	6-A	
3.4 Hide or unhide rows and columns			
3.4.1 Hide or unhide a column	1	3-C	
3.4.2 Hide or unhide a row	1	3-C	
3.4.3 Hide a series of columns	1	3-C	3-4
3.4.4 Hide a series of rows	1	3-C	
3.5 Manipulate Page Setup options for worksheets			
3.5.1 Configure page orientation	1	6-A	6-2
3.5.2 Manage page scaling	1	6-B	6-3
3.5.3 Configure page margins	1	6-A	
3.5.4 Change header and footer size	1	6-A	
3.6 Create and apply cell styles			
3.6.1 Apply cell styles	1	4-E	4-5
3.6.2 Construct new cell styles	1	4-E	
4. Managing Worksheets and Workbooks			
4.1 Create and format worksheets			
4.1.1 Insert worksheets			
4.1.1.1 Single	1	5-A	5-2
4.1.1.2 Multiple	1	5-A	
4.1.2 Delete worksheets			
4.1.2.1 Single	1	5-A	
4.1.2.2 Multiple	1	5-A	
4.1.3 Reposition worksheets	1	5-A	
4.1.4 Copy worksheets	1	5-A	5-2
4.1.5 Move worksheets	1	5-A	5-2
4.1.6 Rename worksheets	1	5-A	5-1
4.1.7 Group worksheets	1	5-A	
4.1.8 Apply color to worksheet tabs	1	5-A	5-1
4.1.9 Hide worksheet tabs	1	5-A	5-2
4.1.10 Unhide worksheet tabs	1	5-A	5-2
4.2 Manipulate window views			
4.2.1 Split window views	1	5-B	5-3

Objective Domain	Level	Topic	Activity
4.2.2 Arrange window views	1	5-B	5-3
4.2.3 Open a new window with contents from the current worksheet	1	5-B	5-3
4.3 Manipulate workbook views			
4.3.1 Use Normal workbook view	1	1-A	1-1
4.3.2 Use Page Layout workbook view	1	6-A	6-1
4.3.3 Use Page Break workbook view	1	6-A	6-1
4.3.4 Create custom views	1	6-A	
5. Applying Formulas and Functions			
5.1 Create formulas			
5.1.1 Use basic operators	1	2-A	2–1
5.1.2 Revise formulas	2	2-A	
5.2 Enforce precedence			
5.2.1 Order of evaluation	1	2-A	
5.2.2 Precedence using parentheses	1	2-A	
5.2.3 Precedence of operators for percent vs. exponentiation	1	2-A	
5.3 Apply cell references in formulas			
5.3.1 Relative and absolute references	1	2-C	2-3
5.4 Apply conditional logic in a formula			
5.4.1 Create a formula with values that match conditions	2	1-D	
5.4.2 Edit defined conditions in a formula	2	1-D	
5.4.3 Use a series of conditional logic values in a formula	2	1-D	
5.5 Apply named ranges in formulas			
5.5.1 Define ranges in formulas	2	1-A	1-1
5.5.2 Edit ranges in formulas	2	1-A	
5.5.3 Rename a named range	2	1-A	1-1
5.6 Apply cell ranges in formulas			
5.6.1 Enter a cell range definition in the formula bar	1	3-B	
5.6.2 Define a cell range	1	3-B	3-2
6. Presenting Data Visually			
6.1 Create charts based on worksheet data	2	3-A	3-1
6.2 Apply and manipulate illustrations			
6.2.1 Insert	2	5-A	5-1
6.2.2 Position	2	5-B	
6.2.3 Size	2	5-A, 5-B	5-1, 5-2
6.2.4 Rotate	2	5-B	
6.2.5 Modify Clip Art SmartArt	2	5-C	5-3

Objective Domain	Level	Topic	Activity
6.2.6 Modify Shape	2	5-B	5-2
6.2.7 Modify Screenshots	2	5-A	
6.3 Create and modify images by using the Image Editor			
6.3.1 Make corrections to an image			
6.3.1.1 Sharpen or soften an image	2	5-A	
6.3.1.2 Change brightness	2	5-A	
6.3.1.3 Change contrast	2	5-A	
6.3.2 Use picture color tools	2	5-A	
6.3.3 Change artistic effects on an image	2	5-A	
6.4 Apply Sparklines			
6.4.1 Use Line chart types	3	4-B	4-2
6.4.2 Use Column chart types	3	4-B	
6.4.3 Use Win/Loss chart types	3	4-B	
6.4.4 Create a Sparkline chart	3	4-B	
6.4.5 Customize a Sparkline	3	4-B	
6.4.6 Format a Sparkline	3	4-B	4-2
6.4.7 Show or hiding data markers	3	4-B	4-2
7. Sharing Worksheet Data with other users			
7.1 Share spreadsheets by using Backstage			
7.1.1 Send a worksheet via Email or Skydrive	3	2-B	
7.1.2 Change the file type to a different version of Excel	1	1-D	1-4
7.1.3 Save as PDF or XPS	3	2-B	
7.2 Manage comments			
7.2.1 Insert	2	6-B	6-2
7.2.2 View	2	6-B	
7.2.3 Edit	2	6-B	6-2
7.2.4 Delete comments	2	6-B	
8. Analyzing and Organizing Data			
8.1 Filter data			
8.1.1 Define a filter	2	2-C	2-4
8.1.2 Apply a filter	2	2-C	2-4
8.1.3 Remove a filter	2	2-C	
8.1.4 Filter lists using AutoFilter	2,	2-C	
8.2 Sort data			
8.2.1 Use sort options			
8.2.1.1 Values	2	2-C	2-4
8.2.1.2 Font color	2	2-C	
8.2.1.3 Cell color	2	2-C	

Objective Domain	Level	Topic	Activity
8.3 Apply conditional formatting			
8.3.1 Apply conditional formatting to cells	3	1-D	1-4
8.3.2 Use the Rule Manager to apply conditional formats	3	1-D	1-5
8.3.3 Use the IF function to apply conditional formatting	3	1-D	
8.3.4 Clear rules	3	1-D	
8.3.5 Use icon sets	3	1-D	
8.3.6 Use data bars	3	1-D	

C | Microsoft Office Excel 2010 Expert Exam 77-888

Selected Element K courseware addresses Microsoft Office Specialist certification skills for Microsoft Office 2010. The following table indicates where Excel 2010 Expert skills are covered. For example, 3-A indicates the lesson and topic number applicable to that skill, and 3-1 indicates the lesson and activity number.

Objective Domain	Level	Topic	Activity
1.1. Apply workbook settings, properties, and data options			
1.1.1. Set advanced properties	3	1-A	1-1
1.1.2. Save a workbook as a template	2	6-D	6-4
1.1.3. Import and export XML data	3	6-C	6-3, 6-4
1.2. Apply protection and sharing properties to workbooks and worksheets			
1.2.1. Protect the current sheet	3	2-A	2-1, 2-2
1.2.2. Protect the workbook structure	3	2-A	2-3
1.2.3. Restricting permissions	3	2-G	2-9, 2-10
1.2.4. Require a password to open a workbook	3	2-A	2-3
1.3. Maintain shared workbooks			
1.3.1. Merge workbooks	3	2-E	2-7
1.3.2. Set Track Changes options	3	2-C, 2-D	2-5, 2-6
2. Applying Formulas and Functions			
2.1. Audit formulas			
2.1.1. Trace formula precedents	3	3-A	3-1
2.1.2. Trace dependents	3	3-A	3-1
2.1.3. Trace errors	3	3-B	3-3
2.1.4. Locate invalid data	3	3-B	3-2
2.1.5. Locate invalid formulas	3	3-B	3-2, 3-3
2.1.6. Correct errors in formulas	3	3-B	3-2, 3-3
2.2. Manipulate formula options			
2.2.1. Set iterative calculation options	4	3-B	3-3

Objective Domain	Level	Topic	Activity
2.2.2. Enable or disabling automatic workbook calculation	2	6-A	
2.3. Perform data summary tasks			
2.3.1. Use an array formula	4	1-A	1-1
2.3.2. Use a SUMIFS function	4	4-C	4-3
2.4. Apply functions in formulas			
2.4.1. Find and correct errors in functions	3	3-B	3-3
2.4.2. Applying arrays to functions	4	1-A	1-1
2.4.3. Use Statistical functions	4	4-A, 4-B, 4-C	1-1, 1-2, 1-3
2.4.4. Use Date functions	4	Appendix A	
2.4.5. Use Time functions	4	Appendix A	
2.4.6. Use Financial functions	4	3-A, 3-B	3-1, 3-3
2.4.7. Use Text functions	4	5-A	5-1
2.4.8. Cube functions	4	Appendix A	
3. Presenting Data Visually			
3.1. Apply advanced chart features			
3.1.1. Use Trend lines	3	4-A	4-1
3.1.2. Use Dual axes	4	6-B	6-2
3.1.3. Use chart templates	4	6-B	
3.1.4. Use Sparklines	3	4-B	4-2
3.2. Apply data analysis			
3.2.1. Use automated analysis tools	3	4-E	4-6
	4	2-A, 2-B, 2-C 2-E, 2-F	2-1, 2-2, 2-3, 2-5, 2-6
3.2.2. Perform What-If analysis	3	4-C, 4-D	4-3, 4-4
3.3. Apply and manipulate PivotTables			
3.3.1. Manipulate PivotTable data	2	4-A	4-1
3.3.2. Use the slicer to filter and segment your PivotTable data in multiple layers	2	4-B	4-2
3.4. Apply and manipulate PivotCharts			
3.4.1. Create PivotChart	2	4-C	4-3
3.4.2. Manipulate PivotChart data	2	4-C	4-3
3.4.3. Analyzing PivotChart data	2	4-C	4-3
3.5. Demonstrate how to use the slicer			
3.5.1. Choose data sets from external data connections	2	4-B	
4. Working with Macros and Forms			
4.1. Create and manipulate macros			
4.1.1. Run a macro	3	1-B	1-2
4.1.2. Run a macro when a workbook is opened	3	1-B	

Objective Domain	Level	Topic	Activity
4.1.3. Run a macro when a button is clicked	3	1-B	
4.1.4. Record an action macro	3	1-B	
4.1.5. Assign a macro to a command button	3	1-B	
4.1.6. Create a custom macro button on the Quick Access Toolbar	3	1-B	
4.1.7. Apply modifications to a macro	3	1-C	1-3
4.2. Insert and manipulate form controls			
4.2.1. Insert form controls	3	Appendix A	
4.2.2. Set form properties	3	Appendix A	

Lesson Labs

Lesson labs are provided as an additional learning resource for this course. The labs may or may not be performed as part of the classroom activities. Your instructor will consider setup issues, classroom timing issues, and instructional needs to determine which labs are appropriate for you to perform, and at what point during the class. If you do not perform the labs in class, your instructor can tell you if you can perform them independently as self-study, and if there are any special setup requirements.

Lesson 1 Lab 1

Customizing Your Workbook

Activity Time: 15 minutes

Data Files:

C:\084678Data\Streamlining Workflow\Travel Expenses.xlsx, enus_084678_01_1_datafiles.zip

Scenario:

The Travel Expenses workbook contains two worksheets: April and May. Both worksheets should follow a specific format. The standards are:

- Draw attention to any monthly total that exceeds $2,000.00 by applying a light red fill to the corresponding cells.
- The value of cells with numeric data should range only from 1 to 20,000.
- The font size of the Totals row must be 14 pts.

Instead of repeating the same task for all sheets in the workbook, you need to find an easier way to automate the task. You then reconsider the large font size and want to reduce it, but you don't want to redo the entire automation task to decrease it to 12 pts.

---

1. Open the Travel Expenses.xlsx file from the C:\084678Data\Streamlining Workflow folder.

---

2. Start recording a macro named "TravelReport" to record the formatting actions performed in the **April** worksheet.

---

3. Apply a light red fill conditional formatting to the cells of the **Totals** rows such that any monthly total for an employee that exceeds $2,000.00 is highlighted.

---

4. Force all cells of the range **B5:D14** to accept values only in the range of 1 to 20,000.

---

5. Increase the font size of the **Totals** row to 14 pts.

---

6. Stop recording the macro.

---

7. Apply the settings to the **May** worksheet by running the macro.

---

8. Edit the macro to decrease the font size of the **Totals** row to 12 pts.

---

9. Apply the modified macro to both the worksheets.

---

10. Save the file as an Excel Macro-Enabled Workbook with the name *My Travel Expenses* and close it.

Lesson 2 Lab 1

Collaborating with Others Using Excel

Activity Time: 15 minutes

Data Files:

C:\084678Data\Collaborating with Others\Loan Amortization.xlsx, enus_084678_02_1_ datafiles.zip

Scenario:

You have two workbooks: Loan Amortization and April May Travel. You have completed work on the Loan Amortization workbook and want to distribute it to five of your colleagues. You want them to modify data in the worksheet using a password.

You have not finished development on the April May Travel workbook and you would like to get some feedback before you certify the file as production ready. You decide to digitally sign the file so that the reviewer can verify its authenticity.

1. Open the Loan Amortization.xlsx and April May Travel.xlsx files from the C:\084678Data\ Collaborating with Others folder.

2. Save the Loan Amortization file as *My Loan Amortization*

3. In Loan Amortization.xlsx, protect the worksheet using the password *P@ssw0rd*

4. Save the workbook with an opening password *password* and close the file.

5. Save the April May Travel.xlsx workbook as *My April May Travel.xlsx* and digitally sign it with your user name.

6. Close the file.

Lesson 3 Lab 1

Auditing a Worksheet

Activity Time: 15 minutes

Data Files:

Australian Division.xlsx, enus_084678_03_1_datafiles.zip

Scenario:

Four sales representatives from Western Australia have sent you a workbook containing sales data. One of the formulas in the workbook, the yearly average cell, isn't properly calculating data. You have to figure out the reason and then fix the issue. Also, you would like to view the yearly totals more easily without the detailed data for each quarter.

---

1. Open the Australian Division.xlsx file from the C:\084678Data\Auditing Worksheets folder.

---

2. Trace precedents for each cell in the range **B12:E12** and remove the arrows.

---

3. Trace the error in cell **F12.**

---

4. Watch the error in the **Watch Window** dialog box as you evaluate and fix it.

---

5. Create an outline for the 1st, 2nd, 3rd, and 4th quarters manually.

---

6. Save the file as *My Australian Division* and close it.

Lesson 4 Lab 1

Analyzing Data in the Expense and Revenue Summary Workbook

Activity Time: 15 minutes

Data Files:

Expense and Revenue Summary.xlsx, enus_084678_04_1_datafiles.zip

Scenario:

The management has given you the Expense and Revenue Summary workbook to project expenses for the year 2010 using the trendline feature. Additionally, they would like to know what would happen to:

- The 2010 profits, if they had increased each revenue stream by 10 percent of the value in 2009 and the advertising budget by 20 percent.

- Each one of the 2010 revenue streams, if the total profit was set to $250,000.

---

1. Open the Expense and Revenue Summary.xlsx file from the C:\084678Data\Analyzing Data folder.

---

2. Create a linear trendline for the chart on the **Total Expenses Projection** worksheet such that the trendline extends out to one point beyond 2009.

---

3. On the **2009** worksheet, create a scenario for 2010 that increases each revenue stream by 10 percent and the advertising budget by 20 percent and display it.

---

4. On the same worksheet, use Solver to project each one of the 2010 revenue streams, if the total profit was set to $250,000 and retain the Solver solution.

---

5. Change the worksheet title to *2010 Expenses and Revenue* and rename the **2009** worksheet as *2010.*

---

6. Save the file as *My Expense and Revenue Summary* and close it.

Lesson 5 Lab 1

Working with Multiple Workbooks in Excel

Activity Time: 15 minutes

Data Files:

Consolidate Sales Totals.xlsx, Consolidate Eco.xlsx, Consolidate Flanders.xlsx, Consolidate Smith.xlsx, Consolidate Sales and Commissions.xlsx, enus_084678_05_01_datafiles.zip

Scenario:

As the regional manager of OGC Bookstores (Southeast region), you want to consolidate data from three of your sales representatives into a single worksheet so that you can see group totals at a glance. You would like to perform the following tasks:

- Create a workspace that incorporates the Consolidate Sales Totals workbook with the individual sales data located in the Consolidate Eco, Consolidate Flanders, and Consolidate Smith workbooks.

- Consolidate data from the individual representatives' files in the Consolidate Sales Totals workbook.

A month after sending the new file off to your senior manager, you decide to rename the Consolidate Sales Totals workbook to Consolidated Totals because the file will contain more information. You contact your manager and ask her to send the original file back to you so that you can edit the link in her file.

---

1. Open the Consolidate Sales Totals.xlsx, Consolidate Eco.xlsx, Consolidate Flanders.xlsx, Consolidate Sales and Commissions.xlsx, and Consolidate Smith.xlsx files from the C:\ 084678Data\Working with Multiple Workbooks folder.

---

2. Create a workspace with the files and name it *My Consolidated Workspace.xlw*

---

3. In the Consolidate Sales Totals.xlsx, consolidate the **Quantity** and **Sales** columns from each of the files.

---

4. Select **Consolidate Sales and Commissions.xlsx** and link it to the **Consolidate Sales Total** cells in the Consolidate Sales Totals.xlsx.

---

5. Change the name of Consolidate Sales Totals.xlsx to *Consolidated Totals.xlsx*

---

6. Edit the link in the file you sent to your manager so that it now points to Consolidated Totals.xlsx.

---

7. Save and close the files.

Lesson 6 Lab 1

Importing and Exporting Sales Data

Activity Time: 15 minutes

Data Files:

C:\084678Data\Importing and Exporting Data\OGC US Sales.xlsx, C:\084678Data\Importing and Exporting Data\Decker.txt, enus_084678_06_1_datafiles.zip, C:\084678Data\Importing and Exporting Data\Property Schema.xsd, C:\084678Data\Importing and Exporting DataProperty Listing Data.xml

Scenario:

You are consolidating the 2010 sales data for your manager. She needs you to:

- Make the contents of OGC US Sales.xlsx available in Microsoft Word.
- Store the contents of Decker.txt in an Excel file.
- Bold format the headings and adjust the width of the columns to fit the contents in the Decker workbook file in order to improve its visual appeal.

---

1. Open the OGC US Sales.xlsx file from the C:\084678Data\Importing and Exporting Data folder.

---

2. Export the contents of OGC US Sales.xlsx to Microsoft Word, and then save the file.

---

3. Import the contents of Decker.txt into a new Excel file.

---

4. Format the file as necessary, and save it as *My Decker* and close it.

---

5. Open a new workbook in Excel and map the contents of the Property Schema.xsd file to the new workbook.

---

6. Import the contents of the Property Listing Data.xml file into the workbook.

---

7. Save the new workbook as *My Property Listing Info*

---

8. Add the data listed below to the mapped region of the workbook.

- 7891 EFG Lane is a Colonial with 2200 square feet of living space and is listed at $275,000.

- 5678 HIJ Lane is a Cape cod with 1200 square feet of living space and is listed at $162,000.

9. Export the XML data as My Property Listing Data.xml.

Lesson 7 Lab 1
Publishing Excel Data to the Web

Activity Time: 15 minutes

Data Files:

Math Web Page.xlsx, enus_084678_07_1_datafiles.zip

Scenario:

The school you work for has decided to post all grades on its website. You have been asked to prepare your grading workbook for publishing on the web. The tasks listed below should be performed to ensure that the web page works as intended.

- Include the teacher's name and the subject name on the web page title.
- Republish the web page every time it is saved.
- Preview the web page in the browser window.

1. Open the Math Web Page.xlsx file from the C:\084678Data\Integrating Excel Data with the Web folder.

2. Change the file name to *My Math Web Page*

3. Publish the workbook as a web page.

4. Change the title of the web page to *Math – Mr.Harris*

5. Set options for autorepublishing the workbook every time it is saved.

6. Preview the web page in a browser.

7. Close all open windows.

Glossary

absolute referencing

Actions will be recorded by taking the absolute position of cells in which actions are performed.

CA

(Certification Authority) A third party certification authority that issues digital certificates.

cell dependent

A cell that contains a formula referring to other cells

cell precedent

A cell reference that supplies data to a formula.

conditional formatting

A formatting technique that applies a specified format to a cell or range of cells based upon a set of predefined criteria.

data consolidation

A method of summarizing data from several ranges into a single range.

data validation

A validation technique to restrict the value or type of data that can be given as input based on a specific set of criteria.

delimited text file

A TXT file that contains data fields separated by certain characters.

dependent workbook

A workbook that contains a link to another workbook.

digital certificate

An electronic file that contains unique information about a specific person.

digital signature

A content authentication tool that authenticates the sender and ensures the integrity of the digital document.

Error Checking

A command that is used to check for errors in a formula.

exporting

The process of sending data that is created in one application to a different application.

external reference

A reference to another workbook or a defined name in another workbook.

file publish

A method of publishing data that has been created in an application to a web page.

importing

The process of capturing data from one application for use in another application.

invalid data

Invalid data is any data that does not conform to the cell's data validation scheme.

IRM

(Information Rights Management) A service that permits users and administrators to define permissions to access presentations, documents, and workbooks.

macro

A task automation tool that executes a set of commands to automate frequently repeated steps.

Microsoft Office SharePoint Server 2010

A collaboration and content management server that is integrated with the Office 2010 suite.

Microsoft SharePoint Foundation 2010

A collaboration software product from Microsoft® that enables individuals to share information and communicate with one another from a central location.

module

A VBA code block containing one or more macros.

outline

A data organizing method in which a set of data is combined to form a group.

relative referencing

Actions are recorded relative to the cell that is selected.

revision tracking

A formatting tool used to track the person, date, and time of any revisions made to a workbook.

scenario

A set of input values substituted for the primary data in a worksheet.

shared workbook

A workbook that is set up and saved to allow multiple users on the same network to view, edit, and save the workbook at the same time.

Solver

A data analysis tool used to set the value stored in a single cell to a specified value by changing the value stored in multiple other cells.

source workbook

The workbook to which a formula refers.

sparklines

It is tiny chart embedded in a cell as representation of the trend for a given range, which can be a row or column.

tracer arrows

Graphics of the flow of data between cells that contain values and those that contain formulas.

trendline

A graphical representation of trends in a data series that allows you to make informed decisions.

Visual Basic Editor

An add-in application you can use to load, view, and edit the VBA code for a macro.

Visual Basic for Applications (VBA)

The programming language used to create macros in Microsoft Office 2010 applications.

web query

A query that allows you to import data that changes regularly.

Windows Live SkyDrive

A service provided by Microsoft that allows users with a Windows Live ID to store and share files on the web.

workspace

An Excel file that contains information on the location, screen size, and screen position of multiple workbooks.

XML map

An Excel component that maps the contents of an Excel workbook to an XML schema.

XML schema

An XML file that sets rules and defines the structure of other XML files of a particular type.

XML

A language that describes data by creating structured text files that are readable and easy to interpret.

Index